MW00848574

Exploring the
NEW TESTAMENT
BOOK BY BOOK

THE JOHN PHILLIPS COMMENTARY SERIES

THE JOHN PHILLIPS COMMENTARY SERIES

Exploring the
NEW TESTAMENT
BOOK BY BOOK

An Expository Survey

JOHN PHILLIPS

KREGEL
MINISTRY

Exploring the New Testament Book by Book: An Expository Survey

© 2009 by John Phillips

Published by Kregel Publications, a division of Kregel Inc., 2450 Oak Industrial Dr. NE, Grand Rapids, MI 49505.

All rights reserved. No part of this book may be reproduced, stored in a retrieval system, or transmitted in any form or by any means—electronic, mechanical, photocopy, recording, or otherwise—without written permission of the publisher, except for brief quotations in printed reviews.

All Scripture quotations, unless otherwise indicated, are from the King James Version. Italics added by the author.

Scripture quotations marked PHILLIPS are taken from The New Testament in Modern English, copyright © 1958, 1959, 1960 J. B. Phillips and 1947, 1952, 1955, 1957 The Macmillian Company, New York. Used by permission. All rights reserved.

All maps are reproduced with the permission of Moody Publishers, 820 N. LaSalle Blvd., Chicago, IL 60610.

ISBN 978-0-8254-3566-9

Printed in the United States of America
5 6 7 8 9 / 29 28 27 26 25 24 23

CONTENTS

The View from the Heights

Some two dozen rules govern Bible interpretation. Two of them, *structural analysis* and *Bible survey*, are of particular significance. *Structural analysis* involves breaking down any given passage of Scripture to its basic components. *Bible survey* involves examining larger portions of the Word of God. The one deals with the microscopic; the other deals with the telescopic.

I. The Microscopic Approach

Hans and Zachari Janssen of Middleburg, Holland, introduced us to the microscope at the end of the sixteenth or the beginning of the seventeenth century. We can well imagine the astonished unbelief of their critics when the Janssens announced the existence of living creatures so small that a single drop of water from a nearby ditch provided an ample ocean for these microscopic creatures.

As time went on, the specimens to be examined became increasingly small. A wag observed,

> Great fleas have little fleas upon their backs to bite them,
> And little fleas have smaller fleas, and so on *ad infinitum*, . . .
> And the big fleas themselves, in turn, have greater fleas to go on; While
> these, in turn have greater still, and greater still, and so on . . .
>
> —Agustus De Morgan,
> *A Budget of Paradoxes*

Nowadays we have electron microscopes, which enable us to see ever more clearly the innate structure of things. Objects as small as certain molecules can be seen and studied. Other wonders, too, have been revealed. Microbes have been discovered that can thrive in extreme environments, immune to conditions that spell instant death for ordinary forms of life. These creatures can thrive in temperatures far above and far below the freezing and boiling points of water.

What the microscope is to the scientist in his laboratory *structural analysis* is to the Bible explorer in his study.

II. THE TELESCOPIC APPROACH

The telescope was invented in 1609 by Hans Lippershey (c. 1570–1619), a Dutch optician. His marvelous invention literally opened up new and vast worlds for us to see. The Italian astronomer Galileo seized upon this marvelous instrument and announced to an unbelieving world that the planet Jupiter had moons. He had seen them! He had but touched the hem, though, of nature's stellar robes.

Now, of course, we have explored far, far beyond our solar system—itself a wonder in an endless infinity of wonders. It is 50 billion, billion times as voluminous as planet Earth, containing one star we call the sun, along with eight planets and 144 moons, millions of asteroids, and more than a trillion comets. It also hosts countless specks of dust, various gas molecules, and sundry atoms.

And so on, *ad infinitum!*

What the telescope is to the astronomer in his observatory, *Bible survey* is to the Bible student in his place of study.

This book is about Bible survey. It is an instrument that enables us to see the big picture, to see how the various parts of the Bible relate one to another. The higher we climb up the mountain, the more of the surrounding countryside can be surveyed.

Xerxes, the powerful Persian emperor, realized the value of a view from a high place. He had marched his vast army to the gates of Greece, had sailed his warships to the beckoning shore. He was ready to realize his dream—the conquest of Greece. Now he wanted to savor his victory to the full.

Should he display his banner on the pavilion where his generals and admirals within were deciding which moves to make? No! He had a better idea. He would get the big picture, the broad view. He would set his seat on high. He would see those great triremes of his make short work of the inferior warships of Greece.

High and lifted up, on his golden throne, he would see it all. And so he did. He saw his mighty fleet sail into the narrow straits between the mainland and the Salamas peninsula. But what did he see? His big battleships were all crowded together while the nimble Greek vessels rammed his, spreading havoc. Flaming arrows set his ships on fire, and Greek warriors swarmed aboard his stricken fleet. Now his army was imperiled. It was high time for him to go, lest he, himself, become a prisoner of war.

A survey view indeed!

It is this survey view of the Bible we will be studying here—the New Testament book by book! It will help us sort things out; see how the Bible fits together. For instance, the lists of names so characteristic of 1 Chronicles actually reflect the gospel of Matthew, which begins with a corresponding list of names. Yet four silent centuries lie between.

Still, Romans 9 is not to be divorced from Exodus 5–14.

The "silent centuries" were not silent at all!

Years ago I saw a most extraordinary copy of the Constitution of the United States of America. It was a pen-and-ink rendering executed by a craftsman of unusual skill. Up close it was difficult to decipher because in places the words were crowded and cramped, almost falling over each other. In other places the words and letters were spaced far and wide. Looking at the manuscript up close, I could see little or no reason for such an arrangement. When I stood back, however, and took a general survey of the work, the writer's purpose became plain; he had not only written out the American Constitution, intact, but he had portrayed a portrait of George Washington—the cramped and crowded sections worked together with the spaced-out sections to form the lights and shadows of the face.

The Bible is like that. God's act of creating all the worlds of space is dismissed in five short words ("He made the stars also," Gen. 1:16). By contrast, the form and function of the tabernacle is spread over some fifty chapters of the Bible. Consider, too, the genealogies. We can scarcely pronounce them, let alone make much sense of them.

Why such choice and arrangement of material? The Holy Spirit has taken the Bible and, in all its pieces and parts, has given to us a perfect portrait of God's beloved Son.

Many centuries ago two sad and discouraged disciples of the Lord Jesus were making their way across the Judean hills. It had been a delightful dream while it lasted. They had known the Christ (as they believed Him to be) very well indeed. They had been awed by His miracles, thrilled by His parables. They had staked everything on Him. They had expected Him to cleanse Jerusalem of its corruption, rid the Promised Land of the Romans, and extend His empire to earth's remotest bounds.

But it was all over now. Their beloved Lord had been crucified and then buried in a Jerusalem tomb. True, certain women were circulating a story of a resurrection and an empty tomb, but there could be nothing to a tale like that! Only memories remained—dreams of what might have been.

Then somewhere on the hills they had been joined in their journey by Jesus, although they did not know it was Him. He joined their conversation. "Ought not Christ to have suffered?" He asked (Luke 24:26). Then beginning at Moses and all the prophets, He expounded to them things concerning Himself (Luke 24). In other words, He gave them a survey of the Scriptures. He put things in perspective. Christ was going to reign. Of course He was. But first He must redeem.

Their hearts burned within them. Suddenly Jesus was known to them. Just as suddenly He was gone. They could not wait until morning. Swiftly they locked up their house and made all speed to tell their tale to all in yonder upper room.

That was what a Bible did for them. That is what it will do for us.

John Dryden was poet laureate of Great Britain in the difficult days of Charles II. He lived in poverty but was buried with pomp in England's Westminster Abby. Dryden wrote these stirring lines about the Word:

> Whence but from heaven could men unskilled in arts,
> In different ages born, from different parts
> Write such agreeing truths?
> Or how, or why, should all conspire to cheat us with a lie?
> Fearful their pains,
> Unwanted their advice,
> Starving their gains
> And martyrdom their price.

Well, write it they did!

And nothing helps us more appreciate this Book of books than a Bible survey.

PART 1
THE PARENTHESIS BETWEEN THE OLD AND NEW TESTAMENTS

CHAPTER 1

THE SILENT YEARS

Between Malachi and Matthew are about four hundred "silent years," during which God had no further revelations to make to His people. The broad outline of these years is given in Daniel 11, but much that meets us when we first turn from the Old Testament to the New Testament is new indeed. We read of sects and parties unknown in Old Testament times: scribes, Pharisees, Sadducees, and Herodians. We find Hebrew a dead language, and Aramaic and Greek the languages of intercourse, culture, and commerce. We find Palestinian cities bearing Greek names, and Persia long replaced by Rome as the power dominating the Land of Promise. We read of "the twelve tribes which are scattered abroad" (James 1:1), otherwise known as the dispersion. We discover that a Greek version of the Scriptures is in common use among the Jews, and that idolatry, the great snare of Israel in the Old Testament, is completely rooted out of the nation. We read of an Idumean reigning as king in Jerusalem and of an official Jewish council known as the Sanhedrin holding some form of religious and political power in the land. Even the temple in Jerusalem is not identical with the one we left in the Old Testament. Far and wide among the Jews, synagogues have come into existence as places of worship. We are curious about all these different things. Indeed, if we are to properly understand the New Testament, we need some information about them.

HISTORY

The Old Testament closed with Palestine still under Persian rule. A remnant of the Jewish people were back in the land, but the majority were dispersed more as colonists than captives throughout the Persian Empire. In 333 B.C., Alexander the Great brought Syria under his control, and Palestine was merged into the growing empire of Greece. Upon the death of Alexander, the land became a pawn in the power struggles of Syria and Egypt, being ruled by whichever power happened to be the stronger at the time. The persecutions of the Syrian king Antiochus Epiphanes provoked the revolt of the Maccabees, who led the Jews in a struggle for independence (167–141 B.C.). This was followed by the rule of the Hasmonaeans, descendants of the Maccabees, until 63 B.C., when Pompey the Great conquered Palestine and brought the country under the iron rule of Rome. Christ was born in Bethlehem in the days of Caesar Augustus. This Caesar confirmed Herod the Great as king of the Jews after the Battle of Actium in 31 B.C., when Augustus overthrew the alliance of Anthony and Cleopatra of Egypt. Herod the Great ruled Judea, Samaria, Galilee, Persia, and Idumea, and was the king responsible for the massacre of the babes of Bethlehem shortly after the birth of Christ. Herod the Great rebuilt the temple in Jerusalem, which had not been ornate enough to suit his tastes. The entire reconstruction took about eighty-five years and was not fully completed until the time of Agrippa II.

SECTS AND PARTIES

We frequently read of the scribes in the Gospels. These men—the interpreters and teachers of the Scriptures—were held in high esteem by the Jewish people. As a class they first came into prominence after the return of the captives from Babylon, Ezra himself being described as both a priest and a scribe. They were bitterly opposed to Christ and were frequently denounced by Him for making the Scriptures of no effect by their traditions.

The Pharisees were an influential Jewish sect that arose in the time of the Maccabees. Originally, this group separated themselves from the ambitious political party in the nation. They were zealous guardians of the law and were conservative in belief, accepting both the supernatural and the concept of an afterlife.

The Sadducees, on the other hand, were rationalists, the liberals of their day, who denied the existence of spirits as well as the resurrection and the immortality of the soul. Numerically, they were a much smaller group than the Pharisees, but for the most part they were wealthy and influential, and the aristocracy of the Jewish nation. They also came into prominence during the days of the Maccabees. Both Pharisees and Sadducees as a group opposed Christ, and those members who did so were condemned by Him.

The Herodians were not a religious cult but a political party. They took their name from Herod and their authority from the Roman government. The Herodians looked upon Christ as a revolutionary and opposed Him on those grounds.

The Zealots were an extremist group who were fanatical defenders of the theocracy and engaged in acts of violence against the Romans. One of Christ's disciples might have been a Zealot (Luke 6:15).

THE SANHEDRIN

In New Testament times the Sanhedrin was the supreme civil and religious body within the Jewish nation. The high priest was its president; twenty-three members composed a quorum. The body that eventually became known as the Sanhedrin probably came into existence during the Greek period of Palestinian history. It was eventually dissolved.

PREPARE THE WAY OF THE LORD

The four hundred "silent years" between the Testaments were actually years of intensive preparation of the world for the coming of God's Son. The Jews of the dispersion did much to spread abroad the basic ideas on which the gospel was to be founded. The Jewish Sabbath, synagogue, and Scriptures became well known, and Jewish separation, while it antagonized some, attracted others. The Jewish messianic hope was kept alive so that when the apostles began to spread the news that the Christ had come, many were ready to believe. The Greeks, in turn, had left an indelible mark upon the ancient world. Greek logic and learning and, above all, Greek language had created a cultural climate that, when the time came, greatly expedited the missionary outreach of Paul. The Romans, too, had done their share. They had hammered the world into one vast empire and had flung their arterial highways across the whole. Indeed, a "Roman peace" had descended on the world, enforced by a central government with a genius for organization and the armed might to make it effective. Added to all this was the bankruptcy of pagan religions, which only served to accentuate the spiritual needs of mankind.

So "when the fulness of the time was come, God sent forth his Son, made of a woman, made under the law, To redeem them that were under the law, that we might receive the adoption of sons" (Gal. 4:4–5).

CHAPTER 2

THE NEW TESTAMENT

The entire teaching of the New Testament is contained in four sketchy memos, one tantalizing brief historical abstract, twenty-one letters, and one short prophetic summary.

For the most part, the New Testament was written in the form of letters. One, Paul's epistle to the Romans, the most important letter ever written, was actually carried in a woman's purse over many a dangerous mile.

It almost seems a frivolous way to commit such weighty documents to posterity, but there was a reason for it. The Christian faith, first and foremost, is not something to be studied in a theological seminary. It is something to be lived and experienced in the rush and bustle of everyday life.

The best way, perhaps, to comprehend the total message of the New Testament is to group the books that make it up according to their major emphases. When we do this, we discover that they concern themselves with the Christian and his beliefs, the Christian and his brethren, the Christian and his behavior.

THE CHRISTIAN AND HIS BELIEFS

What are the cardinal, essential, imperishable truths of the New Testament? What makes up the hard-core imperatives of the faith? Of the fourteen writings that deal with the essentials, some deal with that which is fundamental, others with that which is false, and a few with that which is future. We shall consider them in that order.

That Which Is Fundamental: Matthew, Mark, Luke, John, Romans

The basic truths of the New Testament are contained in these writings. Take away other New Testament writings, and Christianity would be impoverished; take away these and it would be impossible.

In the four gospels we have the facts, in Romans we have the faith. In the Gospels the life is exemplified; in Romans the logic is explained. The Gospels set before us the person of Christ; Romans sets before us the principles of Christianity. In the Gospels we discover *whom* we must believe; in Romans we learn *what* we must believe.

Matthew, Mark, Luke, and John set before us the person of Christ. The writers—a tax collector, a nobody, a physician, and a fisherman! Who would have chosen such an odd assortment of men to pen the most valuable books in the world? The four gospels are mere pamphlets, by no means biographies of Christ, merely memoirs. Yet the world does not contain their equal.

Matthew wrote primarily for the Jews, Mark for the Romans, Luke for the Greeks, and John for the church. They present Christ as sovereign, servant, Savior, and Son of God. Matthew and Mark present Christ in His official capacity as sovereign and servant; Luke and John present Christ in His personal character as Son of Man and Son of God.

The first three gospels are called synoptic because they present the truth about Christ from similar points of view; John is a supplementary gospel because it presents Christ from a totally different point of view. In the Synoptic Gospels we have the earthly, the outward, the Galilean, the public, the humanity; in the gospel of John we have the heavenly, the inward, the Judean, the private, the Deity.

The four gospels tell of the matchless person, the virgin birth, the sinless life, the countless miracles, the magnificent teachings, the atoning death, the glorious resurrection, and the public ascension of the Lord Jesus. This is where it all begins—with Christ.

Romans sets before us the principles of Christianity. It is "the gospel according to Paul." In this book he takes the facts of the gospel and transforms them into the faith of the gospel. The four gospels tell how Christ gave His life *for* us; Romans tells how He now gives life *to* us. It tells of the doctrines of sin, salvation, sanctification, sovereignty, and service. Its key word is righteousness, a word that occurs thirty-six times.[1] It tells how righteousness is required, received, and reproduced.

These five books, then, deal with that which is fundamental. Obviously the enemy could not leave such books unchallenged. Within the life span of the first generation of Christians he threw at the church every possible doctrinal deviation and error his fertile mind could invent. In the wisdom of God this concentrated attack took place during the lifetime of the apostles, so that the aberrations could be dealt with apostolically. The next seven books deal with error.

That Which Is False: 2 Corinthians, Galatians, Colossians, 2 Timothy, Hebrews, 2 Peter, Jude

The attack upon the truth can be considered under two major topics: antagonism to the truth, and apostasy from the truth. One was bad, the other worse.

Four of the letters dealt with antagonism to the truth. Of these, three—Galatians, Colossians, and Hebrews—deal with antagonism toward the principle teachings of Christianity.

The moment these books are opened the atmosphere of controversy is felt. Vital truths have been assailed. The errors that have surfaced, if not dealt with competently and completely, threaten to destroy Christianity. The three errors involved were legalism, Gnosticism, and Judaism. Galatians deals with the first, Colossians with the second, and Hebrews with the third.

Legalism was an attack upon the liberty of the Christian. It is answered in Galatians. Many in the early church thought that Gentiles should have to become Jews in order to become Christians. The idea was that Gentiles should be forced to keep the law of Moses, submit to the rite of circumcision, observe the Sabbath, and adopt the Levitical dietary code.

Such a requirement would have made Jerusalem the mother church; it would have aborted Christianity into a mere Jewish sect, and it would have stifled the faith, making it repulsive to the majority of Gentiles. It was arrogant nonsense and wholly contrary to the mind of the Holy Spirit. Galatians deals with that error in no uncertain terms.

Gnosticism was an attack upon the lordship of the Christ. It is answered in Colossians. Gnosticism was one of the most subtle, dangerous, and far-reaching heresies of the early church. It combined a vaunted mysticism with elements of Judaism, intellectualism, and dead ritualism. The result was a particularly pernicious assault upon the person and work of Christ.

The Gnostics believed that matter was evil, and therefore denied the true humanity of Christ. They believed He was a form of angelic being, sufficiently removed from God that He could adopt a material body without contaminating the deity.

Colossians tells the truth about Christ, about the cult, and about the Christian. It begins with a magnificent declaration of the absolute deity of Christ as the creator and sustainer and owner of the universe.

Judaism was an attack upon the legitimacy of the church, and it is answered in Hebrews. The first Christians were all Jews, and it was very difficult for them to see that Judaism was obsolete, that the shadows of Judaism had been forever replaced by the substance of Christianity, that the church was not an extension of Judaism but a totally new departure in God's dealings with men. The church could not function within the confines of the temple and synagogue.

The book of Hebrews examines the Old Testament in the light of Calvary, and swiftly cuts the ground from under those who wanted to perform a balancing act between Judaism and the Christian faith. It had to be one or the other; it could not be both. Hebrews sets forth the superior person of Christ, the superior provisions of Calvary, and the superior principles of Christianity.

Thus, three of the letters dealing with antagonism toward the truth focus the antagonism to the principle teachings of Christianity. The fourth letter, 2 Corinthians, deals with antagonism toward the principal teacher of Christianity, the apostle Paul. Paul was given the major job of hammering out and enunciating the great truths of Christianity and putting them down in permanent written form.

Because he had so thoroughly espoused the cause of the Gentiles, Paul was disliked by many in the Jewish-Christian community, and detested and persecuted with ceaseless rancor by unbelieving Jews. Galatians takes care of their attacks upon his principles; 2 Corinthians takes care of their attack upon his person.

In 2 Corinthians, the most autobiographical of all his writings, Paul talks about his commission, his converts, and his critics. His critics had accused him of being fickle, proud, boastful, weak, ugly, dishonest, and even insane. The attack upon the man, however, was an attack upon the message. Therefore Paul vigorously defended himself with bluntness and skill.

So, then, four of these letters deal with antagonism to the truth; the remaining three deal with apostasy from the truth. If antagonism was bad, apostasy was worse. Antagonism could be dealt with by means of a good dose of unpalatable medicine; apostasy called for major surgery.

Of the three epistles that deal with apostasy, one deals with the development of apostasy. This is 2 Timothy, the last of Paul's epistles. It was a pastoral epistle, written from Rome, where Paul was expecting execution, warning Timothy not to succumb to the many forces that might pull him away.

Its great, central passage deals with the final great apostasy that will overtake Christendom at the end times. The apostle clearly saw the evidence of its coming— a growing disobedience to parents and a lack of natural affection, the dawning of "perilous times," and the unrestrained wickedness of evil men and seducers.

The other two epistles deal with the dangers of apostasy. These are 2 Peter and Jude, and they cover the ground from the same point of view and in much the same way. Both go back into history to cite proof, from the same body of evidence, that God abhors apostasy, the filthy sins it spawns, and its corruption of society at large. Both demonstrate that, in the end, God always overwhelms an apostate people with catastrophic judgment.

That Which Is Future: 1 Thessalonians, 2 Thessalonians, Revelation

Eschatology is an important part of Christian doctrine. Three New Testament writings are clearly eschatological in character.

First Thessalonians deals primarily with the rapture of the church, the coming of Christ for His own, which is mentioned in every chapter. That event, we are assured, will take place before the coming of the day of wrath.

Second Thessalonians deals primarily with the ruin of the world. Its great, central passage deals with the coming of the Beast, the Devil's messiah, and with his seduction of mankind by means of the strong delusion, the ultimate lie.

Revelation deals with the return of the Lord. Four great visions dominate the book: visions of God, of grace, of government, and of glory. The action is carried by the various series that are conspicuous in the book, notably the seven seals, the seven trumpets, and the seven vials.

We glimpse, in succession, a world ruined by men, ruled by Satan, and rescued by God. Much of the rest of the book is in the form of commentary on the action disclosed under these series.

THE CHRISTIAN AND HIS BRETHREN

God's great instrument for accomplishing His purposes in this age is the church. It is not surprising, therefore, that five New Testament writings should deal with this subject. One book deals with its origins, two with its operation, and two with its officers.

The Origins of the Church: Acts

This book is largely historical and transitional. It bridges the gap between the Gospels and the Epistles. Much that is in the Epistles would be unintelligible apart from this book. But, because it is a transitional book rather than a doctrinal book, we go to the Acts for information rather than doctrine. We obtain our doctrine from the Epistles.

The story of Acts revolves around three men—Simon, Stephen, and Saul. The foundation emphasis of the church is associated with Simon, the forward emphasis with Stephen, and the missionary emphasis with Saul.

The book begins in Jerusalem and ends in Rome. It begins with Jews and ends with Gentiles. It begins in a narrow, upper room, and it ends reaching out to the whole world. It records Paul's three great missionary journeys that turned the world upside down.

It covers a period of about thirty years, the lifespan of a generation. In that time, tens of thousands were converted. If the same rate of progress had been maintained for another generation, no doubt the world would have been fully reached. The secret of such growth lies, of course, in the emphasis on the Holy Spirit. He is mentioned fifty times in the twenty-eight chapters in this book.[2]

The Operation of the Church: 1 Corinthians, Ephesians

These two letters deal with the church in both its local and universal aspects.

In 1 Corinthians we have the community church, the local church to be found in any given community.

The local church at Corinth was a gifted assembly of believers, having in its membership an astonishing array of very able people. Yet it was the most worldly and carnal of all Paul's churches. He thus had to deal with divisions in the church in Corinth. Serious disorders surfaced, some relating to moral issues and others relating to monetary matters. Paul had to deal, too, with matters ranging from those that relate to the personal walk of believers, to matters relating to marriage, and to meats. He had to deal with matters relating to the public witness of believers, notably with the abuse of grace at the table and with the abuse of the gift of tongues.

There was also disbelief in this church. Paul had to emphasize the vital importance of belief in the resurrection. By the time he had finished dealing with all that was wrong at Corinth, he had produced a letter telling local churches ever afterward how to do things right.

In contrast with 1 Corinthians, Paul's letter to the Ephesians deals with the catholic or universal church. The local church is intended to be a miniature, a replica of this universal church. Nobody has ever seen the universal church and nobody ever will until, at the rapture, the entire church is caught up to glory.

Even gifts mentioned in Ephesians are universal gifts—apostles, prophets, evangelists, pastors, teachers—gifts given for the building up of the whole. The illustrations used are likewise universals. The church is a building, a body, a bride.

The Officers of the Church: 1 Timothy, Titus

These two letters give instruction regarding leadership in the local church. Two classes of leaders are envisioned, with high qualifications for each. Elders are to be responsible for the spiritual affairs, and deacons for secular matters.

THE CHRISTIAN AND HIS BEHAVIOR

If there is one thing we learn from the New Testament, it is that Christianity is practical. If we do not have a belief that behaves, then our belief is worthless. The seven remaining New Testament epistles all deal with aspects of this principle. All the epistles are practical, but the ones listed here seem to place special emphasis on behavior.

Dealing with Situations: Philippians

This letter deals with suffering, sacrifice, service, and sickness. Four examples are given: Paul, Christ, Timothy, and Epaphroditus.

Paul's Philippian letter resounds with the note of joy, yet he was writing from prison in Rome. At Philippi he had been beaten to a pulp for preaching the gospel, yet he and his co-worker, Silas, had sung their way into the soul of the prison jailer.

There was at least one man in the Philippian assembly who would shout a loud, "Amen!" as Paul spoke of his bonds in the same paragraph as he spoke of his joy.

The Lord Jesus was Paul's example of sacrifice; indeed, Paul takes us to Calvary for the greatest declaration found anywhere in the Bible concerning the sufferings and consequent glory of Christ.

If Timothy, Paul's most faithful helper, exemplified service, Epaphroditus exemplified the fact that not all sicknesses are healed, and that healing is not an essential part of the atonement. Paul pays this man high tribute. Epaphroditus, Paul says, was so eager to be of help that he did not regard his life. Moule translates the phrase "not regarding his life" as "playing as it were the gambler with his life!"[3]

Dealing with Slavery: Philemon

The greatest social problem of Paul's day was slavery. Philemon was a slave owner. Onesimus was his runaway slave, whose path somehow crossed that of Paul in Rome. There he was won to Christ and sent back to face the consequences of his serious behavior. Paul's attack on slavery was not social but spiritual. He simply instructed Philemon to regard Onesimus as a brother and treat him just as he would treat Paul himself.

Dealing with Sincerity: James

Of all the epistles, James is the one most like the Sermon on the Mount. James was the Lord's brother after the flesh and a late convert. He was an austere man with rigid, almost Pharisaical views. His letter is likely the first of the New Testament writings, and his primary audience was Jewish.

James demands that any profession of Christianity be proven by an evident practice of Christianity. "Faith without works is dead," he writes. It is not that James did not appreciate the doctrine of salvation through Christ alone. He maintains, though, that while we are justified by faith in the sight of God, we are justified by works in the sight of men. In other words, he demands transparent sincerity in the believer's life.

Dealing with Suffering: 1 Peter

The Lord Jesus suffered. Nor does the Bible exempt the believer from suffering. On the contrary, those who live godly lives can expect to suffer. A Christian, however, must not bring suffering on himself by sinful or silly behavior. This is Peter's great theme.

Dealing with Sonship: 1 John

All of John's writings were dated toward the close of the first century of the Christian era. He was an old man when he wrote, and had long pondered the significance of those amazing years he had spent with Jesus, as well as all that had happened since. In his day, heresy had made deep inroads, and Gnosticism was a very real problem.

The keynotes running through John's first letter are those of the new birth and Christian fellowship. While Paul's characteristic words were faith, hope, and love; John's were light, love, and life.

As John sees it, being born into the family of God is not merely a theological proposition; it is a practical transformation. He sees no shades of gray; everything is either right or wrong, true or false, good or evil. It is either Christ or anti-Christ, salvation or damnation. He hews a very straight line.

Dealing with Separation: 2 John

This brief little memo was addressed to an unknown Christian lady (some think a church) to congratulate her on the exemplary behavior of her children. John cautions this excellent woman not to entertain in her home those who bring divisive and devilish doctrines. Christian charity does not include extending a helping hand to heresy.

Dealing with Strife: 3 John

Three people are addressed in this next equally brief memo. Set forth is the prosperity of Gaius, the praise of Demetrius, and the pride of Diotrephes.

This latter person evidently regarded himself as a little pope in the local assembly. He even ranted against the beloved apostle. John promised to deal with him the next time they met. The epistle was thus written to warn against strife and against the proud haughty spirit from which it grows.

PART 2
THE NEW TESTAMENT

CHAPTER 3

THE FOUR GOSPELS

Down through the centuries many attacks have been made on the trustworthiness of the four gospels. The same people who will believe without question what Josephus wrote about the Jews, what Plutarch wrote about the Romans, and what Seutonius wrote about the Caesars, will not believe what Matthew, Mark, Luke, and John wrote about Jesus Christ. Many who accept the writing of secular authors at face value treat with scorn and skepticism the works of sacred writers. Such an attitude is not only unfair, it is fatal. For if the New Testament documents be true, then those who neglect or reject their message are making the biggest mistake possible to man.

One of America's greatest lawyers was Simon Greenleaf (1783–1853). His work *A Treatise on the Law of Evidence* was unsurpassed for nearly one hundred years, and probably has to be ranked as one of the most important works on the subject ever to appear in the English language. It ran through sixteen editions. When he was a mature lawyer at the age of sixty-three, just seven years before his death, Simon Greenleaf published the work in which he examined the testimony of the four evangelists to Jesus Christ, using the same laws of evidence employed in courts of justice in the civilized world. He said, "Our profession leads us to explore the mazes of falsehood, to detect its artifices, to pierce its thickest veils, to follow and expose its sophistries, to compare the statements of different witnesses with severity, to discover truth and separate it from error."[1] In this extensive work, Simon Greenleaf came to the conclusion that the Gospels are absolutely trustworthy, and that the four evangelists could not possibly have lied about Jesus Christ, for their testimony rings true. Paul put it this way: "This statement is completely reliable

and should be universally accepted—*Christ Jesus entered the world to rescue sinners*"
(1 Tim. 1:15 PHILLIPS, emphasis added).

The four gospels give us four views of Christ, written by different men at
different times for different audiences and from different perspectives. Matthew,
Mark, and Luke are known as the Synoptic Gospels because they present Christ
from a similar viewpoint, while John is known as the Autoptic Gospel because it
has a different emphasis from the other three.

Some important differences can be pointed out between the first three gospels
and the fourth. In the first three, most of the action takes place in Galilee; in John
it is mostly in Judea. Had we only the first three gospels, we might easily come to
the conclusion that Christ's public ministry lasted only a year, but John, with his
repeated chronological notes (he mentions three Passovers), shows that the ministry
extended over a little more than three years. The first three gospels concentrate on
Christ's works; John concentrates on His words. Even where the first three devote
space to what Jesus said, they record messages quite different from those found in
John. The synoptic writers concentrate mostly on Christ's parables; John gives no
parables but, instead, records a number of lengthy discourses. But taken together,
the four gospels make up a harmonious whole.

MATTHEW

Matthew was a Jew and wrote primarily for the Jewish people. He answered the
kinds of questions a Jewish person would ask about Jesus of Nazareth: Could Jesus
trace His ancestry back to David to prove that He was the rightful king of Israel?
What relationship did Jesus have to the law and the prophets? Did He uphold the
law? Did He fulfill the Old Testament prophecies concerning the Messiah? To answer these questions Matthew traced the ancestry of Jesus back to David through
the legal line of Joseph, His foster father. Matthew constantly quoted Old Testament
Scriptures to prove that Jesus of Nazareth was the Son of David and Israel's rightful
Messiah. He shows that Christ had come, indeed, to found a kingdom.

MARK

Mark's gospel, written primarily for the Romans, sets forth Christ as the Servant
of Jehovah. It is short and to the point and written in the coarse Greek of the slave
market. Mark explains Jewish customs, which would not be understood by his
Roman readers. His emphasis was on the doings of Jesus rather than on His sayings, for he wished to impress the businesslike Romans that Jesus was essentially a
Man of action. The words "immediately" and "straightway" are key words in Mark.
Things that one would expect to be of interest to a servant are prominent in Mark's
gospel: clothing, food, utensils, service, trade, boating, fishing, and animals. It is a
down-to-earth gospel.

LUKE

Luke was probably a Greek. He was a physician by profession, a close companion of the apostle Paul, and a scholar. His gospel, written especially for Greeks, presents the Lord Jesus as the perfect Man, and does so with simplicity and dignity. Luke tells us that he carefully examined all the facts before he began to write. He traced the ancestry of the Lord Jesus back to Adam, the first man, showing us that Jesus is "the last Adam" and "the second Man." His gospel arrests the individual, for it is full of human interest: it deals with sympathy and forgiveness; it brings women and children before us more than any other gospel. Luke showed us Jesus as the Savior of sinners. His key verse is, "For the Son of man is come to seek and to save that which was lost" (Luke 19:10). Typical of the beautiful simplicity of Luke's style is that each word in this verse contains only one syllable.

JOHN

John, known as "the disciple whom Jesus loved," wrote much later than the synoptic writers and mainly for believers, to emphasize the deity of Jesus and to combat heresy, which was making inroads into the church. He gave us the reactions of belief and unbelief to the ministry of Jesus. His material supplements what the others wrote. While the discourses he records are different from those in the other gospels, half of his gospel is made up of the actual words of Jesus. John also selected certain miracles of Jesus that he set forth as "signs" of Christ's deity.

Here then are the four gospels. Without doubt they are the most important documents in the world. They are not "a life of Christ" but are more like memoirs. They are brief and are as remarkable for the things they omit as for the things they contain. The emphasis of each one is heavily weighted toward the death of Christ. Matthew gives eight chapters, or two-sevenths of his gospel, to the Passion Week; Mark gives six chapters, or three-eighths of his gospel; Luke gives five and one-half chapters, or one quarter of his gospel; while John gives ten chapters, or about one-half of his gospel, to the Passion Week. The reason for this is obvious: important as the life of Christ is, it was through His death on the cross at Calvary that He wrought redemption for lost sinners. Jesus did not die as a martyr for a noble cause. He died as a Redeemer for sinful men, and His death was not an accident but an accomplishment (Luke 9:31).

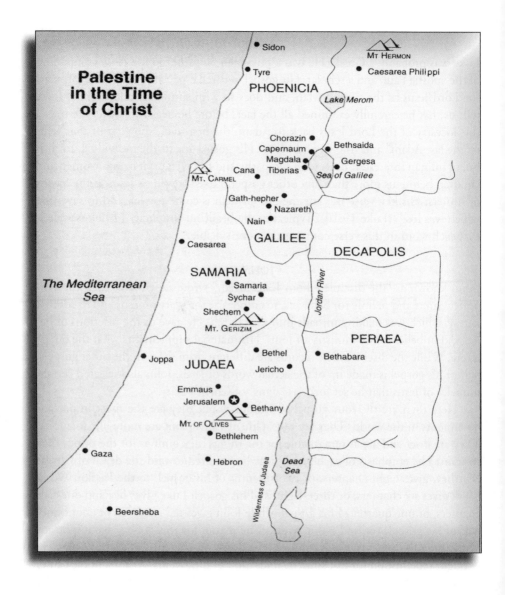

CHAPTER 4

MATTHEW

Behold Thy King

Matthew was a Palestinian Jew whose Hebrew name was Levi. When we first see him, he was a customs officer sitting at the toll road near Capernaum on the Great West Road from Damascus to the Mediterranean, or perhaps he is levying taxes from the profitable fishing business on the Sea of Galilee. Shortly after meeting Jesus, Matthew invited all his friends to come and meet his new Master. Thereafter he renounced his former despised profession of "publican" (tax collector for the Romans) and became a committed disciple of the Lord Jesus. Traces of his former occupation come out in his frequent references to money—he was evidently a man used to handling money, especially money of the highest value.

He wrote his gospel particularly for the Jews—not just Palestinian Jews, but for the Jews scattered abroad throughout the world. In all probability, although Matthew knew Hebrew and Aramaic, he wrote in Greek—the *lingua franca* of the ancient world. While we cannot be certain exactly when he wrote, it was probably about A.D. 58, some dozen years before the fall of Jerusalem. References to "the Holy Place," "the temple," "the city of the great King," and "the Holy City" point to a time before the destruction of Jerusalem and the temple.

Matthew's aim was to convince the Jews that Jesus was their Messiah. He quotes frequently from the Old Testament—there being about 130 quotations from, and allusions to, the Old Testament in his gospel, mostly from the Psalms, the book of Deuteronomy, and the prophecy of Isaiah. Of the 130 references to the Old Testament, no less than 89 are made by the Lord Himself. Some of the references are to the Hebrew Bible and some are to the Septuagint (the Greek version of the Old Testament Scriptures). Of the 1,068 verses that make up Matthew's gospel, 644 contain actual words of the Lord Jesus, so that more than three-fifths of Matthew's gospel is made up of words spoken by Jesus Himself.

About thirty sections in Matthew are peculiar to his gospel, most of them having some bearing on Matthew's main theme—the King and His kingdom. Words and expressions that are peculiar to Matthew have the same purpose. Note the many appearances of such expressions as "the kingdom of heaven" (which occurs not once in any of the other gospels); "Father in heaven" (repeatedly in Matthew and only twice in Mark); "son of David"; "that it might be fulfilled which was spoken" (appearing in none of the other gospels); "that which was spoken" or "it was spoken" (in Matthew and nowhere else). Matthew never lost sight of his audience, which was made up primarily of Jews trained to believe that when the Messiah came He would conquer all Israel's foes and make Jerusalem the capital of a Jewish world empire. Most Jews believed in the Christ but did not believe that *Jesus* was the Christ.

Matthew's gospel does not follow a strict chronological order. His method was to accumulate evidence for the messiahship of Jesus. He records, for instance, twenty specific miracles of Jesus (out of the three dozen recorded altogether in the four gospels), and half of them are lumped together in chapters 8 and 9. Moreover, these miracles, thus grouped together, follow three chapters of discourse. Matthew's aim was to produce cumulative proof that Jesus was the Messiah.

He tells us *what Jesus taught*, then *what Jesus wrought*, then *what people thought*. That seems to be his overall plan—and he concentrates on things that would interest the Jewish people: Did Jesus claim to be the Messiah? Was He of the line and lineage of David? Did He uphold the law? Did He fulfill the Old Testament prophecies about the Messiah? Had He come to establish a kingdom? What has happened to that kingdom? What was His relationship to the Establishment? In pursuing this objective, Matthew hammers home over and over again that Jesus fulfilled the Old Testament prophecies concerning the Messiah. Twelve times he says, "That it might be fulfilled," and follows up with an Old Testament quotation. Twelve times he uses the parallel expression "which was spoken . . ." and follows it up with an Old Testament quotation.[1]

The outline of Matthew shows clearly that Jesus is the long-awaited Son of David, King of Israel, and God's promised Messiah.

I. The King Is Revealed (chaps. 1–9)
   A. His Person (1:1–4:11)
      1. The Messiah's Ancestry (1:1–17)
      2. The Messiah's Advent (1:18–2:23)
      3. The Messiah's Ambassador (chap. 3)
      4. The Messiah's Adversary (4:1–11)

B. His Purpose (4:12–7:29)
  1. The King's Men (4:12–25)
  2. The King's Mandate (chaps. 5–7)
C. His Power (chaps. 8–9)
II. The King Is Resisted (10:1–16:12)
  A. The Resistance Foretold (chap. 10)
  B. The Resistance Felt (chap. 11)
  C. The Resistance Focused (12:1–14:12)
    1. The Malice of the Pharisees (chap. 12)
    2. The Mysteries of the Kingdom (chap. 13)
    3. The Murder of John (14:1–12)
  D. The Resistance Fades (14:13–36)
  E. The Resistance Fanned (15:1–16:12)
III. The King Is Rejected (16:13–27:66)
  A. The Shadow of That Rejection (16:13–25:46)
    1. The Private Discussions (16:13–20:34)
    2. The Public Disputes (chaps. 21–23)
    3. The Prophetic Discourse (chaps. 24–25)
  B. The Shape of That Rejection (chaps. 26–27)
    1. The Forming of the Plot (26:1–5)
    2. The Forecast at Bethany (26:6–13)
    3. The Falseness of Judas (26:14–16)
    4. The Feast of the Passover (26:17–30)
    5. The Fearfulness of Gethsemane (26:31–56)
    6. The Framing of the Trials (26:57–27:26)
    7. The Facts of the Crucifixion (27:27–56)
    8. The Finality of the Burial (27:57–66)
IV. The King Is Raised (chap. 28)
  A. The Light Dawns (28:1–10)
  B. The Lie Develops (28:11–15)
  C. The Lord Dominates (28:16–20)

I. THE KING IS REVEALED (CHAPS. 1–9)

Matthew begins with a revelation of His person.

A. His Person (1:1–4:11)

Matthew's first concern is to satisfy the Jews' curiosity.

1. The Messiah's Ancestry (1:1–17)

Matthew in effect goes back to the temple records, runs his unerring finger down the family tree, gives proof from the carefully preserved genealogical records that Jesus was the Son of David. That, in itself, was an important piece of evidence. Every Jew at least knew this—the Messiah *had to be* of the tribe of *Judah* and of the family of *David*.

It is important in writing a book to catch the attention of your audience as quickly as possible. Matthew did. He started to write down names—Abraham, David, Solomon, Rehoboam, Hezekiah, Josiah, Zerubbabel. Such a beginning would bore anyone but a Jew, but such a beginning would immediately arrest the attention of a Jew to whom these were much more than names. They were histories. These were names that could point in only one direction. These were names leading directly to a *Messiah*.

This listing of names would have a special significance to Jews raised on a knowledge of the Bible. The Jewish Bible contains the same books that we find in our Old Testament, but they are not in the same order. The last book in the Jewish Bible is not Malachi, although it is in there. The last book is Chronicles. The book of Chronicles begins with nine chapters of names, chronologies designed to show the Jews that, despite the Babylonian captivity and the disappearance of David's throne, the royal line was still intact. Matthew simply continues that royal line down through the silent centuries, showing that the royal line was not only still there but that it came to an end with Jesus. "Who shall declare his generation?" was Isaiah's prophetic challenge to the Jews who would murder the Messiah (Acts 8:33). Matthew dared them to investigate the genealogical claims of Jesus to be the Son and Heir of David. An hour or two with the archives in the temple would have been enough to prove Christ's claim. Matthew produces the proof that the Jews had neglected to obtain for themselves.

The genealogy of Christ as given by Matthew is not the same as that given by Luke. Matthew gives the regal line ending in Joseph, the foster father of Jesus, and showed Christ to be the Son of David and the Son of Solomon. Luke gives the legal line through Nathan, a brother of Solomon (2 Sam. 5:14), and ends with Mary, the Lord's mother.

2. The Messiah's Advent (1:18–2:23)

Every Jew knew that Messiah had to be born in one place and only one. A man might be a Jew of royal descent but if he was born in Jerusalem or in Athens or in Rome he could not possibly be the Messiah, no matter how pure his pedigree. He had to be born in Bethlehem. Jesus was. That was another piece of evidence that would impress the unbiased Jew. And this Man was born under auspicious circumstances. A new star appeared in the sky. Wise men came from the distant east, stirring Jerusalem and frightening the Idumean usurper on the throne. They asked, "Where is he that is born King of the Jews?" (2:2). The subsequent massacre of the babes of Bethlehem was a corroborating, incidental fragment of evidence. It had been foretold.

3. The Messiah's Ambassador (chap. 3)

Every Jew knew, too, that the Messiah had to be preceded by a prophet. God had promised to send Elijah and, behold, one coming in the spirit and power of Elijah had indeed announced the messiahship of Jesus. John the Baptist had come. He had hammered at the conscience of the nation and had insisted that the kingdom of heaven was at hand. He had told people to repent, and revival had broken out. The Jewish leaders scorned the whole thing, but the common people knew better. They believed that John was a prophet and more than a prophet, and John had said that *Jesus* was the Lamb of God come to take away the sins of the world.

4. The Messiah's Adversary (4:1–11)

But what kind of a *person* was He—this Messiah? Was He a good man? Was He not called "the holy one of God" by the prophets? What was His attitude toward sin?

Matthew records the Lord's temptation by Satan and shows that Jesus met Satan as *Man*, not as *God*. When Satan said, "If thou be *the Son of God*, command that these stones be made bread," Jesus answered, "It is written, *Man* shall not live by bread alone" (vv. 3–4).

Satan presented Jesus with the same great primeval temptations with which he overthrew the human race in the garden of Eden. He tempted Him with the lust of the eye, the lust of the flesh, and the pride of life, but failed to make any impression whatsoever upon Jesus. This temptation was permitted by God, not to see whether or not Jesus would sin, but to demonstrate that He could not sin. Any thought of disobeying His Father was alien to His nature. The very idea of sin was abhorrent to him.

B. His Purpose (4:12–7:29)

The temptation was over. John the Baptist was in prison. Jesus went at once to Galilee and picked up John's message: "Repent: for the kingdom of heaven is at hand" (4:17).

The King's men are introduced, particularly Peter and Andrew, James and John, along with a brief note about *the King's miracles*, which resulted in His being followed by enormous crowds. Matthew, however, was more interested in *the King's mandate*, the famous "Sermon on the Mount," which occupies three astonishing chapters. It was not so much that Jesus taught the people new things—although He promulgated the most demanding set of laws ever given on earth—He demanded a new spirit in keeping these laws. He took the great edicts of the law of Moses and the lessons of the prophets and lifted them to the plane of absolute perfection. He saw adultery in the lustful look, murder in the angry thought, theft in the covetous wish.

Those who think they can get to heaven by living a good life must live the Sermon on the Mount, something that is utterly impossible for sinful man. The only person who ever lived it was the One who gave it. Christianity is not copying Christ. Christianity *is* Christ—"Christ in [me], the hope of glory," as Paul put it (Col. 1:27). Nobody can even come close to keeping the edicts of the Sermon on the Mount apart from spiritual rebirth and the indwelling and filling of the Holy Spirit. Even then failure is all too evident because of the works of the old nature! Only Jesus lived the life of the Sermon, and He did so flawlessly all His life.

As we have noted, Matthew has a tendency to group his material so as to produce a cumulative effect. Five sections can be discerned in his gospel (4:12–7:28; 8:1–11:1; 11:2–13:53; 13:54–19:1; 19:3–26:1), all ending with the phrase "and it came to pass, when Jesus had finished. . . ." Each section ends with a discourse that reflects the Jewish manner of teaching in Bible times.

The Sermon on the Mount is one of these concentrated passages where Matthew aims for a cumulative effect. The Sermon on the Mount is peculiar to Matthew. Luke records many of the Lord's sayings on this occasion, but they are scattered throughout his gospel. The Sermon on the Mount as recorded by Matthew is one of the most revolutionary passages in the Bible. In sweeping statements the King revealed His concept of the kingdom as spiritual, otherworldly, and yet intensely practical. He boldly lifted the law of Moses to a higher plane and, brushing aside all cumbersome traditions and evasive interpretations, faced men with laws of behavior that, humanly speaking, are impossible to obey. Yet He practiced the life He preached, living it out day by day, moment by moment, for thirty-three and a half magnificent years.

C. His Power (chaps. 8–9)

No king who ever lived had such power as Jesus. He had power to command the leper to be clean, power to still the storm with a single word, power to raise the very dead. He had power over demons, over disaster, over disease, over death, over distance. Matthew piles up instance after instance. For just such a Messiah was promised by the prophets of old.

And not just naked power to awe and frighten, but the kind of miracles that showed He was *Savior* as well as *Sovereign*. For His miracles were parables, each with a spiritual message underlying the physical deed. He cleansed the *leper* to show His power over the corrupting, contaminating, crippling power of sin; He gave sight to the blind to show that sin's power to shut men's eyes to the truth ended with Him; He made the deaf to hear to prove that He could heal man's natural inability to hear God's voice; He made the fever flee to show that He could still the restlessness of the soul; He healed the man with the withered hand and the man who was lame to show that men could be set free to work for God and walk in His ways; He raised the dead to prove that He could speak life to a sin-deadened soul.

II. THE KING IS RESISTED (10:1–16:12)

A. The Resistance Foretold (chap. 10)

One would have thought that the world would go delirious with delight—to know that at last One had come who could conquer all earth's ills. But no, the world resisted Him. When the Jewish leaders discovered He had not come to perpetuate the system and confirm them in power, they rejected Him. As soon as they realized that the kingdom He offered was in truth the kingdom of *heaven*, that to get into that kingdom one must verily be born from above, that "except a man be born again, he cannot see the kingdom of God" (John 3:3), and that the citizens of His kingdom must repent of their sins, surrender to the Savior, be controlled by the Spirit of God, and live in newness of life, it was very strong medicine indeed. That kind of a king did not interest them at all. What *they* wanted was a king who would smash the power of Rome, make Israel an empire, Jerusalem capital of global power, and themselves heirs apparent to it all.

In chapter ten, Matthew tells how Jesus sent His twelve disciples across the country to spread the gospel of the kingdom, armed with power to work miracles. He told them they could expect severe opposition: "Behold, I send you forth as sheep in the midst of wolves," He said (v. 16). He foretold the hostility they would face. That hostility came to a final head in the period covered by the book of Acts when the nation of Israel, at home and abroad, confirmed its opposition to Christ and His church.

B. The Resistance Felt (chap. 11)

Matthew now records the imprisonment of John the Baptist by Herod and tells of John's doubts about his ministry. He records, too, the Lord's gentle solicitude for His brave forerunner and His high regard for him. The same opposition John had faced He would face. The significant expression, "this generation" (v. 16), is introduced for the first time into the Gospels, a reference primarily referring to the wicked generation that rejected Jesus as Messiah.

C. The Resistance Focused (12:1–14:12)

The turning point in this gospel comes in chapter twelve where Matthew tells how the Jews blasphemed the Holy Spirit. They accused Jesus of being in league with the Devil and of performing His miracles in the power of Satan. Jesus turned His back on them, walked out of their affairs, and prepared for the journey home.

But first, He enunciated the parables of the kingdom of heaven (chap. 13). These parables were intended to conceal the truth from the Christ-rejecting crowd and to reveal the status of the kingdom of heaven while the King is absent from heaven. In a sense, the kingdom has gone underground. The manifestation of the kingdom is now postponed until the time of the King's return, and its affairs on earth are discernible only by those who are in on the secret.

The growing opposition to the new age, now being introduced, came to a sudden focus in the murder of John the Baptist and the Lord's temporary retirement from the public eye.

D. The Resistance Fades (14:13–36)

The crowds, however, soon found Him in His place of retirement and thronged Him again. The feeding of the five thousand that followed led to a momentary break in the resistance to Jesus. The crowds would welcome *this* kind of a king— one who would load them with temporal benefits.

E. The Resistance Fanned (15:1–16:12)

But now the scribes, the Pharisees, and the Sadducees took offense at Him again and began to oppose Him every possible way, because Jesus poured scorn upon the rabbinical traditions and refused to give them the sign they demanded. "A wicked and adulterous generation seeketh after a sign," He said (16:4).

III. THE KING IS REJECTED (16:13–27:66)

A. The Shadow of That Rejection (16:13–25:46)

Matthew traces that rejection first in the *private discussions* of Jesus. He records those heart-to-heart talks Jesus had with His disciples, especially after Peter's great confession. The Lord made it increasingly clear that He was now heading directly for the cross. The idea horrified them. Peter remonstrated and was roundly rebuked. Then, on the Mount of Transfiguration, Moses and Elijah appeared—and the topic of their discussion with Jesus was, again, the decease He would accomplish at Jerusalem.

Matthew then tracks the rejection in the *public disputes* of Jesus (chaps. 21–23). We witness, for instance, the *triumphal entry* and the cleansing of the temple followed by verbal attacks upon Him by the various religious classes of the nation— the priests and elders, the Herodians, the Sadducees, and the Pharisees. These attacks called forth the fearful denunciation of the Jewish religious leaders by Jesus.

As His public preaching had begun with eight beatitudes of blessing, so it closed with eight terrible woes. Then, in a final gesture of dismissal, He gathered up all the martyrdoms of God's people in the Old Testament and heaped the blood-guiltiness of the world on the heads of the generation that rejected Him and plotted against Him. The crime they were about to commit—the crime of crucifying their King— was so great that they might as well be guilty of every crime. This crime swallowed up all lesser crimes. It still does. God does not send people to hell because they kill and steal and commit adultery and wallow in foul forms of sexual perversion. He sends them to hell for rejecting His Son.

As the shadow darkens, the Lord's private discussions and public disputes give way to the *prophetic discourses* of Jesus (chaps. 24–25). This is His last great sermon in Matthew. The first was given on a mountain, so was this last one. The first we call the Sermon on the Mount, this one we call the Olivet Discourse; the first was given in Galilee, this one in Jerusalem; in that one we have *precepts*, in this one *prophecy*; the first had to do with *His rule*, this one with *His return*; then the kingdom was in *prospect*, now it is *postponed*.

With swift strides, the Lord Jesus hurries us down the centuries, lingering a little longer over our own times, pointing out the salient features of the present age and focusing on end-time events. He answers the great, overriding question of the disciples when it dawned on them at last that the kingdom was now in abeyance: "*What shall be the sign of thy coming?*" (24:3). He said, "*Watch the fig tree*" (see 24:32). Watch Israel! When the nation of Israel comes back to life again, *then* you can expect My return.

And with the conclusion of this great prophetic discourse, the Lord was through. Just two more days were left—then the cross.

B. The Shape of That Rejection (chaps. 26–27)

The plots against Christ deepened. The palace of Caiaphas, the high priest, became the center of a conspiracy to do away with Jesus, and Jesus again and again warned His disciples of what was coming. Then Judas decided to cash in on the situation and salvage what he could from this sinking ship. He made his treacherous arrangements with the priests to betray Jesus into their hands.

In the upper room, the Lord Jesus kept His last Passover. He and His disciples feasted upon the slain lamb, and His thoughts were filled with the deep, symbolic significance of it all. Then Peter made his proud boast that he, at least, would never deny his Lord and was quietly told that he most certainly would, and that before the crowing of the cock.

Then Matthew takes us into *Gethsemane* to show us what passed during those dark hours when the King prepared Himself for betrayal and death. As the hymn writer puts it,

Three times, alone, in the garden
He prayed, Not My will, but Thine—
He shed no tears for His own griefs
But sweat drops of blood for mine.
—Charles H. Gabriel,
"I Stand Amazed in the Presence"

And all the time Peter, James, and John slept.

Then came the mob led by Judas, who betrays the King with a traitor's kiss. The King is about to be arrested when Peter draws a sword, and with a wild, slashing sweep he prepares to defend his King. He is quietly told to put up his sword. Not thus is the King to be defended. Even at that very moment, yonder in the glory, there were twelve legions of angels with drawn swords. They waited only a word, one word from Him, and they would stamp flat the high hills of Judah, turn to blood the waters of the seven seas, and usher in *Armageddon* then and there. But no word came. Not thus, not yet, was the kingdom to come.

Matthew does not record all the trials. He does not tell of all the comings and goings. He is concerned just to show us the guilt of both Jew and Gentile, to show Jewish mockery and Gentile mistrial. First the Sanhedrin condemned Jesus. It put Him under oath, and under oath He solemnly told the Jewish leaders that indeed He was the Son of God. They accused Him then of blasphemy, spat on Him, mocked Him, sentenced Him to death, and handed Him over to Pilate.

But Pilate did not know what to make of Him. He had faced many a vociferous prisoner, loudly protesting his innocence—but here was a Prisoner who said nothing. It is Matthew who best records the Roman's dilemma: "What shall I do then with Jesus which is called Christ?" and the obdurate answer of the Jews: "Let him be crucified" (27:22).

And so it was. Matthew tells us how the King was mocked, how they arrayed Him in a scarlet robe, crowned Him with thorns, bowed the knee before Him, made fun of Him, spat on Him, and hit Him on the head with the reed they had given Him for a scepter. The King endured all this brutal horseplay, His back one vast congealing wound from the brutal scourging He received.

Then came the journey to Calvary, and the last dastardly act. The horrible details of the actual crucifixion are mentioned only in passing. Our attention is directed by Matthew to the title on the cross: This is Jesus of Nazareth, the King of the Jews. It is Matthew who tells us that the Jews mocked Him with the words, "If He be the King of Israel, let Him now come down from the cross and we will believe Him" (see 27:42). They should have remembered the noble answer of Nehemiah when his enemies, in his day, tried to tempt him down from the wall: "I am doing a great work . . . why should the work cease, whilst I leave it, and come down to you?" (Neh. 6:3).

Matthew, too, tells us how Christ reigned as a *King* on that cross. He tells us how Jesus put out the sun, how He rent the temple veil, split open creation's rocks, burst wide the tombs, shook the place with an earthquake, and converted the centurion and his men.

And, when it was all over, Matthew says there came a man named Joseph, Joseph of Arimathea, a very rich man (reputed, indeed, to be one of the wealthiest men in the land), who begged the body of Jesus from the shaken and humbled governor. And so the King was buried with a degree of dignity for, after His death, none but the hands of His friends ever touched Him again.

IV. THE KING IS RAISED (CHAP. 28)

It is Matthew who emphasizes that this astonishing event marked "*the end of the sabbath*" and that it was "as it began to dawn toward the *first day of the week*" (v. 1). That was a note for the Jews. The end of the Sabbath! Judaism was obsolete; the rent veil signaled that. And now "the end of the Sabbath" had come. There was to be a new day, a new age, a new dispensation, something centered in the first day of the week.

It is Matthew, too, who records the stubborn, persistent unbelief of the Jewish leaders in propagating the lie that the disciples had stolen the body of Christ—thus to give some feeble explanation for the empty tomb.

It is Matthew, too, who tells of the great commission. Now the gospel is to go forth and spread throughout the world—to all nations. No longer is the message to be kept inside the cramping confines of the Jewish fold; it has become a message for all mankind.

And it reaches us here, today. The *King* is alive! He confronts us where we are. And, like the Jews of Jesus' day, we have the same choice: to *crucify Him* to ourselves, or to *crown Him* Lord of our lives. Neutral we cannot be.

CHAPTER 5

MARK

Behold My Servant

John Mark was the son of that Mary who lived in Jerusalem and whose home was one of the meeting places of the early church (Acts 12:12). John was his Jewish name, Mark his Roman name. When Paul and Barnabas set out on their first missionary journey, John Mark went along to minister to them in the capacity of a servant (Acts 13:5). No sooner did the missionaries reach the mainland of Asia Minor, however, than Mark abandoned the enterprise, sowing the seeds of a later serious quarrel between Paul and Barnabas. Afterward Mark made good in the Lord's work and was even commended by Paul, who had felt so strongly about Mark's desertion. It would seem that Mark came under the influence of Peter and that, between the ministry of Barnabas and Peter, Mark was recovered to the work of the Lord.

There are some interesting traditions about Mark. One is that he founded the church in Alexandria in Egypt, and that he was martyred there in A.D. 68. His body is said to have been removed by a merchant and taken to Venice, where a great church stands in his honor. He had a nickname—"Mark of the short finger." According to one version of the Vulgate, Mark deliberately cut off one of his fingers after he became a Christian so as to disqualify himself for the Jewish priesthood. Another version of the Vulgate says he was born with this defect. In any case, it is generally accepted that the tradition is true that Mark had a mutilated hand. Be that so or not—he certainly turned his hand to good account when he wrote this gospel.

He wrote it before the fall of Jerusalem, some think as early as A.D. 50, which would make it the earliest of the New Testament documents. He is generally believed to have written it at Rome. The language he uses is not elegant, and some of his Greek words and phrases would not be used by strict grammarians, but they would be just the kinds of words used by the slaves and freedmen who made up the earliest congregations of the church in Rome.

There seems little doubt, either, that Mark was inspired by the Spirit of God to give us the gospel as it was preached by Peter, especially as recorded in Acts 10:34–43. Further, in proportion to the other synoptics, Mark mentions Peter the most. Mark's gospel begins at the point where Peter became a disciple, and pays special attention to the Lord's Galilean ministry and especially to His activities around Capernaum, where Peter lived. Mark tells us about Peter's mother-in-law's being healed by Jesus, that it was Peter who drew the Lord's attention to the withered fig tree, that it was Peter and his brother who asked Jesus about the destruction of the temple, and that it was one of the missions of the angels at the resurrection to send a special word of encouragement to Peter.

Generally speaking, however—as we might expect if Peter had a large influence in the writing of this gospel—things that are favorable to Peter are omitted, and things that depreciate Peter are included. It has been said that if the hand that wrote the gospel was Mark's, the voice that speaks is Peter's. In other words, the main source of information upon which Mark drew for this gospel was Peter, who, of course, was able to give firsthand facts about the ministry of Jesus.

When Peter was first sent to the Gentiles, it was to the house of Cornelius, a Roman centurion living in Caesarea. We have an account of Peter's sermon on that occasion. He told the story of Jesus to this Roman and his household, beginning with the ministry of John the Baptist and ending with the ascension (Acts 10:34–43). In essence, Peter gave the substance of the gospel message that the evangelists were preaching everywhere. Mark's gospel follows the exact same ground. Mark fills in the details, but in essence his gospel is an expansion of Peter's sermon to that noble Roman. We are not surprised, therefore, to find that, while Matthew wrote for Jews, Mark wrote for Romans. He has a Roman audience in mind from beginning to end.

We note, for instance, that Mark presents the Lord Jesus at work—for the Romans were a practical people; they got things done. They would not be much interested in the religious questions that so interested the Jews. They would be interested in what Jesus *did* more than in what Jesus *said*. Mark's gospel, therefore, has fewer Old Testament quotations than either Matthew or Luke—he quotes about 63 times from the Old Testament but of these, all but 18 are quotations used by Jesus.

With his Gentile audience in mind, Mark often interprets and explains Jewish words and customs for the benefit of his readers. He explains the meaning of words and names such as Gehenna, Golgotha, Abba, and Bartimaeus. He explains Jewish customs; he gives the location of the Mount of Olives; he explains when the Passover was killed; explains that Jordan is a river. None of these explanations would have been necessary for a Jewish audience. He mentions that the father of

Alexander and Rufus was Simon the Cyrenian, the man who carried the cross for Jesus. This would be of particular interest to the Roman believers since these two men were in their church.

Since the Romans were the masters of the world and had made slaves of millions of people, Mark presents Jesus as a slave! Not the slave of a Caesar, of an empire, or of some social system, for no man was ever His master. He was the slave or the servant of God.

It is Mark who picks up Isaiah's challenge: "Behold my servant" (Isa. 42:1; 52:13). It is particularly interesting that Mark should be the one to present Christ in this light, for he, himself, had singularly failed as a servant. He had gone with Barnabas and Saul to be their servant or their "minister," and he had failed. He shows us One who did not fail. He shows us One always busy, always at work, never tiring, carrying on patiently right to the end.

The key verse in Mark is 10:45: "The Son of man came not to be ministered unto [not to be served], but to minister [to serve], and to give his life a ransom for many." On that verse we can split the gospel. One of the world's missionary societies has as its logo a picture of an ox. On one side is a plow, on the other side an altar. Underneath are the words, *Ready for either*. Such is the gospel of Mark. On the one side of the Lord Jesus is the plow—"The Son of man came not to be ministered unto, but to minister"; on the other side is the altar—"and to give his life a ransom for many." And emblazoned across the whole, *Ready for either*.

Mark's specialized presentation of Jesus as God's perfect Servant comes out in other ways quite apart from his selection of material. For instance, Jesus is addressed as "Lord" no less than 73 times in the other three gospels (by His disciples 37 times and 35 times by others), yet He is addressed that way only twice in Mark.

Here is the way Mark put his gospel together.

I. The Servant Gives His Life in Service (chaps. 1–10)
    A. The Servant's Work (chaps. 1–3)
        1. The Work Begun (chap. 1)
            a. The Servant's Credentials
            b. The Servant's Character
            c. The Servant's Companions
            d. The Servant's Competence
        2. The Work Belittled (2:1–3:6)
            a. Finding Fault with His Method
            b. Finding Fault with His Men
            c. Finding Fault with His Ministry
        3. The Work Blessed (3:7–19)
        4. The Work Blasphemed (3:20–35)

B. The Servant's Words (chaps. 4–5)
   1. Exact in Purpose (4:1–34)
   2. Executive in Power (4:35–5:43)
C. The Servant's Ways (6:1–8:26)
   1. The Attitude of Others to God's Servant (6:1–29)
   2. The Attitude of God's Servant to Others (6:30–8:26)
D. The Servant's Worth (8:27–9:13)
E. The Servant's Will (9:14–29)
F. The Servant's Wisdom (9:30–10:52)
   1. Perfect Wisdom (9:30–50)
   2. Penetrating Wisdom (10:1–31)
   3. Practical Wisdom (10:32–52)
II. The Servant Gives His Life in Sacrifice (chaps. 11–16)
A. By Precipitating the Crisis of Calvary (chaps. 11–12)
   1. By What He Did (11:1–26)
   2. By What He Declared (11:27–12:44)
B. By Portraying the Cross of Calvary (13:1–14:31)
   1. In Public (chap. 13)
   2. In Private (14:1–31)
C. By Paying the Cost of Calvary (14:32–15:47)
   1. The Will of God (14:32–41)
   2. The Wickedness of Man (14:42–15:15)
   3. The Way of Sacrifice (15:16–47)
D. By Proving the Crime of Calvary (chap. 16)
   1. By Conquering the Grave (16:1–14)
   2. By Conquering the Globe (16:15–20)

I. THE SERVANT GIVES HIS LIFE IN SERVICE (CHAPS. 1–10)

A. The Servant's Work (chaps. 1–3)

1. The Work Begun (chap. 1)

Every servant is expected to produce some testimonials. When someone applies for a job, one of the first questions asked of the potential employee is, "Who can recommend you?" Mark tells us that Jesus was no exception, and he mentions Jesus' *credentials*. John the Baptist tells, in fact, the world, coming in the spirit and power of Elijah to announce that One far greater than he is here.

Mark mentions next Jesus' *character*. For that, too, is important in a servant, especially one to be employed in a position of great trust where he is likely to be exposed to a great deal of temptation.

When I left school I worked for a large bank. Inquiries were made into my character and I was put to work where it could be observed by those in authority. Soon I was moved to a smaller branch, where I was given greater responsibilities, including control over one of the keys to the vault. Obviously, character was an important factor in being employed in a place of trust where large sums of money and all kinds of negotiable securities were daily to pass through one's hands.

Mark tells us how Jesus, in His position of great trust, faced temptation. He does not go into many details, but he does add one interesting sidelight: Jesus was "with the wild beasts" (that's the one extreme), and "the angels ministered unto Him" (that's the other extreme [v. 13]). On the one extremity we see the wild beasts and Satan; on the other we see Jesus and the angels of God.

Then Mark mentions Jesus' *companions*. When a person is to be placed in a position of trust, the kind of company he keeps is of great account. We see this Servant choosing companions from the ranks of working-class people, those who were busy in the heat of the day. After all, the time would come when these people would have to carry on His work. It was important that they were not afraid of work themselves.

Then Mark shows us Jesus' *competence*. This, too, is of prime importance in a servant. Can he get the job done? We are left in no doubt about the competence of this Servant. He plunges right away into the gigantic task of clearing up the mess Satan has left behind him in his occupation of this planet. In the very first chapter, Jesus is seen busy, casting out an evil spirit, healing Peter's mother-in-law, touching and cleansing a leper. The work has begun.

2. The Work Belittled (2:1–3:6)

Introduce a new man on the job, a man who is not afraid of work, who is prepared to tackle any task, who is obviously far more competent and efficient than anyone else around, who shows up instantly the utter incompetence of those who have previously been dabbling with the job—and there is a man who will earn the active dislike of the others. They will sneer at him and belittle him. Mark gives us four examples of what the old crowd said about Jesus, four examples of the kind of malicious gossip that was circulated about Him in and around the place where He exhibited what a perfect Servant of God He was.

They found fault with His *method*: "How is it that he eateth and drinketh with publicans and sinners?" (2:16). They found fault with His men: "Why do the disciples of John . . . fast, but thy disciples fast not?" (2:18). "Behold, why do they [His disciples] on the sabbath day that which is not lawful [pluck and eat the ears of corn]?" (2:24). In other words, they found fault with what they *didn't* do, and they found fault with what they *did* do. They found fault with His *ministry*: "Why doth this man thus speak blasphemies? who can forgive sins but God only?" (2:7).

Their tongues were soon belittling Him, trying to undermine His work. We can hear them: "Look at the kind of company He keeps. A fine credit He is to the work of God—why, He even went into a tavern." "The Sabbath is our day off, we're supposed to take it easy on that day, but look at Him and His people—they actually *work* on the Sabbath. And look at the outrageous claims He makes for Himself!" We can hear them any time a Christian comes onto the job and refuses to go along with the go-slow, feather-bedding system applauded by others. Just so, Jesus' work was belittled.

3. The Work Blessed (3:7–19)

We read, "And great multitudes followed Him from Galilee and from Judea and from Jerusalem and from beyond Jordan, and they about Tyre and Sidon, a great multitude, when they heard of what great things he did, came unto him" (see 3:7–8). It is hard to argue with success. People saw what Jesus could *do*. So they came to Him. Why go to the old crowd? All the old crowd did was put them off with the same old dry-as-dust formulas that did not work and never had worked. Let's try this new Man. And so they did, to the increasing fury of the old crowd, as we can well imagine.

The work was blessed. Jesus had the crowds. Nor did He disappoint them. He gave His life in *service*, such service as this poor old world has never seen before or since.

4. The Work Blasphemed (3:20–35)

The blasphemy came first from His own *family*: "He is beside himself," they said (v. 21)—just because He was so busy He would not stop His work for lunch. Then by His *foes*: "He hath Beelzebub, and by the prince of the devils casteth he out devils," they said (v. 22). He had so thoroughly exposed their own incompetence and unfitness to be the servants of God that all they could do was slander His character.

B. The Servant's Words (chaps. 4–5)

For this Servant had a great deal to say to those to whom He had come to minister. And His words were precise.

1. Exact in Purpose (4:1–34)

Mark does not dwell long on the discourses of Jesus, but he gives us samples enough to see that this Servant knew what He was talking about. In keeping with the purpose of his gospel, however, Mark is far more concerned to show that, when this Servant spoke, His words had authority.

2. Executive in Power (4:35–5:43)

He spoke and it was done! He spoke words that had power to still the storm, power to instantly dismiss evil spirits, power to heal cases no doctor could cure, power to raise the very dead. What servant of Caesar ever spoke with such authority as Jesus?

C. The Servant's Ways (6:1–8:26)

1. The Attitude of Others to God's Servant (6:1–29)

Mark now records various reactions to the ministry of this marvelous Servant. Back in the synagogue of Galilee people depreciated Him: "Is not this the carpenter?" they said (6:3). His own disciples knew better, of course. Jesus sent them forth, armed with His own authority to preach the word and to work miracles. In his palace, wicked King Herod was smote in his conscience. He imagined Jesus to be John the Baptist risen from the dead.

2. The Attitude of God's Servant to Others (6:30–8:26)

Mark again plunges us into a round of activity. He tells how Jesus fed the five thousand and walked upon the waves, how He cared for other people's happiness, hunger, hardships, and health. He even tells us how He cared about their hypocrisy. He reasoned with the Pharisees over their legalistic, traditional teachings, especially on the matter of ritual versus real cleanliness. His heart went out to the Syrophoenician woman, He delivered a dumb man, fed the multitudes again, gave sight to a blind man. He was always busy, looking out for others, filled with compassion for them, eager to help them.

D. The Servant's Worth (8:27–9:13)

Mark records two great, unforgettable instances in the life of Peter and the Lord. He records the highlight of *what Peter said*—the magnificent exclamation of Peter: "Thou art the Christ" (8:29). Peter, as spokesman for the disciples, shows the Lord that, no matter what others might say about Him, His closest followers knew His worth.

Mark records, too, the highlight of *what Peter saw*. Jesus took Peter, James, and John and was transfigured before them. Then came Moses and Elijah to talk with Jesus about His impending death. Peter knew His worth. Years later he summed it all up: "We have not followed cunningly devised fables, when we made known unto you the power and coming of our Lord Jesus Christ, but were eyewitnesses of his majesty. For he received from God the Father honor and glory, when there came such a voice from the excellent glory, This is my beloved Son, in whom I am well pleased. And this voice which came from heaven we heard, when we were with him in the holy mount" (2 Peter 1:16–18).

E. The Servant's Will (9:14–29)

They came down from the mount. In the valley below was a vignette of the world—a demon-possessed boy, a distracted father, a disillusioned multitude, a demoralized "church." Faced with this situation, which they instinctively felt they should have been able to handle, the disciples were not only powerless but overwhelmed. Then Jesus came. There was something about Him that struck one and all with utter astonishment—*ekthambeō* is Mark's word for it, a word used only here and in 14:33 and 16:5–6, suggesting that people sensed they were in the presence of the supernatural, in touch with another world. Jesus at once took charge, asserted His sovereign will, delivered the lad, silenced the critics, and enlightened His disciples to the true sources of spiritual power.

F. The Servant's Wisdom (9:30–10:52)

Mark now gives some examples of the wisdom of God's perfect Servant. It was, of course, *perfect wisdom* (9:30–50). He foretold His coming death, burial, and resurrection; showed His disciples the path of true greatness; warned them of the perils of hell's fire. It was, indeed, a wisdom not of this world. It was also *penetrating wisdom* (10:1–31). Jesus talked about a man and his wife (vv. 1–16) and gave some straight talk about divorce and its consequences. He talked about a man and his wealth (vv. 17–31) and exposed the peril of riches. His disciples were astounded. "Who then can be saved?" (v. 26). If a rich man finds it so hard, then what chance has anyone else? Whoever heard of riches being a spiritual liability? "And what about us?" they wanted to know. "We have left all to follow you" (see v. 28). You have invested for eternity, Jesus told them. Your investment will earn ten thousand percent. His wisdom, moreover, was *practical wisdom* (10:32–52). Again He forced the disciples to face the inevitable fact of His coming crucifixion. When James and John, still imbued with thoughts of personal grandeur in the day of His glory, asked for places of signal honor, He warned of the high cost that must be paid for such posts of honor.

II. THE SERVANT GIVES HIS LIFE IN SACRIFICE (CHAPS. 11–16)

The Lord Jesus refused to trim His sails to suit those who considered themselves to be the true servants of God. Indeed, with time running short, He intensified His efforts, knowing full well that—in the end, the rage and resentment of the high priests and rabbis, of the Pharisees and Sadducees—all the corporate conglomerate of religion would not stand for being so thoroughly exposed as Jesus exposed them, and not retaliate.

In the second part of Mark's gospel, we trace five distinct provocative movements.

A. By Precipitating the Crisis of Calvary (chaps. 11–12)

He did a number of things to bring to a head the growing opposition to Himself and His work.

1. By What He Did (11:1–26)

He did three dramatic things. First He rode in triumph into Jerusalem to fulfill an Old Testament prophecy about the Messiah (Ps. 118:25–26). He thus provoked His opponents along *religious* lines. Then He symbolically cursed the fig tree—a well-known symbol for the Jewish nation. He thus provoked His opponents along *political* lines. Then he chased the money-changers out of the temple, infuriating the Sadducees who had a monopoly of the lucrative concessions that did business there. He thus provoked along *financial* lines. Offend people along those three lines—the religious, the political, and the financial—and you won't have to seek your trouble.

2. By What He Declared (11:27–12:44)

When speaking to His opponents the parable of the vineyard, for instance, He exposed the *rottenness of their government*. And in telling them to pay tribute to Caesar, He endorsed the *reality of Roman government*. It would be hard to think of two more provocative things calculated to infuriate them than that—to tell them that their government was a *fraud* and that Roman government was a *fact*.

B. By Portraying the Cross of Calvary (13:1–14:31)

1. In Public (chap. 13)

Next we have Mark's account of the Olivet Discourse—that grand and sweeping statement of Jesus in which He portrayed the results, for the world, of the murder of the Messiah—war, persecution, deception, the great tribulation. Without Him to manage God's affairs on earth, it is inevitable that chaos will eventually descend upon the world. But be of good cheer! He's coming back!

2. In Private (14:1–31)

He kept the Passover. First, however, while in the house of Simon of Bethany, He received the homage of a woman who came to anoint Him with costly ointment in anticipation of His burial.

Then, with His disciples, He kept the Passover—His last Passover. The only people who keep the Passover now as it was kept in Jesus' day are the Samaritans. They take their lamb, slay it, and impale it. A piece of wood is driven through it lengthwise and another from side to side. It is then roasted, impaled upon the cross of wood.

This last Passover of Jesus was marred by the presence of Judas the traitor, loudly protesting his loyalty to the end.

C. By Paying the Cost of Calvary (14:32–15:47)

Mark takes us to *Gethsemane* and tells of the agony in the garden, of Peter's boast, and how Peter went to sleep. Mark takes us to *Gabbatha* and shows us the mock trial of Jesus, and Peter warming himself at the world's fire, and denying the Lord with oaths and curses. Then Mark takes us to *Golgotha* and describes the crucifixion, the conversion of the centurion, and the governor's astonishment when Joseph came and begged for the body. How could He be dead so soon? And what would motivate one of the richest and best-known Sanhedrin Jews to come begging for the body of a Man the Sanhedrin had forced him to crucify?

D. By Proving the Crime of Calvary (chap. 16)

1. By Conquering the Grave (16:1–14)
Wicked men might thus summarily dismiss this Servant from His sphere of service—but He comes back! And the nail prints in His hands condemn them as they condemn us and all mankind. Here was the crime of crimes. And when this case is brought to trial in a coming day, the only ones who will be able to stand will be those who have come in repentance and taken those pierced hands into theirs by faith, and sued for His forgiveness.

2. By Conquering the Globe (16:15–20)
"Go ye into all the world, and preach the gospel to every creature" (v. 15). And forth they went, with the signs He promised following them here, there, and everywhere.

Such is the gospel of the Servant. Years ago, a Bedford tinker sat in the city jail and dreamed those marvelous dreams we know as *Pilgrim's Progress*. He tells of a pilgrim fleeing from the City of Destruction with a burden on his back—a burden of sin, which grew heavier the longer he read in the Book of God. That burdened pilgrim was a picture of the lost children of Adam's ruined race. To these there comes a glorious Man with scars in His hands and the light of heaven in His face with the blessed promise of rest. For when Bunyan's Pilgrim came at last to Calvary, the burden was loosed from his back, rolled down a steep place, and disappeared into an open tomb. Then Pilgrim went on his way, rejoicing, a song in his soul:

> Blest cross! Blest sepulcher,
> But blessed rather be
> The One who there was put to shame for me.
> —John Bunyan

This, then, is the great burden of Mark's gospel. The Servant has come to lift our intolerable burdens. He has carried the great burden of human sin and sorrow to Calvary, His mighty shoulders bowed beneath the weight of the whole world's sin. He has come to set us free. Now all that remains is for us to tell the good news to all mankind.

CHAPTER 6

LUKE

Behold the Man

L uke is referred to by name only three times in the New Testament (Col. 4:14; 2 Tim. 4:11; Philem. 24). From these three references we learn that Luke was a physician, that he was one of Paul's fellow workers, and that he was with Paul during his last dreadful imprisonment in Rome, when almost all the world had abandoned him. It is practically certain that Luke was a Gentile. The consensus of opinion seems to be that he was born in Antioch in Syria. William Ramsay, that great scholar and archaeologist, acknowledged to be one of the world's leading authorities on the life of the apostle Paul, had a different idea. He believed that Luke was "the man from Macedonia" who walked into Paul's camp the morning after the great vision that turned the gospel westward toward Europe.

Luke, then, was probably a Gentile and most likely a Greek. He was certainly a medical man. In his day there were three great university cities to which a man could go to get his degree in medicine: Athens, Alexandria, and Tarsus. The appealing idea is that Luke took his medical training at Tarsus, which was the birthplace of Paul, and that he and Paul, being much the same age, went to the same university, and it was there that they met and forged the first links in their lifelong friendship.

It is certain that Luke and Paul traveled together and that Luke was greatly influenced by Paul's grasp of the gospel and by Paul's understanding of the significance of the cross. We first see the two together on Paul's second missionary journey, where Luke first shows up right after Paul's vision at Troas. He accompanied the missionary party as far as Philippi. On Paul's third missionary journey, the two were together again. He meets up with Paul at Philippi and stays with him all the way to Jerusalem. He shared Paul's journey to Rome, his shipwreck, and the exciting experiences of that momentous journey.

Theories abound about Luke. Some have theorized that he was one of the seventy disciples of Jesus sent out by Christ on an evangelistic mission, that he was one of the two disciples on the Emmaus road, that he had been a slave in the household of a wealthy government official in Antioch by the name of Theophilus, that Theophilus had him trained as a doctor, that Luke led Theophilus to Christ, and that Theophilus thereafter gave him his freedom. It has been speculated, too, that Luke and Titus were brothers. Some have even speculated that Luke wrote the epistle to the Hebrews, which hardly seems likely if Luke were a Greek.

Internal evidence strongly suggests that Luke wrote for Gentiles and particularly for Greeks; to the Greeks belonged Homer and Plato and Aristotle. He explains Jewish customs and locates Jewish places—something that would not be necessary if he were writing for Jews. He quotes from the Old Testament but says little or nothing about fulfilled prophecy. He tends to substitute Greek names for Hebrew names.

In writing his gospel, Luke uses two writing styles. His introduction (1:1–4) is written in elegant and idiomatic Greek. He changes suddenly to Hebraistic Greek. Then he returns to the Greek style.

He tells us that he relied on sources for his material. Doubtless he met such people as Mark and Mary and probably he met all the apostles. He knew Philip the Evangelist, very likely he talked to people like Zacharias and Elisabeth, the parents of John the Baptist, as well as to Martha and Mary, and to others of like nature. Above all he talked about these things over and over again with his dear friend, Paul, who, while not one of the original disciples of the Lord Jesus, had been to Jerusalem often enough and personally knew many of the people who belonged to the infant church.

Opinion is divided as to when he wrote his gospel, but for various reasons it seems that Luke's gospel was written either at Caesarea or at Rome sometime between the dates of A.D. 58 and A.D. 63. In A.D. 64 Nero burned Rome, in A.D. 68 Paul was martyred, and in A.D. 70 the Romans reduced Jerusalem to rubble. In all likelihood Luke's gospel was written before any of these things took place.

Luke wrote for the Greeks as Matthew wrote for the Jews and Mark for the Romans. The Greeks were the custodians of the world's culture, language, art, science, and philosophy. They were the intellectuals of the ancient world, their great ideal being perfect manhood; their Olympic games were intended to display such manhood. They made their gods in the image and likeness of man, and then peopled Mount Olympus with gods like fallen men. They projected the lines of fallen humanity into infinity with the result that their gods were fallen supermen and their religion was carnal and debasing and wholly unsatisfying to even the emptiest human heart. Luke gives back to the Greeks a perfect Man. He says to them, in effect, "Here's the perfect Man you have been seeking. His name is Jesus. Project the lines of *His* personality into infinity and you will find that unknown God for whom you have been looking so long." Jesus is God in focus!

The key verse in Luke's gospel says, "For the Son of man is come to seek and to save that which was lost" (19:10). The gospel of Luke, then, presents to us Jesus as Savior and as the Son of Man. Luke's gospel contains many beautiful portraits, and its pages are crowded with people. It is also the gospel of womanhood. We meet Elisabeth and the Virgin Mary; Anna; Martha and her sister, Mary; Mary Magdalene. These constant references to women in this gospel are all the more remarkable since they occur in a gospel for the Gentiles—where in general women were often degraded. Thus, this gospel emancipated womanhood.

It is the gospel of sympathy. We see the heart of Jesus reaching out in pity to all in need. He is the friend of sinners. It is the gospel for those in all ages for whom the world had no gospel—the poor, the sick, the aged, the insane, the widowed, the orphaned, the maimed, the criminal, the blind.

It is the gospel of forgiveness. Luke tells of Peter's asking whether forgiving someone seven times would be adequate, only to be told that seventy times seven would be more appropriate. It is Luke who records the Lord's prayer on the cross: "Father, forgive them; for they know not what they do" (23:34).

It is the gospel of song. Four hymns are found, in fact, only in Luke's gospel— the Magnificat of Mary (1:46–55), the *Benedictus* of Zacharias (1:64–79), the *Nunc Dimittis* of Simeon (2:29–32), and the *Gloria in Excelsis* of the angelic hosts (2:14). All have to do with the birth of Christ—an event that indeed brought "joy to the world."

It is the gospel of prayer. As Man, dependent on the Father, the Lord is constantly seen in prayer (3:21; 5:16; 6:12; 9:18, 29; 11:1; 22:32, 41; 23:34, 46). On six specific occasions, Luke shows us the Lord praying; seven times he makes mention of glorifying God in praise. Seven of the Lord's prayers are recorded only by Luke.

It is the gospel of the home. We are in and out of homes throughout the book— that of Simon, Zaccheus, Simon the Pharisee, the home of the two Emmaus disciples.

It is the gospel of angels, which are referred to twenty-three times.[1] They were sent to Zacharias, to Mary, to Joseph, to the shepherds. They carried poor Lazarus to Abraham's bosom. They constantly ministered to the Lord.

It is the gospel of salvation. It contains the word "sinner" more often than all the other gospels put together. The writer is fond of Pauline words such as grace, forgiveness, salvation, repentance, mercy, faith.

I. Introduction (1:1–4)

Luke begins by telling us that many "have taken in hand" (*epicheireō*) the task of narrating (*diēgēsis*) the great truths connected with the gospel. At once he uses two of those medical words that are such a marked feature of his writings. The first is found, for instance, in Acts 9:29 and 19:13 connected with the idea of failure; the other word, occurring only here in the New Testament, was used by the celebrated physician Galen of a medical textbook.

Luke tells us that his gospel was prepared specifically for one *Theophilus* (v. 3, a common-enough Roman name meaning "beloved of God"), who Luke calls "most excellent Theophilus," a title indicating social status. He says that his method was to draw up a statement derived from his personal investigation and interviews with those who were "eyewitnesses" (another medical word, *autoptai*, from which we derive our word autopsy) and "ministers of the word" (v. 2).

II. Events Relating to the Savior's Coming (1:5–4:13)

A. His Birth at Bethlehem (1:5–2:39)

Luke gives us the fullest account of the Christmas story and does so with delicacy, feeling, and much human interest. We never tire of reading of the visits of the herald angel, of the sweet confidences that passed between Mary and her cousin Elisabeth, of the birth of John the Baptist, of the humble birth of God's beloved Son, of the worship of the shepherds, and of the glad messages of Simeon and Anna.

Both Matthew and Luke make it quite clear that the Lord Jesus was virgin born; that He had a human mother but no human father. In Him deity and humanity were combined. The Son of God became the Son of man so that the sons of men might become the sons of God. He entered into human life to become near of kin to our ruined race so that He might be able to redeem us to God by His blood so that we might be allowed to enter into His family.

B. His Boyhood at Nazareth (2:40–52)

Only Luke records the remarkable incident that occurred when Jesus was twelve years of age—an important age in Jewish life, when a boy assumed responsibility for his behavior. He was taken to Jerusalem for the Passover and tarried there in the temple when everyone else headed for home.

How that temple gripped His young heart! It was His Father's house. When the sorrowing Mary and Joseph found Him in the midst of the doctors, Mary rebuked Him: "Thy father and I have sought thee sorrowing," she said (v. 48). We have then the first recorded words of Jesus: "Wist ye not that I must be about my Father's business?" (v. 49). Joseph was not His father. They knew it; He knew it. His Father's business was not the work of a carpenter; it was the work of the cross. He knew that, too. His first recorded word introduced that wonderful word *Father* into human speech as a glorious and significant name for God.

Then "he went down with them, and came to Nazareth, and was subject unto them" (v. 51)—an object lesson for all entering the difficult teenage years of life.

C. His Baptism in Jordan (3:1–22)
Luke carefully and meticulously dates the ministry of John the Baptist. His ministry was designed to awaken the nation to a sense of its sin, and a people to their need of a Savior in view of the imminence of the Lord's coming. Tremendous interest was aroused around the country. Then Jesus came and identified Himself with the race He had come to save by being baptized in the Jordan.

Soon afterward Herod Antipas arrested John for preaching against his theft of his half-brother Philip's wife Herodias.

D. His Background in History (3:23–38)
In keeping with his purpose, Luke traces the Lord's ancestry right back to Adam. He does not stop with David, founder of the Hebrew royal family, or with Abraham, founder of the Hebrew racial family. By going back to Adam, he shows the Lord's relationship not just to the *Hebrew* family but to the *human* family. Jesus was the last Adam, the second Man. Luke traces the Lord's ancestry through Mary, a descendant of David and Bathsheba, not through the main line from Solomon but from a collateral line through Nathan. The marriage of Joseph and Mary brought both lines together.

E. His Battle with Satan (4:1–13)
The Lord's temptation was precipitated by the Holy Spirit, who had just anointed Him for service as a sequel to His baptism. Luke tells us that the period of forty days Jesus spent alone, fasting in the wilderness, was one long period of testing and temptation. The culmination came in the effort to get the Lord to step outside the will of God, act in independence, and seek to achieve His life's goals in some way other than that ordained by God.

Of particular interest is Luke's report of the temptation that sought to persuade Jesus to win the crown without the cross. Luke says, "And the devil, taking him up into an high mountain, showed unto him all *the kingdoms* of the world in a moment of time. And the devil said unto him, All this *power* will I give thee, and the *glory* of them. . . . If thou therefore wilt worship me" (vv. 5–7). He offered Him the kingdoms, power, and the glory. But Jesus had not come to receive "kingdoms," the war-torn divided kingdoms of this world; He had come to receive *The* kingdom. Nor was He about to trade "the glory that he had with the Father before the worlds began" (see John 17:5) for the tarnished and tinsel glory of this sin-cursed world. And as for the "power," it was not *dunamis* (untrammeled, unhindered, absolute power) that Satan offered, but *exousia*, "power subject to another power," that is, delegated authority.

No wonder Jesus instantly turned it down. Such an offer He simply scorned quite apart from the perjured character of the tempter, the "father of lies."

And, it is worth noting, in each of the temptations there was an *if.*

III. Events Relating to the Savior's Career (4:14–21:38)

A. The Work in Galilee: His Anointing in Focus (4:14–9:50)

1. The Work Is Commenced (4:14–5:16)

Luke hurries us from place to place. First we see the Lord in the synagogue of Nazareth, where He had been raised as a boy. There He formally announced His anointing and deliberately told the people of Nazareth some home truths, which infuriated them. They made the first of those repeated attempts, instigated by Satan, to kill Him.

Next we see Him in the synagogue of Capernaum, a town on the Sea of Galilee, where He had now taken up residence. There, an evil spirit, who possessed a man, acknowledged Him to be "the Holy One of God" (4:34) and was silenced and cast out—something that made a deep impression on the people.

Then we see Him in Simon Peter's home, where He healed Peter's mother-in-law. That same evening, He performed many miracles of healing.

Later, having preached in various Galilean synagogues, He is seen at the seaside teaching people from Simon's boat. There, He also rewarded Peter for the use of his boat, producing a large and miraculous catch of fish.

Then He is in "a certain city" (5:12), probably one of those like Chorazin or Bethsaida, in which "most of His mighty works were done," where He healed a man "full" (one of Luke's medical words) of leprosy.

2. The Work Is Criticized (5:17–6:11)

Luke gives four instances of Jesus' receiving criticism. The first took place at a conference of doctors of the law, convened from all the cities of the three major regions of the country. The Lord healed a man in their presence, but first He forgave the man his sins. Then, knowing their thoughts (highly critical of Him for, in their mind, He had blasphemously usurped a prerogative belonging only to God), He read them a lesson in omnipotence as well as omniscience, which sent them away amazed, glorifying God, filled with fear, and perplexed.

The conversion of Levi (Matthew) provoked the next burst of criticism, for the Lord at once accepted Matthew's invitation to come and meet his publican friends—something no self-respecting Jew desirous of protecting his reputation would think of doing. "I came not to call the righteous, but sinners to repentance" (5:32), was the Lord's devastating reply to their caustic comments.

The third incident arose when the Lord's disciples plucked and husked some corn on the Sabbath day—something forbidden by rabbinical tradition and teaching. The Lord defended His disciples by bypassing the foolish rabbinical restrictions and referring His critics back to the Bible.

On another Sabbath, this time in a synagogue, He deliberately healed a man with a withered hand. He knew His enemies were watching Him, now actively looking for an occasion to use against Him. His probing, infuriating question about doing good on the Sabbath, followed, as it was, by a deliberate healing, filled the scribes and Pharisees with anger.

3. The Work Is Climaxed (6:12–9:50)

Luke now gives four quick glimpses of the Lord, before turning attention to the mounting opposition Christ had to face.

We see a *dependent Savior*, One engaged in prayer before making the full and final choice of those twelve men. To them, He would entrust the future of His cause on earth.

We see a *dynamic Savior*, going about doing good, healing the sick, raising the dead, casting out demons, feeding the multitudes, empowering His disciples, stilling the storm, teaching with grace and power, triumphing everywhere. The evidence that He was all He claimed to be was overwhelming.

We see a *divine Savior*, challenging His disciples to declare who He really was, the Christ of God; giving His first intimation that the cross lay ahead for Him; revealing Himself to the inner circle of His disciples on the mount of transfiguration. Then, after coming down from the mount, He healed a poor demoniac boy possessed of a particularly violent demon who defied all attempts by the disciples to exorcize him.

We see a *discerning Savior*. Fully conscious now that Calvary was coming closer, He seeks to teach His disciples the path of quiet humility and cooperation with those who "followeth not with us" (9:49) but whose love for God was very evident, indeed.

B. The Way to Golgotha: His Adversaries in Focus (9:51–21:38)

The turning point now comes. Luke says, "And, . . . when the time was come that he should be received up, he steadfastly set his face to go to Jerusalem" (9:51).

Luke has shown us the Savior at work, but we do not read far into Luke's gripping account of Christ's ministry before we meet the Lord's enemies, who coldly criticize Him on religious grounds. These enemies of Christ are prominent in Luke's gospel. But Luke sweeps us on, showing us the dynamic Christ—dynamic in His words and in His works, in His ways and in His walk, in His wisdom and in His will. Distance cannot prevent the going forth of His power, as the centurion whose servant was sick discovered; neither can death, as the widow of Nain found out. Neither the tempest nor the terrorist can thwart His will, for the dynamic Savior is also divine.

But Christ had His enemies—many of them—and Luke dramatically shifts the emphasis to them and shows how the perfect Man handled all His foes. The *scholastic approach* was tried by a certain lawyer who "stood up, and tempted him, saying, Master, what shall I do to inherit eternal life?" (10:25). Certainly this man was convicted when the Lord told the parable of the Good Samaritan and then drove the point home.

The *slanderous approach* drew forth a terrible warning of the unpardonable sin from the lips of God's Son. To blaspheme the Holy Spirit shall not be forgiven.

The *sophisticated approach* was tried by a certain Pharisee. He invited Jesus to dinner, then sneered at Him secretly for not washing His hands.

The *systematic approach* was tried next. We read, "The scribes and the Pharisees began to urge him vehemently, and to provoke him to speak of many things: Laying wait for him, and seeking to catch something out of his mouth, that they might accuse him" (11:53–54). Of course they failed.

The *sermonic approach* was tried by the ruler of the synagogue. He was indignant because Jesus healed a crippled woman on the Sabbath day. "There are six days in which men ought to work," carped this man. "In them therefore come and be healed, and not on the sabbath day" (13:14). Jesus bluntly and publicly told this man he was a hypocrite.

The *scare approach* was tried next, as some warned Jesus that Herod would kill Him. Jesus' answer was to call Herod a fox.

The *subtle approach* was tried by one of the chief Pharisees. This man invited Jesus home with him to break bread on the Sabbath, but waited to pounce should Jesus heal a man afflicted with dropsy.

The *sarcastic approach* was used by the Pharisees and scribes on yet another occasion. They sneered, "This man receiveth sinners, and eateth with them" (15:2). This sarcastic thrust only drew forth the three priceless parables of the lost sheep, the lost silver, and the lost son.

The *scoffing approach* was also evident. We read that "the Pharisees . . . derided him" (16:14) for His teaching on covetousness.

The *selfish approach* was manifested in the ingratitude of the nine lepers. Their neglecting to thank Him deeply hurt the Lord.

The *snobbish approach* is apparent in the Pharisees' demand. They asked Him, "When will the kingdom of God come" (see 17:20)?

The *straightforward approach* of Christ's enemies became increasingly prominent after the triumphal entry into Jerusalem. "The chief priests and the scribes . . . sought to destroy him," we read (19:47).

The *seductive approach* was the last recorded. They threw questions at Him, which were "loaded" both politically and religiously, and then hired Judas for his act of treachery.

Books could be written about all these approaches. All we can do here is expand on a few examples.

The scholastic approach (9:51–10:42) shows us only what passes for scholarship. For to reject Christ is not scholarship at all. It is a species of insanity. The Lord Jesus, we remember, was tackled by a man the Holy Spirit describes as "a certain lawyer" (10:25). This man wanted to know what he should *do* to *inherit* eternal life. Jesus told him to read his Bible. After all, he was supposed to be an expert in Levitical law. Jesus told him to start by fulfilling the second great commandment. Then the man wanted to know, "Who is my neighbor?" (10:29). And Jesus told him the story of the Good Samaritan, forced him to confess that the despised Samaritan was a better neighbor than either priest or Levite, and concluded with the barbed thrust, "Go, and do thou likewise" (10:37). Of course the man would need a new heart for that!

And the scholarly lawyer went away very much put out. For Jesus had deliberately put *him* in the story. One of the men who had passed by the robbed and wounded wayfaring man was a lawyer, a Levite. And as for the good Samaritan, the Levite would not have fellowshipped with him at any price. The scholar rejected Christ because Christ identified Himself with the hated Samaritan. There was nothing rational or logical or sane or sensible about this "scholastic" rejection of Christ. It was simply a case of prejudice. Jesus did not say the right kind of things.

Of the systematic approach (11:53–13:9), we read that after the Lord denounced the Pharisees for their religious hypocrisy "the scribes and the Pharisees began to urge him vehemently, and to provoke him to speak of many things: Laying wait for him, and seeking to catch something out of his mouth, that they might accuse him" (11:53–54). This was a systematic, deliberate, intentional, calculating rejection of Christ.

There are still people like that. They will comb the Bible, looking for errors and contradictions. And, when they think they have found one, they think themselves very clever and make that their excuse to go to hell. Their real problem is their love of sin and their hatred of Christ for exposing it and pointing to Himself as their only hope of salvation.

The Lord followed up this attempt to gang up on Him. His fresh and fervent denunciations of the leaders of Israel for their rejection of Himself were accompanied by warnings and revelations concerning His coming again.

The Sabbath provided an ironically appropriate day for the sermonic approach (13:10–30). The Jews of Jesus' day had woven around the Sabbath such a knotted tangle of traditional interpretations, such a web of dos and don'ts, that the whole thing had become a solemn but burdensome farce. That which God had intended to be a great *blessing* to men—a day of rest from labor and toil, a day set apart for Himself in which men could gather and worship Him—had become instead a great *burden*. People had come to loathe and dread the Sabbath. You couldn't do this, you couldn't do that, you couldn't go here, you couldn't go there. It was the Sabbath Day.

Jesus was where you might expect to discover Him on the Sabbath, in the local synagogue. Into that synagogue came a poor woman bent double with curvature of the spine. She had been like that for eighteen years. When Jesus saw her His heart went out to her, and He called her to Him. As we can imagine, every eye was on Him. There was a sudden stillness in that synagogue, and one could feel the tension in the air. "Woman," He said, "thou art loosed from thine infirmity" (v. 12). And, giving added force to His words, He put His hands on her. Instantly she straightened up and began to praise and glorify God. Of course she did! Here was a crooked woman made straight by Jesus.

Now listen to the instant rejection of Christ by the leader of the synagogue. He stood up and addressed the people. "There are six days in which men ought to work," he said. "In them therefore come and be healed, and not on the sabbath" (v. 14). This pious fraud had nothing good to say about Jesus and nothing to say about the good Jesus had just done. The petty rules of his denomination had been broken, and he began to lecture the people on their religious duty.

Jesus cut him short, "You hypocrite!" He said. "You've got a donkey, haven't you? On the Sabbath day—the Sabbath day, mark you—you loose your donkey from the stall and lead it away to get a drink. *You do that on the Sabbath*. And here is a poor woman. Satan has bound her for eighteen long, miserable years. Why should she not be loosed on the Sabbath?" (see vv. 15–16).

There are many people like that leader. They cover up their rejection of Christ with a great deal of religious cant. But it is rejection just the same, rejection as deep and as bitter and as damning as any other kind. In many ways it is, in fact, worse, for there is no opposition to the gospel more vehement than that sponsored by dead religion.

For the sarcastic approach (15:1–32), we read, "And the Pharisees and scribes murmured, saying, This man receiveth sinners, and eateth with them" (v. 2). Of course He did! That was why He came. They indignantly pulled their robes around them and looked down their noses at the harlots, the publicans, the openly vile who Jesus had come to save. In answer to their jibe, He told the matchless stories of the lost sheep, the lost silver, and the lost son. Men are lost by following natural tendencies, or by a sudden fall. Jesus told how God loved the lost and how God had sent Him to seek and to save that which was lost.

Then He added a postscript to the story. He painted a picture of the prodigal's older brother, painting him into the picture, using deft strokes. He put into the lips of the older brother the sneers and snobbery that boiled like a witch's cauldron in their own shallow souls: "Thou never gavest me a kid. . . . But as soon as this thy son was come, which hath devoured thy living with harlots, thou hast killed for him the fatted calf" (vv. 29–30).

God is not impressed by sarcastic jibes. Yet, wonder of wonders, He loves the poor, carping hypocrites just as much as the wayward prodigal. He would have them come and join the feast as well. But they had no interest in coming on terms such as that—they would rather reject Him than associate with such a low-bred crowd as He would include in His kingdom.

And so it went on and on. Chapter after chapter of it. Jesus rejected of men. For one shallow reason or another. Until, in the end, they threw off all pretense and came out openly and boldly as His enemies, determined to get rid of Him and live their lives without Him.

IV. EVENTS RELATING TO THE SAVIOR'S CROSS (CHAPS. 22–24)

A. The Table (22:1–38)

First we gather with the Lord and His disciples in the upper room for that last sad Passover. Judas was there with Satan in his heart (22:3) and the silver in his purse. He had been bought for a paltry thirty pieces of silver, and Satan was now in full possession of his property. Judas thought he had sold Jesus when, all the time, he had sold himself.

"He took bread, and gave thanks." What a revelation of the heart of the Savior. Having given thanks for the bread, He "brake it" and said "This is my body" (v. 19). There, in the upper room, He gave thanks for the breaking of His body soon to take place. "Hallelujah! What a Savior!" He gave *thanks*, well knowing all that lay ahead for Him in the next few hours.

B. The Tears (22:39–53)

Luke takes us next to dark Gethsemane. It is Luke, the physician, who tells us that so great was His agony that "his sweat was as it were great drops of blood falling down to the ground" (v. 44). Some think that Satan tried to kill Him there.

C. The Trials (22:54–23:31)

Luke takes us first to the palace of the high priest, where the Lord overheard Peter's sad denials, was mocked and smitten, and then "put to the question"—a question He answered unequivocally with an absolute claim to be the Son of God.

We are taken then to Pilate's judgment hall, hurried off to Herod who, being unable to persuade Jesus to perform a miracle and being faced with a stony silence, mocked Him. This was the Herod who had murdered John. To him Jesus had nothing to say.

Then we are taken back to Pilate's judgment seat. There, we witness Pilate's three futile appeals to the Jews and his capitulation before their dreadful demand for Christ's death.

We are taken out onto the Calvary road next. Simon the Cyrenian is forced to carry the cross for Jesus and to hear the Lord warn the daughters of Jerusalem that judgment was on the way.

D. The Tree (23:32–49)

It is in Luke we find the word "Calvary" (v. 33, the Greek for "Golgotha," literally "a skull"). We are so familiar with the word from our hymnbooks we tend to think it one often used in the Bible. In the beloved King James text, it occurs only this once.

Luke tells us of the mocking and of the malefactors, of the darkness and of Christ's death, of the confession of the centurion, and of the dismay of the crowds. Like all the evangelists, Luke treads lightly over this ground and passes over with but the barest possible words the harrowing details of death by crucifixion.

E. The Tomb (23:50–56)

Luke draws our attention to "a man named Joseph"—a "good man" is his description of him—a counselor, a member of the Sanhedrin, a dissenter from the majority vote, which consigned Jesus to the death of the cross.

This notable counselor had the respect of Pilate, who instantly released the body of Jesus to his custody. Joseph had a tomb ready for his own burial, a tomb he surrendered to Jesus. Thus the life of the Lord Jesus on earth is bounded by two Josephs—one to serve Him when He was *born*; the other to serve Him when He was *buried*. Two more honorable men could scarcely be found.

F. The Triumph (chap. 24)

Death could not hold its prey! Luke tells us of the early morning visit of Mary Magdalene, Mary the mother of James, Joanna, and other women to the tomb. He tells us the interesting story of the incident on the road to Emmaus. He takes us into the upper room to show us the risen Christ appearing in the midst of His disciples, and adds that fascinating touch about Jesus eating a meal to prove to the disciples that His body was real, that He was not just a ghost.

Then Luke, taking us farther than the others, leads us out to the Mount of Olives to witness the Lord Jesus ascending bodily into heaven. He leaves us witnessing the joy and wonder of the disciples as they were "continually in the temple, praising and blessing God" (v. 55).

Then he puts down his pen with one last resounding "Amen!" only to pick it up again soon thereafter to write the equally fascinating book of Acts.

CHAPTER 7

JOHN

Behold Your God

John declares his purpose in writing his gospel. It was to present the Lord Jesus as God, to tell of His impact on humanity, and of the twofold reaction to Him— belief on the one hand and unbelief on the other. In John's gospel, Jesus calls God His Father 156 times. The word *believe* occurs 100 times, and the word *know* occurs 142 times. Other key words are the characteristic words of John—love, life, and light. His gospel was written in the last decade of the first century, when Christianity had already taken firm root in the world, and when various heresies were already on the rise.

John's emphasis is entirely different from that of the other three gospels. There is no genealogy, no birth, no boyhood, no temptation, no Gethsemane. There are no scribes, no lepers, no publicans, and no demoniacs. John does not relate a single parable. The miracles he records are almost all different from those in the Synoptics. John looks at things in sharp tones of black and white with no shades of gray. In John it is light and darkness, life and death, spirit and flesh, heaven and earth, truth and error, love and hate, Christ and the Devil, God and the world, faith and unbelief.

The only incidents John records in common with the other evangelists are the work of John the Baptist, the Last Supper, the anointing at Bethany, the passion, the resurrection, and two miracles—the feeding of the five thousand and the walking on the Sea of Galilee. The Synoptic Gospels place great emphasis on Christ's ministry in Galilee, but John concentrates on Jerusalem and Judea, hence the Lord's visits to the feasts are given special prominence (2:13–3:21; 5:1; 6:4; 7:10; 10:22; 11:55). It is from John's gospel that we determine the length of the Lord's public ministry—approximately three and a half years.

Dr. Graham Scroggie[1] points out that Luke's gospel and John's dovetail the one into the other in a most remarkable way. It is just as if two halves of a broken jug were to be brought together so that every indentation of the one corresponds to every protuberance of the other, as John carefully avoids relating incidents related by Luke.

I. Prologue (1:1–18)
   A. The Divine Life in Its Essence (1:1–5)
   B. The Divine Light in Its Evidence (1:6–13)
   C. The Divine Love in Its Experience (1:14–18)
II. The Signs of the Son of God: The Lord's Deity in Focus (1:19–12:50)
   A. His Deity Is Declared (1:19–4:54)
      1. The Testimony of John (1:19–51)
         a. Its Faithfulness (1:19–34)
         b. Its Fruitfulness (1:35–51)
      2. The Triumphs of Jesus (2:1–4:54)
         a. The Wine at the Wedding: Triumph over Life's Sudden Disappointments (2:1–12)
         b. The Traffic in the Temple: Triumph over Life's Secular Debasements (2:13–25)
         c. The Night with Nicodemus: Triumph over Life's Spiritual Deceptions (3:1–21)
         d. The Jews and John: Triumph over Life's Saddening Discouragements (3:22–36)
         e. The Woman at the Well: Triumph over Life's Sordid Defilements (4:1–42)
         f. The Faith of a Father: Triumph over Life's Sorrowful Disablements (4:43–54)
   B. His Deity Is Disputed (5:1–10:42)
      1. The Impact of His Life (5:1–6:71)
         a. In Urban Jerusalem (5:1–47)
            (1) The Impotent Man Challenged (5:1–15)
            (2) The Impenitent Men Challenged (5:16–47)
               (a) The Indictment Raised (5:16)
               (b) The Indictment Refuted (5:17–38)
                  i. The Witness of His Own Father (5:17–32)
                  ii. The Witness of His Own Forerunner (5:33–35)
                  iii. The Witness of His Own Fruits (5:36–38)
               (c) The Indictment Reversed (5:39–47)
         b. In Rural Galilee (6:1–71)

      (1) Christ's Claims Revealed (6:1–40)

        (a) In His Power (6:1–21)

          i. Publicly: The Breaking of the Bread (6:1–15)

          ii. Privately: The Walk upon the Waves (6:16–21)

        (b) In His Preaching (6:22–40)

      (2) Christ's Claims Resented (6:41–71)

    2. The Implications of His Life (7:1–10:42)

      a. His Exposition of the Word of God (7:1–8:1)

        (1) The Animosity of His Family (7:1–10)

        (2) The Arguments of the Jews (7:11–29)

        (3) The Antagonism of the Rulers (7:30–8:1)

      b. His Exposure of the Wickedness of Men (8:2–9:41)

        (1) Convicting Them (8:2–11)

        (2) Contradicting Them (8:12–59)

        (3) Confounding Them (9:1–41)

          (a) Delivering the Blind Man (9:1–34)

          (b) Defending the Blind Man (9:35–41)

      c. His Explanation of the Way of Life (10:1–42)

        (1) His Death in Focus (10:1–21)

          (a) The Two Systems (10:1–10)

          (b) The True Shepherd (10:11–21)

        (2) His Deity in Focus (10:22–42)

          (a) His Response to Their Challenge (10:22–30)

          (b) Their Response to His Challenge (10:31–42)

  C. His Deity Is Disowned (11:1–12:50)

    1. Some Examples of His Rejection (11:1–12:36)

    He is rejected in spite of:

      a. His Feat of Power (11:1–12:11)

      b. His Fulfillment of Prophecy (12:12–19)

      c. His Fervor in Prayer (12:20–36)

        (1) The Visit of the Greeks (12:20–26)

        (2) The Voice of God (12:27–36)

    2. Some Explanations of His Rejection (12:37–50)

III. The Secrets of the Son of God: The Lord's Disciples in Focus (13:1–17:26)

  A. The Talk in the Upper Room (13:1–14:31)

    1. The Background of the Talk (13:1–30)

      a. The Table (13:1–3)

      b. The Towel (13:4–17)

      c. The Traitor (13:18–30)

    2. The Burden of the Talk (13:31–14:31)

       a. Another Commandment (13:31–35)

       b. Another Coming (13:36–14:7)

       c. Another Commission (14:8–15)

       d. Another Comforter (14:16–31)

    B. The Walk on the Gethsemane Road (15:1–17:26)

      1. He Talked to Them About the Father (15:1–16:33)

      2. He Talked to the Father About Them (17:1–26)

IV. The Sorrows of the Son of God: The Lord's Death in Focus (18:1–20:31)

    A. He Is Falsely Condemned (18:1–19:15)

      1. He Is Arrested (18:1–12)

      2. He Is Arraigned (18:13–19:15)

       a. Before the Priests (18:13–27)

       b. Before the Procurator (18:28–19:15)

    B. He Is Finally Crucified (19:16–42)

      1. An Act of Government (19:16–24)

       a. The Sentence (19:16–18)

       b. The Superscription (19:19–22)

       c. The Soldiers (19:23–24)

      2. An Act of Grace (19:25–27)

      3. An Act of Greatness (19:28–30)

       a. Deliberately He Received the Sponge (19:28–29)

       b. Deliberately He Released His Spirit (19:30)

      4. An Act of God (19:31–42)

       a. The Protection of His Bones (19:31–37)

       b. The Provision for His Burial (19:38–42)

    C. He Is Fully Conqueror (20:1–31)

      1. Revelations at the Empty Tomb (20:1–18)

       a. The Wondering Disciples (20:1–10)

       b. The Weeping Disciple (20:11–18)

      2. Revelations in the Upper Room (20:19–31)

       a. All Distress Banished (20:19–23)

       b. All Doubts Banished (20:24–31)

  V. Epilogue (21:1–25)

    A. The Same Dynamic Life (21:1–14)

    B. The Same Determined Love (21:15–17)

    C. The Same Discerning Light (21:18–25)

John's special viewpoint of the Lord Jesus comes out everywhere in his gospel. It was the last gospel to be written, one of the last books of the New Testament to be written. The apostolic age was almost over. John stood alone, looking back now over the century, which had begun with the birth of Jesus. Gnosticism was already taking fast root in the church despite the warning voices raised against it. Half a dozen epistles warned against all kinds of error, heresy, and apostasy. John raised his voice in a gospel, in three brief epistles, and an apocalypse. Matthew wrote for the Jews, Mark for the Romans, Luke for the Greeks. John wrote for the church. Jesus was and is God, over all, blessed for evermore. He was truly Man, man in every sense of the word, but He was also God. John studiously avoids recording what has already been written about Christ. He saw no point in laboring points already made. No! What was needed was a definitive answer to mounting attacks upon the person of Christ. What was needed was a gospel that would say again, once and for all, that the Lord Jesus Christ was God manifest in flesh.

John selects his material with care. In John's gospel, for instance, the Lord is never depicted as praying to the Father, as He is in the other gospels, but always as speaking to Him. The English word "pray" found in John 16:26; 17:8–9, 15, 20 is from the word *erōtaō*, which literally means "to ask," and implies familiarity, even equality. The usual word for prayer is *proseuchomai*. Prayer was appropriate for a king, a servant, a man dependent on God at all times. But in John's gospel, Jesus is God. He talks to His Father, never acts in independence, tells us much of the unique relationship between Himself and His Father, assures us that the works He does are His Father's works. While the other gospels—which all emphasize aspects of His humanity—show the Lord Jesus in prayer on various occasions, He is never so shown by John. Talking to the Father? Yes. All the time. Praying to Him? No! Not in the usual sense of the word.

I. Prologue (1:1–18)

John's three characteristic words are life, light, and love—just as Paul's characteristic words are faith, hope, and love. John's gospel, in the original, has a vocabulary of about six hundred words—the vocabulary of a seven-year-old. But, if John's words are few, they are of great worth. John's vocabulary does not go in much for small change. He uses words minted of gold and of high denomination.

A. The Divine Life in Its Essence (1:1–5)

John says nothing about the manger but instead carries us right up to the throne. He shows us One who *transcends all thought*: "In the beginning was the Word, and the Word was with God, and the Word was God" (v. 1). That was not a *start* but a *state* (the word *was* is in the imperfect tense). He was God. He was also *with* God. Those two statements affirm His essential deity and His distinct personality. He was the "Word" (the *Logos*). As the spoken word reveals the invisible, inscrutable thought, so the living Word is the perfect expression of the invisible God. All that God is—in His nature, person, and personality—so Jesus is. He is the articulated, visual expression of the invisible God. This is a thought beyond all thought.

John shows us One who *transcends all time*: "The same was in the beginning with God" (v. 2). He goes back beyond the beginning of all things. Astronomers postulate a beginning for the universe, a time, in the remote past, when all the matter in the universe was concentrated in an inconceivably small, dense mass. Then came "the big bang." It was the beginning of time. Before that—they refuse to go. The Holy Spirit takes us that one step beyond. Jesus was there.

John shows us One who *transcends all things*: "All things were made by him; and without him was not any thing made that was made" (v. 3). Every sun and star, every cloud and continent, every speck of dust drifting in the coldness and the darkness of outer space, every blade of grass, every living creature, every human being—He made them all. He is the source and sum of all life. His is eternal, un-created, self-existing life. He is coequal and coeternal with the Father and the Spirit. His life is God's life. Thus John begins.

B. The Divine Light in Its Evidence (1:6–13)

"There was a man sent from God, whose name was John. The same came for a witness, to bear witness of the Light, that all men through him might believe" (vv. 6–7). That was John the Baptist, who is mentioned twenty times[2] in this gospel. John's great work was to bear witness to the Light, which had now come into the world with the advent of Jesus. At once, the evangelist pays down one of his gold-minted coins of vocabulary—"that all—might *believe*." This is the gospel of belief.

C. The Divine Love in Its Experience (1:14–18)

"And the Word was made flesh, and dwelt among us, (and we beheld his glory, the glory as of the only begotten of the Father,) full of grace and truth" (v. 14). This is a marvelous description of the Lord Jesus and about as close as John ever comes to the cradle. The word for *dwelt* is, literally, "tabernacled." That is, He pitched His tent, so to speak, among us. The tabernacle in the Old Testament spoke throughout of Christ. There was nothing very beautiful about it on the outside, but it was all glorious within—where everything was of gold; richly dyed fabric—scarlet, blue, purple; fine-twined linen; the Shechinah glory cloud bathing all in the light of an-other world. The glory of the Lord Jesus was thus. It was a covered glory. The glory was there, but it was veiled by His flesh. Thus John, in four words, describes the incarnation, where Luke uses 2,500.

At once, John brings us to the essence of the new dispensation. "The law," he says, "was *given* by Moses, but grace and truth *came* by Jesus Christ" (v. 17). In the days of Moses there was grace (Exod. 34:6–7, and particularly the book of Deuteronomy), and the law itself was the embodiment of truth. But in Jesus we see truth incarnate (14:6), and in His life and death such an exhibition of grace and love as this world has never seen before or since.

II. THE SIGNS OF THE SON OF GOD: THE LORD'S DEITY IN FOCUS (1:19–12:50)

A. His Deity Is Declared (1:19–4:54)

1. The Testimony of John (1:19–51)

Having introduced the Eternal Word made flesh, John gets right down to his theme—showing how John the Baptist faithfully witnessed to Jesus both as the Lord and as the Lamb. He showed how the disciples of the Baptist "heard him speak, and they followed Jesus" (1:37). He told how they recognized Him as Messiah, and how Nathanael confessed Him as "Son of God" and "King of Israel" (v. 49).

2. The Triumphs of Jesus (2:1–4:54)

Most of the well-known miracles of the Synoptic Gospels are missing in John's gospel. Instead, we have specially selected proofs of Christ's deity in what John calls "signs." The first of these was at Cana, where we have *the wine at the wedding*, the first miracle of Jesus and one performed not only to relieve an embarrassing social situation but to convince His disciples of His claims. This took place in Cana of Galilee.

Next we find Jesus in Jerusalem for "the Jews' passover" (2:13). "The Jews" is a characteristic expression in John, and a pointed way of highlighting the consequences of Israel's rejection of the Messiah. Instead of "Israel" they are now called "the Jews," the name by which they were known to the Gentiles. It was "the Jews' Passover," no longer God's. Similarly, we read of "the feasts of the Jews" (5:1; 6:4; 7:2; 11:55; 19:42) instead of "the feasts of the Lord" as they were called in the Old Testament.

In Jerusalem the Lord confronted *the traffic in the temple*. The Sadducees had a controlling interest in the temple. They profited from the concessions in the court, where ordinary money was changed into money for the temple tax and where animals for sacrifice could be purchased. Jesus accused the Jews of turning His Father's house into a common marketplace and proceeded to clean it up, much to the surprise and annoyance of those concerned, and who responded with a vehement demand for an explanation.

Then followed *the night with Nicodemus* and the Lord's definitive teaching on the need for being born again. In this section occurs the text of texts, John 3:16—perhaps the greatest single statement on salvation in the Bible. We can observe the ten contrasting words that make up this famous text: God and the Son; the world and whosoever; loving and giving; believing and having; perishing and everlasting life.

John inserts here a parenthesis, *the Jews and John*, to show John the Baptist's glorious humility and happiness in the success, so far, of Jesus' ministry. Far from being discouraged because he was now being eclipsed by Jesus, he saw this as right and proper.

There follows the lovely story of Jesus and *the woman at the well*. We can underline the different words she used to describe this unusual Stranger who asked her for a drink and then offered her living water—Jew, Sir, Prophet, Christ. The whole story is a masterpiece of soul-winning. We should note the Lord's statement: "God is a Spirit: and they that worship him must worship him in spirit and in truth" (4:24)—in *spirit* because of what He is, in *truth* admitting what we are. The woman was a Samaritan. Most Jews would go miles out of their way to avoid Samaria. Not Jesus! He went into their city, stayed there two days, and won numbers of the Samaritans to faith in Himself. He saw "the fields . . . white already to harvest" (4:35).

The final incident in the series concerned *the faith of a father*—a nobleman (i.e., a royal officer, probably of the court of Herod Antipas) whose son was sick. He dared to believe that Jesus could heal, even from a distance, and his faith was rewarded. This second sign was also performed in Galilee.

B. His Deity Is Disputed (5:1–10:42)

1. The Impact of His Life (5:1–6:71)

a. In Urban Jerusalem (5:1–47)

There was first the case of *the impotent man* at the pool of Bethesda. The waters of the pool had a reputation for healing, a healing that was said to take place at certain times when the waters were disturbed. Popular belief explained the whole thing in terms of angelic activity. The man in question certainly believed the common tradition, so did many others. This poor man had patiently waited for thirty-eight years for a miracle to happen to him. Time and again, when the waters surged, people all about him had flung themselves into the pool. Not him. He needed help to get in. He had been there more than half a lifetime, abandoned by all. Except Jesus. Jesus healed him, told him to take up his bed and walk—and that on the Sabbath day.

Then there was the case of *the impenitent men* who were infuriated with Jesus for having dared violate the Sabbath—the Sabbath, that is, as it was supposed to be kept according to rabbinical teaching and tradition.

There followed one of those long verbal skirmishes Jesus had with the Jews, especially with the leaders of the nation. He referred them to His Father: "My Father worketh hitherto, and I work," he said (5:17). This is one of the many times in this gospel that God is called His "Father" (the expression "the Father" and "my Father" occurs over 150 times). "The Jews sought the more to kill him," says John, "because he not only had broken the sabbath, but said also that God was his Father, making himself equal with God" (5:18).

b. In Rural Galilee (6:1–71)

John now takes us back to Galilee, to the feeding of the five thousand (the only miracle recorded in all four gospels) and to the miraculous walk upon the waves. It was close to Passover time, John says. The day after these signs, came the Lord's great discourse on the bread of life.

The Lord's claim that "I am the bread of life" is the first of the seven great "I am" sayings of Jesus in this gospel. "I am the bread of life" (6:35, 41, 48, 51); the light of the world (8:12; 9:5), the door (10:7, 9); the good shepherd (10:11, 14); the resurrection and the life (11:25); the way, the truth, and the life (14:6); and the true vine (15:1, 5). Jesus was deliberately claiming to be the I AM, the Jehovah of the Old Testament. His teaching on the Bread of life was so strong that many of His disciples left Him. "Then said Jesus unto the twelve, Will ye also go away? Then Simon Peter answered him, Lord, to whom shall we go? thou hast the words of eternal life" (6:67–68). But there was one whose heart was already estranged. "Have not I chosen you twelve, and one of you is a devil?" Jesus said (v. 70).

2. The Implications of His Life (7:1–10:42)

Back and forth the scene swings, between Galilee and Jerusalem. Jerusalem drew Him like a lodestone. It was there, He knew, He must die.

John records the Lord's visit now to Jerusalem to celebrate the joyous week-long Feast of Tabernacles. This long section contains many of the Lord's disputes with the authorities who were becoming more and more outraged with this Jesus of Nazareth.

One notable passage concerns "the last day, that great day of the feast" (7:37) when Jesus cried, "If any man thirst, let him come unto me, and drink. He that believeth on me, as the scripture hath said, out of his belly shall flow rivers of living water" (7:37–38). This heralded a coming change in dispensations—the dispensation of the Holy Spirit, which would begin on the day of Pentecost.

Another passage describes the Lord's encounter with the scribes and Pharisees over the matter of the woman taken in adultery. How incisive He was in dealing with these hypocritical men who tried to bring Him, in all His love, compassion, and grace into conflict with the death penalty demanded by the Mosaic Law (8:1–11). This is the only place in the Bible where we read of Jesus writing—and what He wrote is forever blotted out! How wonderfully mercy and truth met together in

His kind word to the woman: "Neither do I condemn thee: go, and sin no more" (v. 11).

In this section, too, is the story of the man born blind (9:1–41) and the altercation with the Pharisees because Jesus restored the man's sight on the Sabbath day. Here, too, we have the Lord's wonderful teaching about the Good Shepherd and the Door. "I and my Father are one," He declared (10:30). "Then," we read, "the Jews took up stones again to stone him" (v. 31).

The implications of His life became increasingly clear. He claimed to be, He proved Himself to be, "the Word made flesh"—and they hated Him for it.

C. His Deity Is Disowned (11:1–12:50)

This section begins with what, perhaps, was the greatest of all His miracles—the raising of Lazarus from the dead after he had been dead and decomposing for four days. This miracle caused a notable stir. Many believed on Him. The chief priests and Pharisees, however, were greatly concerned. Caiaphas made his remarkable statement, "It is expedient for us, that one man should die for the people" (11:50). It was made in unbelief and in order to justify the murder of Jesus, but proved to be a prophetic utterance regarding the substitutionary nature of Christ's death.

Soon after this the Lord rode in triumph into Jerusalem in fulfillment of Daniel 9:25–26. It is John who points out that the raising of Lazarus played its part in the Lord's enthusiastic welcome by the crowd at this time. The frustrated Pharisees threw up their hands in rage: "The world is gone after him" they exclaimed (12:19). But within the week He was dead.

III. THE SECRETS OF THE SON OF GOD: THE LORD'S DISCIPLES IN FOCUS (13:1–17:26)

A. The Talk in the Upper Room (13:1–14:31)

John now records those long, heart-to-heart talks Jesus had with His disciples in view of His impending death. He gathered with them in the upper room to celebrate the last Passover with them and—as soon as Judas the traitor had been warned and had left—He began to prepare the others for what lay ahead. He revealed to them the soon-coming ministry of the Holy Spirit, who would take His place and lead them into all truth.

B. The Walk on the Gethsemane Road (15:1–17:26)

It was no part of John's purpose to describe the agony in the garden. Instead, he revealed some of the Lord's conversation on the way to Gethsemane—*how He talked to them about the Father*, revealed Himself as the true Vine, added more information about the Holy Spirit, and warned them of the severe ordeal of the next few hours and days. And *how He talked to the Father about them* in that magnificent high priestly prayer in which are revealed the great mysteries of the new relationships of life in Christ.

IV. THE SORROWS OF THE SON OF GOD: THE LORD'S DEATH IN FOCUS (18:1–20:31)

It is John who tells how, when Judas came with the cohort to arrest Jesus in Gethsemane, the Lord put forth the power of His deity in announcing Himself to be the I AM (18:5). They fell backward to the ground before Him. He was demonstrating the truth of His declaration, "No man taketh [my life] from me, but I lay it down of myself" (10:18).

Having demonstrated their inability to arrest Him, however, He let them take Him. John describes His trial before Annas and Pilate, and Peter's sad denial and the significant crowing of the cock, which stabbed through to Peter's heart and heralded the dread day of the crucifixion. John describes Pilate's fear of Christ and his even greater fear of Caesar.

The dark scene on Golgotha he touches lightly but does record how the Lord sent His mother away from the scene in John's charge. John, too, tells how Nicodemus and Joseph of Arimathea secured the body from Pilate and laid the Lord's remains reverently to rest in Joseph's new tomb.

Then came that wondrous first day of the week. John gives us three resurrection scenes at the empty tomb and in the upper room. One concerned himself and Peter and shows how the resurrection challenged *the mind*; the second concerned Mary Magdalene and shows how it challenged *the heart*; the third concerned doubting Thomas and shows how the resurrection challenged *the will*.

V. EPILOGUE (21:1–25)

John's final picture brings life, love, and light back into focus. The scene is set back in Galilee and revolves around Peter's frustrated declaration, "I go a-fishing" (v. 3). We see how the Lord recalled Peter's failure, recaptured Peter's fervor, and reshaped Peter's future.

John's last word is challenging: "There are also many other things which Jesus did, the which, if they should be written every one, I suppose that even the world itself could not contain the books that should be written" (v. 25).

Thus ends the writing of the four gospels—the most important books ever written in the history of mankind. Happy are those who have these books in their mother tongue, who read them, believe them, obey them. Foolish are those who have them but ignore them, neglect them, disbelieve them, and toss them aside. These very books will be opened against them in the day of judgment.

CHAPTER 8

ACTS

The Early Church in Action

The apostolic period lasted seventy years—from A.D. 30 to A.D. 100. Nowhere, in all of history do we find such a momentous generation. During this period, Judaism was rendered obsolete, its temple destroyed, its people scattered. Christianity arose, superseded Judaism, and flung its outposts across the world. Its roots went down so deeply that not all the might and power of imperial Rome could uproot and destroy it. Moreover, during this period, twenty-seven books were written, which have had a greater impact on mankind than any other literature ever penned.

When God chose Israel to be His instrument for the spiritual education of mankind, He first *separated* the nation from all other nations of the earth. He did this so that Israel might be grounded in the truth of God. Then He *scattered* the nation among all other nations of the earth so that the truths they had learned might be spread abroad. Israel, however, utterly failed to understand the purposes of God in her election. The Jews cultivated a spirit of exclusivism, pride, and bitter intolerance toward the Gentiles. Above all, they not only crucified their Christ but persisted in unbelief. The gospels tell us how Israel rejected the ministry of the *Savior*; Acts tells us how they rejected the ministry of the *Spirit*. As a result, the Jewish people were cast off as a nation, for the present age, during which the church is God's instrument for communicating His mind and will to men.

The book of Acts is a book of *people, places, and principles*. Its pages are crowded with seventy or more characters and, as we travel down its twenty-eight chapters, we encounter some fifty or more places.

The writer of Acts was Luke. The book has the same introductory address as his gospel and resumes the history where that document leaves off. The book does not really describe the "acts of the apostles"—for only a few of them are given any degree of prominence—but the acts of the risen and ascended Lord through the Holy Spirit.

The Holy Spirit is named a number of times in the book.[1] It is a worthwhile study to look up every reference in the book to the Spirit of God and study these in their context and in view of the transitional character of the book of Acts. It should be remembered that Acts is essentially a book of history. We do not go to Acts for our doctrine, we go to the epistles for that. Indeed, much modern confusion about the Holy Spirit could be avoided by keeping this hermeneutical principle in mind.[2]

Luke used a number of sources for his information, and some of his facts are firsthand. The "we" sections of the book (16:10–17; 20:5–15; 21:1–18; 27:1–28:16) indicate that he was in the company of the apostle Paul.

The book traces the history of the church from its origin on the day of Pentecost to its spread throughout the western part of the Roman Empire; from its being a small Jewish minority to its becoming a populous group, predominantly Gentile. The key to the book is 1:8—"But ye shall receive power, after that the Holy Ghost is come upon you: and ye shall be witnesses unto me both in Jerusalem, and in all Judea, and in Samaria, and unto the uttermost part of the earth."

The book of Acts is in three parts, each with a different emphasis. The first describes God's man, Simon Peter; the second deals with God's martyr, Stephen; and the third displays God's missionary, Saul. Around these three men the three movements of the book are centered.

First we have the *foundation* emphasis, which centers around the person and ministry of *Simon*; then we have the *forward* emphasis, which revolves around the ministry and martyrdom of *Stephen*; finally we have the *foreign* emphasis, which is related to the conversion and world vision of *Saul*.

    I. The Foundation Emphasis: Simon (chaps. 1–5)
       A. Transition (chap. 1)
          1. Walking with the Savior (1:1–11)
          2. Waiting for the Spirit (1:12–26)
       B. Testimony (chap. 2)
          1. The Wind of the Spirit (2:1–4)
          2. The Witness of the Saints (2:5–47)
       C. Triumph (chaps. 3–4)
       D. Treachery (chap. 5)
    II. The Forward Emphasis: Stephen (chaps. 6–12)
       A. New Voices (chaps. 6–8)
          1. The First Martyr (chaps. 6–7)
          2. The First Missionary (chap. 8)

The story begins with the beginning of the church.

I. The Foundation Emphasis: Simon (chaps. 1–5)

A. Transition (chap. 1)

The first chapter is preliminary and preparatory. We see the believers in the Lord Jesus (about ten dozen of them) doing two things.

1. Walking with the Savior (1:1–11)

For forty days the Lord Jesus appeared from time to time in their midst, revealing Himself to them in resurrection power, convincing them that it was all gloriously true, preparing them for things to come.

We see Him hammering home the Great Commission: "Ye shall be witnesses unto me both in Jerusalem, and in all Judaea, and in Samaria, and unto the uttermost part of the earth" (v. 8). We see Him raise His hands in parting blessing and then bodily rise into the clouds, promising, as He did so, that He would most certainly return.

By the time those forty days were over, the little band of believers had no doubts at all about the *resurrection*, the *rapture* and the *return* of Christ.

2. Waiting for the Spirit (1:12–26)

We see them in the upper room, where they are praying together. Then we see them casting lots to see who should succeed Judas, choosing a man of whom we never hear again instead of waiting for God to add the apostle Paul. They spend ten *days* in this way, waiting for the Spirit. All this was transition.

B. Testimony (chap. 2)

At last the days of waiting were over. The "day of Pentecost was fully come" (v. 1). It had come many times before—annually, for some fifteen hundred years. Over and over again the day had dawned and the required ritual had been enacted, all richly symbolic, all typical of what actually took place in the upper room. Then the day "fully came," and phenomenal signs accompanied the coming of the Spirit on that, the true day of Pentecost.

1. The Wind of the Spirit (2:1–4)

The Holy Spirit came like a mighty, rushing wind and with cloven tongues as of fire. With this coming of the Spirit, half a dozen things took place that mark out the uniqueness of the church age and set it apart both from the Old Testament legal age and the future promised millennial age.

First, the Holy Spirit came to *baptize*. About 120 individual believers in the Lord Jesus ascended the steps to the upper room; one body, the church, came down.

Of the seven direct references to the baptism of the Holy Spirit in the New Testament, only one is doctrinal (1 Cor. 12:13; cf. Matt. 3:11; Mark 1:8; Luke 3:16; John 1:33; Acts 1:5; 11:16). The baptizing work of the Holy Spirit is that work of the Spirit of God that takes an individual believer in the Lord Jesus and makes that person a member of the church, the mystical body of Christ. *All* true believers are thus baptized with the Holy Spirit.

Then the Holy Spirit came as God's *gift* to all believers (Acts 2:38) and as such He *indwells* all believers (Rom. 8:8–9), so that the individual believer's body becomes the actual *temple* of the Holy Spirit (1 Cor. 6:19). Since the Holy Spirit is a person, we receive Him in His totality and entirety the moment we are saved. One cannot receive a person by installments. It is the gift and the indwelling of the Holy Spirit that makes the Christian life possible, for the Holy Spirit's great work is to reproduce the life and loveliness of the Lord Jesus in us.

The Holy Spirit came to *seal* (Eph. 1:13) and thus indelibly mark each believer as God's purchased possession. He came to be the *earnest* (Eph. 1:14), the guarantee of God's intentions toward us and of our inheritance in the world to come. He came to *fill* (Eph. 5:18), but the filling of the Spirit, unlike those ministries of the Spirit mentioned above, is conditional. It depends on us. The baptism, the gift, the indwelling, the seal, and the earnest are all sovereign acts of God, unconditionally and impartially bestowed on all believers; the filling depends upon us maintaining a continuing relationship with an ungrieved Holy Spirit.

He came to *anoint* (1 John 2:20). In the Old Testament, prophets, priests, and kings were inducted into their spheres of specialized service by anointing. The anointing or "unction" of the Holy Spirit is for service, and it is that ministry of the

Spirit particularly that enables the Lord's servant to use God's Word in unique ways with God's blessing attending its use.

All this was inherent in what took place on the day of Pentecost. The doctrine of it was developed later by Paul. In the post apostolic age, we come into the good of what took place in the upper room the moment we are saved. The special signs that first accompanied the coming of the Holy Spirit were temporary and were directed toward the nation of Israel.

2. The Witness of the Saints (2:5–47)

In the mighty, transforming power of what had happened in the upper room, the saints of God began to blaze forth the news of the gospel to the world. They spoke with other tongues. People from a score of lands were in Jerusalem, and each and every one heard the message *in his own native tongue*. As a result, three thousand people were saved and added to the church. The church was not only launched that day, but she weighed anchor and set forth before the wind with all sails set.

C. Triumph (chaps. 3–4)

A golden opportunity was followed by a growing opposition. Peter and John healed a man lame from birth in the power of the saving name of Jesus. Then, as the people came running, they preached the gospel of Christ. The Jewish authorities, who had been stunned by all this, reacted at once. Peter and John were arrested and told to stop preaching in the name of Jesus. They lost no time in telling the Sanhedrin that they had absolutely no intention of obeying such an order. "Neither is there salvation in any other," they said, "for there is no one other name under heaven given among men, whereby we must be saved" (v. 12).

D. Treachery (chap. 5)

Satan, having failed to stop the growth of the church by force from without, now tried fraud from within. Ananias and Sapphira lied to the Holy Spirit. They pretended to have given a greater sum to the Lord's work than they actually had, and the Holy Spirit struck at once. He did something Christ never did—smote two people with death. The fear of God descended on the church and on the world so that pretenders backed off.

II. The Forward Emphasis: Stephen (chaps. 6–12)

A. New Voices (chaps. 6–8)

1. The First Martyr (chaps. 6–7)

Stephen was one of the seven deacons appointed by the early church to "wait on tables" (see 6:2). He was a man "filled with the Holy Spirit" (see 6:5), a requirement for any kind of service or office in the New Testament church.

He was also able so successfully to present the cause of Christ that his opponents—and it is likely that one of them was the brilliant Saul of Tarsus—decided that since they could not defeat him, the best thing would be to destroy him. And so they did. He was taken before the Sanhedrin, given a biased trial, and handed over to the executioners. Saul of Tarsus lent a hand in the stoning of this first martyr of the church.

Far from stemming the rising tide of belief in Christ, the martyrdom of Stephen seemed to give it impetus. At his death, the believers scattered far and wide from Jerusalem, taking the good seed of the gospel wherever they went.

2. The First Missionary (chap. 8)

Philip the evangelist now steps forward to take the lead in church affairs. He was another of the seven deacons. He carried the gospel down to Samaria, where none of the apostles seemed inclined to go. Samaria was not a popular place with the Jews, but Philip took seriously the Lord's command: "Ye shall be witnesses . . . in . . . Samaria." Prejudice against the Samaritans was of ancient vintage, but it could not stand before the gospel. A tremendous revival broke out, so much so that the Jerusalem church decided to send its two leading apostles, Peter and John, to see what was going on.

Philip then left to carry the gospel to a traveling black man, the Treasurer of Ethiopia. Thus the gospel was taken to Africa, and Philip became the first foreign missionary of the infant church.

B. New Victories (chaps. 9–11)

The time had come for the gospel to be taken without let or hindrance to the Gentile world. We note three things that happened in this regard.

1. A Gifted Messenger for the Gentiles Saved (9:1–31)

The Lord Jesus reached down from heaven and converted Saul of Tarsus. The conversion of Saul was probably one of the most important events in the history of the church. Saul was a Jew by birth, breeding, and background; a Greek by enlightenment and education; a Roman by citizenship. Here was a man with a mind and heart to write the greater part of the New Testament, being the foremost thinker and theologian of the church. It was he who coined the very vocabulary of New Testament truth, and it was he who blazed gospel trails across the frontiers of the pagan world. If he was about thirty-five years of age when he was saved, then he was about twenty-eight when Christ died. Soon it would be abundantly evident that in Saul, or Paul as he is more generally called, the church had a new apostle.

When converted, he was on his way north to Damascus, armed with warrants for the arrest of any Christians he could find, when he came face-to-face with the living Son of God. He was converted on the spot, and thereafter flung himself enthusiastically and tirelessly into the evangelization of the lost.

2. A Good Man of the Gentiles Saved (9:32–11:18)

About this time, Peter was sent to Caesarea to open the door of the church to the Gentiles once and for all. Peter was reluctant to go. All his native-born prejudice against the Gentiles militated against any such mission. God had to speak to Peter three times in a thrice-repeated vision before he stopped saying, "Not so, Lord" (10:14).

Finally he went to the house of a Gentile centurion named Cornelius, taking some witnesses with him. What occurred there might be called a second Pentecost! The "middle wall of partition" (Eph. 2:14) between Jew and Gentile was flung down, and the Gentiles entered the church. Before long, Jews would become a permanent minority in its communion.

In these past three chapters, three people were saved—in chapter 8 it was a black man, a man from Ethiopia; in chapter 9 it was a Jew named Saul of Tarsus; in chapter 10 it was a Roman named Cornelius. In these three chapters God saved a descendant of *Ham*, then a descendant of *Shem*, then a descendant of *Japheth*, thus uniting all the world's families in the family of God.

3. A Great Multitude of the Gentiles Saved (11:19–30)

The scene moves north to Antioch. There the gospel was first taken to the Gentile world in such a way that many, many Gentiles became Christians. Soon Antioch became the new center of the faith, and the center of gravity began to move away from Jerusalem to the Gentile world. Jerusalem became increasingly less and less important, a mere appendage to a faith that would blaze in a hundred cities of the world.

C. New Violence (chap. 12)

The scene shifts temporarily back to Peter and Jerusalem. Herod Agrippa I, grandson of Herod the Great, decided that persecuting the leadership of the church was a good way to ingratiate himself with his Jewish subjects. Accordingly, he martyred James and imprisoned Peter.

God, however, threw open the prison doors and set Peter free, and followed this up with summary judgment on Herod. The king was celebrating a festival of thanksgiving at Caesarea for the safe return of the imperial puppet Claudius from his farcical expedition to Britain. Herod made a speech, and the crowd applauded, carried away by the pomp and splendor of this petty little puppet prince. The people called Herod God! Herod drank in the adulation and worship, but then the angel that saved Peter smote Herod, and he died a dreadful death.

III. THE FOREIGN EMPHASIS: SAUL (CHAPS. 13–28)

A. Paul the Pioneer (13:1–21:26)

When Saul of Tarsus was converted on the Damascus road in A.D. 37, the church was restricted to Jerusalem, Judea, and Samaria. In A.D. 44 the church at Antioch sent Paul and Barnabas to the mission field to evangelize "the regions beyond" and to tell the untold millions the story of Jesus. By the time Paul was arrested in A.D. 58, just fourteen years later, churches in city after city of the Roman Empire were gathering for the worship of Christ. Paul went on three missionary journeys. Each one is a model for missionary work, each had a different emphasis, and each should be studied as a pattern for world evangelism.

1. Exploration: Paul's First Missionary Journey (13:1–15:35)

Paul was the greatest missionary of all times. When he and Barnabas were sent on the work of world evangelism by the church at Antioch, Barnabas at first took the lead. Leaving Antioch, the missionaries went to Cyprus. There, God blessed their ministry. They then went to the mainland of Asia Minor (modern Turkey) and, with Paul now taking the lead, they went on into Galatia and saw a number of churches established. When they returned to Antioch, they found the church in a turmoil because Jewish teachers were insisting that all Gentile converts be circumcised and keep the law of Moses. Paul and Barnabas were soon embroiled in

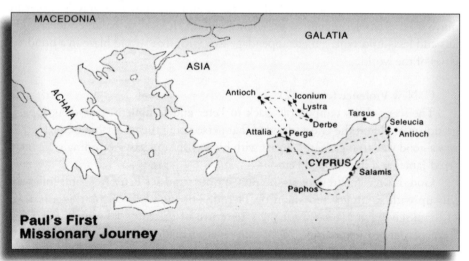

the dispute and led a deputation to Jerusalem, where the issue was settled at a great conference. Gentile emancipation from Judaism in all its forms was endorsed by the leaders of the Jerusalem church.

The problems encountered during this first missionary journey were those typical of all pioneer mission work in raw pagan lands. We see Paul and his companions facing those in high places of government, facing danger, hardship, idolatry, entrenched superstition, organized hostile religion, and persecution. We see him winning souls, daring dangers, deliberately coming back to places where he had been manhandled in order to strengthen and encourage new believers and to set up proper church government.

2. Expansion: Paul's Second Missionary Journey (15:36–18:22)

Paul's second missionary journey began on a sad note, for he and Barnabas quarreled over John Mark, a young man who had deserted them on their first missionary journey. Parting with Barnabas over this issue, Paul took Silas with him and revisited the churches that had been founded on his first missionary journey. Then, moving ever westward until he came to Troas, he received the "Macedonian call" and invaded Europe for Christ. Soon a trail of churches was founded in Macedonia and Greece—Philippi, Thessalonica, Berea, and Corinth. Hurrying back to Jerusalem, Paul paid a flying visit to Ephesus on the way. This was to be the scene of some of his greatest triumphs in the gospel on his third journey.

The experiences that accompanied Paul's second missionary journey are the kind that accompany every missionary enterprise where expansion of existing work into new fields is the goal. We see Paul and his friends going back over ground plowed and planted before, but not tarrying there.

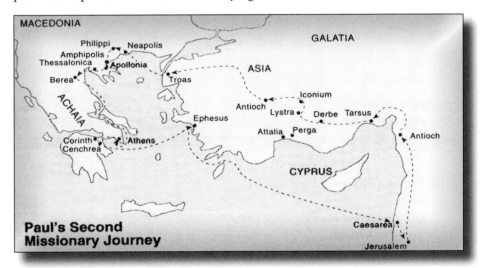

We see him planting churches, challenging unbelief. We see him facing with equal poise high-placed government officials, furious religious fanatics, sophisticated intellectual snobs, hard-working artisans. City after city was invaded, and a trail of blessing followed him everywhere he went.

3. Exhortation: Paul's Third Missionary Journey (18:23–21:26)

Paul's third journey was largely occupied with teaching, establishing, and exhorting the churches founded before, except for his stay at Ephesus, where he founded one of his most important churches. Ephesus was an influential city in western Asia Minor, and Paul spent considerable time there on this, his last recorded missionary journey. A strong and thriving church was established, which became a beacon to all the surrounding countryside.

What a tireless ambassador Paul was! He was a sick man, in constant need of medical attention. He bore in his body the marks of the physical abuse to which he had been subjected time and time again. He traveled 5,580 miles on foot through some of the most difficult, dangerous territory in the world, and 6,770 miles by sea in cockleshells of boats, often in danger of storms, frequently shipwrecked. As recorded in Acts, he covered 12,350 hair-raising miles to tell people about Jesus.

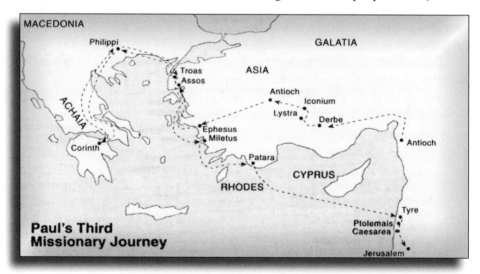

Paul's Third Missionary Journey

B. Paul the Prisoner (21:27–28:31)

1. His Treatment as a Prisoner (21:27–23:35)

Paul arrived back in Jerusalem at the end of his third missionary journey. With him he carried gifts of money, which had been donated for the poor saints in

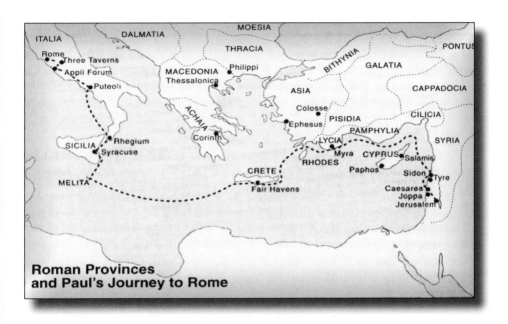

**Roman Provinces
and Paul's Journey to Rome**

Jerusalem by the Gentile churches he had planted far and wide. He seems to have received little or no thanks. Instead, the narrow-minded Jerusalem church leaders insisted that Paul make some gesture in support of their Jewishness. He complied, and as a result was mobbed in the temple courts and had to be taken into protective custody by the Roman authorities. Thus began a long period of imprisonment, first at Caesarea and then at Rome. In all this period Paul seems to have been most courteously treated by the Gentiles, especially after his Roman citizenship became known. He was hounded by the unbelieving Jews and seems to have been studiously ignored by an ungrateful Jerusalem church.

2. His Triumphs as a Prisoner (chaps. 24–26)

While being detained at the Roman city of Caesarea on the Palestinian coast, Paul was given the opportunity to bear testimony before both Felix and Festus, the local Roman governors. His case was grossly mishandled by Festus, who wanted to curry favor with the Jewish authorities in Jerusalem. Paul felt obliged to appeal his case to Caesar. This put Festus in an awkward situation, for he knew Paul had not done anything serious enough to have his case referred to the supreme court. Nero would not take kindly to having his time wasted with such a frivolous case. Accordingly, Festus took advantage of a visit from King Agrippa II (the last of the Herods and the last king of the Jews noted in the New Testament) to have Paul's case reviewed by this expert on Jewish affairs. If Festus hoped to get help in phrasing his reasons for sending Paul to Rome, he must have been disappointed.

Agrippa bluntly told Festus that Paul should have been released. But it was too late now. Once the appeal to Caesar had been made, all lower courts ceased to have jurisdiction.

3. His Travels as a Prisoner (chaps. 27–28)

So off to Rome Paul was sent, and an exciting journey it proved to be. The story is told by Luke with considerable attention to detail.

Once at Rome, Paul wasted no time, despite his chains, in making contact with Roman Jewry and with the church in the capital. We learn from his epistles, especially Philippians, how wonderfully fruitful Paul's captivity turned out to be.

For Satan could not stop Paul from *witnessing*. He witnessed boldly, fearlessly, to everyone who came across his path. It mattered not to Paul whether it was a Felix or a Festus, the high priest of the temple or the last king of the Jews. He witnessed faithfully, fearlessly, and forcefully. He made converts of his jailors, and his fame spread throughout the palace and the Praetorian guard.

He witnessed as boldly as a prisoner as he ever did as a pioneer. He preached the gospel in Jerusalem, the religious capital of the world, and was mobbed; he preached the gospel in Athens, the cultural capital of the world, and was mocked; he preached the gospel in Rome, the political capital of the world, and he was martyred. The Devil could lock him up but he could never shut him up!

Nor could the Devil stop him from *writing*. From out of that prison came some of the greatest of all Paul's epistles. To this day, the Devil must be furious with himself for putting Paul in prison and giving him the time and incentive to write those magnificent, Christ-exalting letters of Ephesians, Colossians, Philippians, and Philemon. Page after page poured from his pen, and the church and the world are forever indebted to Paul for these letters.

The book of Acts is evidently an unfinished document, for Luke never wrote, and could not write, the end of the story. It is still being written today.

Here we are today, some two millennia later, and names are still being written in the Lamb's Book of Life; members are still being added to the church, the mystical body of Christ. One of these days, however, the Holy Spirit will turn the last page, write the closing paragraph, add the final few lines, record the last name, and put a final *AMEN!* to the book, and hand it over to God. Then Jesus will get up from His throne and fulfill the pledge made at the beginning of this book. This same Jesus will come back in like manner as He went.

Then the book of the *Acts of the Holy Spirit* will be opened in heaven. And we shall hear it read, all the way through. And find our own names written down on the page.

CHAPTER 9

ROMANS

Theology of the Gospel

Before beginning a survey of Romans, we should first get a clear picture of the relationships of the various New Testament books. The chart on the following page will help.

If for the purpose of memorization, we count Revelation with the epistles, then we have nine church epistles (Romans to 2 Thessalonians) followed by four pastoral-personal epistles (1 Timothy to Philemon) followed by nine general epistles (Hebrews to Revelation). This pattern is easily memorized (9 + 4 + 9). Taking the church and general epistles (each section containing nine books), we observe the following similarities and differences. Both sections begin with a major doctrinal treatise (Romans and Hebrews). Both sections close with an unveiling of the future (2 Thessalonians and Revelation). Both sections were written to special groups, the first to Gentiles and the second to Hebrew Christians.

Concentrating now on the Pauline church epistles, the following pattern, based on 2 Timothy 3:16, is evident:

A. Doctrine and Instruction: Romans
   B. Reproof (for practical failure): 1 and 2 Corinthians
      C. Correction (for doctrinal error): Galatians

A. Doctrine and Instruction: Ephesians
   B. Reproof (for practical failure): Philippians
      C. Correction (for doctrinal error): Colossians

A. Doctrine and Instruction: 1 and 2 Thessalonians

CATEGORIES OF NEW TESTAMENT BOOKS			
NARRATION	**EXPLANATION**		**CONSUMMATION**
	Paul's Epistles	**General Epistles**	
Matthew Mark Luke John Acts	**To Churches** Romans 1 Corinthians 2 Corinthians Galatians Ephesians Philippians Colossians 1 Thessalonians 2 Thessalonians **To Individuals** 1 Timothy 2 Timothy Titus Philemon	Hebrews James 1 Peter 2 Peter 1 John 2 John 3 John Jude	Revelation

Paul wrote three epistles that are pivotal and that unfold doctrine and instruction. In Romans he expounded the mystery of Christ's *cross*; in Ephesians, the mystery of Christ's *church*; in the Thessalonians, the mystery of Christ's *coming*. The Thessalonian epistles come last, though written first, and there are no "church" epistles beyond these because no higher truth can be taught; the consummation is reached.

Paul had not been to Rome when he wrote his epistle to the church there, but he planned to go as soon as occasion presented itself (1:10, 13; 15:23–24, 28). He wrote from Corinth (16:1) while on his third missionary journey during the "three months" referred to in Acts 20:3, just before his final visit to Jerusalem. As we have seen, Paul's great ambition to preach in Rome was fulfilled in an unexpected way. He went there as a prisoner.

Some of the key words in Romans are law (78 times), all (71 times), righteousness (66 times), faith (62 times), sin (60 times), death (42 times), in Christ (33 times), flesh (20 times), impute (19 times), and God forbid (10 times).[1] Matthew, Mark, Luke, and John gave the facts about Christ's sojourn on earth, but Paul gave the meaning of it, so that in Romans we actually have *the gospel according to Paul.*

More Old Testament quotations appear in Romans than in all the other epistles put together—some seventy quotations from fourteen Old Testament books. In this way Paul showed that the gospel message is the same throughout all ages.

   I. God and the Human Family (chaps. 1–8)
      A. How God Sees Us (1:1–3:20)
         1. Guilty—Without Excuse (1:1–3:8)
            a. The Prologue (1:1–17)
            b. The Pagan (1:18–23)
            c. The Pervert (1:24–28)
            d. The Prodigal (1:29–32)
            e. The Pretender (2:1–16)
            f. The Pious (2:17–3:8)
         2. Guilty—Without Exception (3:9–20)
      B. How God Saves Us (3:21–4:25)
         1. It Is a Free Salvation (3:21–31)
         2. It Is a Faith Salvation (chap. 4)
      C. How God Secures Us (chap. 5)
      D. How God Sanctifies Us (chaps. 6–8)
  II. God and the Hebrew Family (chaps. 9–11)
      A. God's Past Dealings with Israel (chap. 9)
      B. God's Present Dealings with Israel (chap. 10)
      C. God's Promised Dealings with Israel (chap. 11)
 III. God and the Heavenly Family (chaps. 12–16)
      A. The Christian and His Life (chap. 12)
      B. The Christian and the Law (13:1–10)
         1. The Law of Government (13:1–7)
         2. The Law of God (13:8–10)
      C. The Christian and His Lord (13:11–14)
      D. The Christian and His Light (14:1–15:7)
      E. The Christian and the Lost (15:8–33)
      F. The Christian and His Love (16:1–16)
      G. The Christian and the Lie (16:17–20)
      H. The Christian and His Lot (16:21–27)

   In the first three chapters of Romans, Paul paints a black picture of human sin. Jew and Gentile alike are condemned before God and, without exception, are found to be both without excuse and without escape and facing the wrath of God. Then Paul turns to the question of salvation and shows that when God forgives, He does so fully, freely, and forever. Paul sees man's case as hopeless apart from the sovereign grace of God. He traces human sin back to Adam and shows that "in Adam all die," and then shows that God has a second federal Head for the human race, Christ, in whom all are made alive. By natural birth we are children of Adam, but by being born again we become children of God and, for Christ's sake, we are adopted out of Adam's family of ruined men into God's family of the redeemed. The key to salvation is faith in Christ, and human good works are totally excluded as a means of procuring the favor of God.

With Paul, salvation meant eternal security but certainly not freedom to sin. In chapters 6 through 8 he showed that God saves from the power of sin as well as the penalty of sin, and that through the indwelling of the Holy Spirit, sin, self, and Satan can all be subdued in practical daily Christian living.

With this brief summary in mind, we can now look more closely at some of the details.

I. GOD AND THE HUMAN FAMILY (CHAPS. 1–8)

A. How God Sees Us (1:1–3:20)

1. Guilty—Without Excuse (1:1–3:8)

a. The Prologue (1:1–17)

There can be no doubt of Paul's passion to visit Rome. Rome was the center of the world. In the center of the Imperial City at the heart of the empire, stood the golden milestone from which all roads radiated out to the four points of the compass. A man could travel for hundreds upon hundreds of miles along those roads, going from land to land, never having to cross Customs, never having to learn another language if he knew Greek. Along those roads marched the iron men whose invincible might kept the vast empire at rest. It was said that all roads led to Rome. Paul felt that since all roads led to Rome, all roads led *from* Rome. So let him do a work for God at Rome and the world would feel its impact.

As Paul intimated to the Romans, he had boldly written the word *Rome* at the top of his missionary itinerary again and again. Again and again the Holy Spirit had said, "Not yet, Paul." At last he wrote the Holy Spirit a blank check. "*By any means*," he said (v. 10), "let me see Rome." The Holy Spirit cashed that check and sent Paul to Rome—in chains.

That is just another proof of the wisdom of God, for if Paul had gone to Rome the first time he wrote that magic word on his itinerary—well, we might never have had Paul's epistle to the Romans, and we would be greatly impoverished. Matthew, Mark, Luke, and John introduce us to the person of Christ, but Paul, in Romans, introduces us to the principles of Christianity.

b. The Pagan (1:18–23)

In these opening chapters we have a court scene. The Holy Spirit is the Prosecutor of the human race, and the court recorder is Paul. Five kinds of people are arraigned and, in these five, all people are arraigned. The first is the pagan.

The question is often asked, "Are the heathen lost?" Romans 1 says they most certainly are. God has a universal witness to Himself in creation. Suns, stars, and seasons unite their voices to proclaim God's eternal power. Creation is "God's oldest testament." There is enough revealed of God in what we call "nature" to make the heathen guilty, and that without excuse, for their ignorance and for their idolatry.

In His indictment of the pagan, the Holy Spirit marks down idolatry and the worship of graven images as a deliberate repudiation of the light of God in creation. "Professing themselves to be wise [*sophos*], they became fools [from the noun *moros*]," (v. 22). In other words, they became sophisticated morons. To bow down to a graven image of wood, metal, or stone is intellectual and moral insanity.

c. The Pervert (1:24–28)

Anyone who thinks that sodomy is an acceptable alternate lifestyle has evidently not studied God's evaluation of that sin as stated in these verses.

Three times it is stated here that God gave people up. He gave them up to uncleanness, to vile affections, and to a reprobate mind. In other words, God gave them over to the three things so prevalent in our society today. He gave them over to *vile passions*—He abandoned them to a sexually explicit and morally filthy lifestyle. He gave them over to *vile perversions*—He abandoned them to the sins of Sodom, to dragon lusts—to what the Holy Spirit calls here "passions of infamy" (see v. 26). He says of such people that they "burn with lust" (see. v. 27) and that their practices are "against nature" (see v. 27). He adds that they receive *recompense* from God for their vileness—the word literally means "retribution." Doubtless the horrible diseases that attack these people are part of that retribution. He gave them over to *vile persuasions*—He abandoned them to what He calls "a reprobate mind" (v. 28). The mental gymnastics whereby they justify their behavior is completely spurious. So far as the pervert is concerned, God says they are without excuse because "they did not like to retain God in their knowledge" (v. 28). They give God up; God gives them up.

d. The Prodigal (1:29–32)

The rest of Romans 1 catalogs the kinds of behavior characteristic of "the far country." Every kind of sin and wickedness is listed. God sees behavior of the human race as one long list of sins: fornication, covetousness, envy, murder, disobedience to parents, unthankfulness, pride—the list goes on and on.

We are a race of prodigals and we are without excuse. God says of such that "knowing the judgment of God, that they which commit such things are worthy of death, not only do the same, but have pleasure in them that do them" (v. 32).

e. The Pretender (2:1–16)

God is not impressed by the man who says, "I thank thee that I am not as other men are." The moralist who imagines he is better than those who openly sin is as guilty, in God's sight, as those who wantonly commit the sins listed in Romans 1.

The Holy Spirit wastes no time in telling the hypocrite that God intends one day to judge his secrets. The person exposed to God's wrath in this section has his unforgettable picture painted for him by the Lord Himself in the story of the prodigal's elder brother (Luke 15:25–32).

f. The Pious (2:17–3:8)

The pious or religious man is represented by the Hebrew in this indictment. He is the man with a Bible in his hand, a book inspired by God, intended to lead him to Christ—to a Christ he forthwith rejects. This is the worst state of all.

So, then, the human race is arraigned, jointly and severally, and found to be guilty—without excuse.

2. Guilty—Without Exception (3:9–20)

The Holy Spirit now summarizes His case against mankind. He speaks of man's *vile thoughts*, of man's *venomous tongue*, and of man's *violent temper*. He says, "There is none that doeth good, no, not one" (v. 12). He reinforces that blanket statement: "There is none righteous, no, not one" (v. 10). He finds the whole world guilty before God—every mouth stopped, every excuse silenced. Be it the king upon his throne, the priest in his temple, the thief in his den, the child in his crib, the policeman on his beat, the monk in his cloister—*all* have sinned and come short of the glory of God.

B. How God Saves Us (3:21–4:25)

He saves us on the basis of what *He* does, not on the basis of what *we* do.

1. It Is a Free Salvation (3:21–31)

"Being justified freely by his grace . . ." (v. 24). Grace, in the Bible, is unmerited favor, getting something we don't deserve. God saves us on that principle. He knows we cannot do anything to merit His favor, that we are totally depraved, that our best efforts are touched and tainted by our sin nature. Since there is no way we can earn God's favor, if we are to be saved at all it must be freely.

In any case, all the doing has been done. It was done by the Lord Jesus, who so lived as to satisfy every demand of God's law, God's holiness, and God's throne, and who so died that His blood can be the propitiation for our sin.

2. It Is a Faith Salvation (chap. 4)

In chapter 4, two outstanding men are brought onto the witness stand to testify. One is Abraham, the founder of the Hebrew racial family; the other is David, the founder of the Hebrew royal family. In some respects, Abraham might be considered the *chief of saints* in the Old Testament since he is called "the Friend of God" (James 2:23), and "the father of all them that believe" (Rom. 4:11). In some respects, David might be considered the *chief of sinners* in the Old Testament because he sinned against enormous light and privilege. He committed two capital offenses, and was condemned to death by the law for adultery of the most aggravated sort and for murder of the most callous, cold-blooded, and contemptible kind. He escaped the full penalty of his sin only because there was no one in a position to execute the law's sentence. But God forgave him because he repented.

Both these men, Abraham and David, are exhibited by the Holy Spirit to show that salvation is not by works but by faith. Both men (Abraham in his righteousness and David in his rottenness) were driven to the place where they realized that their only hope of heaven was by putting their faith and trust in God.

Salvation is by faith. God says, "I have a salvation for you; it is centered in My Son. All you have to do is *trust Me* and *take Him*. If you can't trust Me to save you, then there is no hope for you at all." For the final insult is to say to God, "I can't trust You."

C. How God Secures Us (chap. 5)

Five times in this remarkable chapter we have the words "much more" (vv. 9, 10, 15, 17, 20). God sees the human family lined up under two federal heads—Adam and Christ. By natural birth we were born into Adam's family; by new birth we are born again into Christ's family. Adam is federal head of ruined humanity; Christ is Federal Head of redeemed humanity. In Adam all die; in Christ all are made alive. In Adam sin reigns, Satan reigns, death reigns; in Christ, Jesus reigns.

The principle expounded in Romans is that, embodied in the Old Testament trespass offering whereby, when a guilty person sought to get right with God because of some wrong he had done, he had to first get right with the person he had wronged. He did this by restoring the full amount he had stolen and by adding to the principal an extra twenty percent. Thus the injured party became the gainer. Calvary has made it possible for both God and the redeemed sinner to become gainers—hence the repetition of the expression "much more."

D. How God Sanctifies Us (chaps. 6–8)

Having told us that we have eternal life through Jesus Christ our Lord, the apostle raises a natural question. If this is so, if a believer is eternally secure, does that mean he can do as he likes, get away with sin, live to please himself? To which he responds with a resounding, "God forbid" (v. 2). Or, as J. B. Phillips renders it, "What a ghastly thought!"

The *principle* of victorious Christian living is stated in Romans 6, where Paul teaches that the old nature in the believer has been put to death by God in the death of Christ. The three key words are *know, reckon,* and *yield.* We are to actively count on the truth of God's assurance that "the old man" (the man of old, the man we used to be) is "crucified with him" (6:6). In the moment of temptation we are to yield, not to the temptation, but to the new life within.

The *problem* with all this is studied in Romans 7. We learn by personal experience that it is possible to know the secret of victory and yet not experience it practically. Romans 7 revolves around a discussion of the spiritual man (vv. 1–6), the natural man (vv. 7–13), and the carnal man (vv. 14–25). All the failure in chapter 7 stems from a reliance on self-effort as a means of producing the kind of life God expects. Paul mentions himself forty-five times in the discussion! No wonder he reaches the end of the chapter with a wail of despair.

The *practice* of victorious Christian living is the subject of Romans 8—one of the greater chapters in the New Testament and one in which the Holy Spirit is repeatedly mentioned. The chapter begins with "no condemnation" and ends with "no separation." In this magnificent eighth chapter, the Holy Spirit lifts us higher and higher until we see ourselves as more than conquerors through Him who loved us.

II. GOD AND THE HEBREW FAMILY (CHAPS. 9–11)

The Jew occupies a special place of privilege in God's purposes for this world. The Jewish nation was selected, separated, and schooled to be a testimony to the true and living God to all mankind. For two thousand years, if God had anything to say, He said it to a Jew. The Jew was blessed with a special covenant relationship with God. He was given the land and the law, wonderful precepts and divine promises, he was given both the Scripture and the Savior. Jesus came into the world, born of a Jewish mother, raised in a Hebrew home—the crown of all Israel's past.

The Jews responded by murdering Him. What, then, has happened to all God's exceeding great and precious promises to the Jewish people? Since the Jews so criminally reacted to their *messianic* hope, what has happened now to their *millennial* hope? Has God cast away the Jew? Again Paul uses his resounding "God forbid"—perish the thought! (11:1).

Paul had a special sympathy for, and understanding of, the Jewish dilemma, for he himself was a Jew. For years he had resisted Christianity, fully alive to its basic challenge to Judaism. In chapters 9 through 11 Paul dealt with the effect the Christian gospel has on God's unique promises to the nation of Israel.

In Romans 9 he looks at God's *past dealings* with the nation of Israel; the key is found in the *sovereignty* of God. Throughout the past, God always had a small believing remnant, the true Israel of God, in the midst of an otherwise rebellious and apostate nation. God's sovereign election was concerned with this remnant.

In Romans 10 Paul looks at God's *present dealings* with the nation of Israel, and he shows that today God's *salvation* is offered to the individual Jew on the same basis that it is offered to the individual Gentile: "Whosoever shall call upon the name of the Lord shall be saved" (Rom. 10:13).

In Romans 11 Paul looks at God's *promised dealings* with the nation of Israel, discussing Gentile and Jew in the place of religious privilege. He shows that, while the Hebrew nation today is cut off from its former place of privilege—as the custodian of God's purpose, revelation, and blessing—when the present age is over the Jewish nation will again be restored (grafted in) as God's chosen people, and God's promises to Abraham and to David will be reinstated. The *sincerity* of God is the key to God's promises. The Christian gospel does not cancel the purposes of God with Israel as a nation. Those promises are merely postponed—and not because God has changed His mind but because Israel refuses to believe.

III. GOD AND THE HEAVENLY FAMILY (CHAPS. 12–16)

A. The Christian and His Life (chap. 12)
The Christian is expected to hand his life—body and soul—over to his Master in heaven. He is to present his body a living sacrifice. That will have a profound effect on his relationship to his *brethren*. He will take the gifts and abilities God has given him and use them to minister to the people of God.

It will also have an immediate effect on his *behavior* to all men. He will be diligent in business. He will be happy, patient, prayerful, generous, sympathetic, impartial, and unconceited.

B. The Christian and the Law (13:1–10)
The Christian is confronted by two legal codes, both of which have a direct bearing on his behavior.

1. The Law of Government (13:1–7)
The Christian recognizes that "the powers that be are ordained of God" (v. 1), so he obeys them who have the rule over him. He honors those who have the right to rule, no matter what their politics. The Christian knows nothing of civil disobedience or of activism against constituted authority. He renders unto Caesar the things that are Caesar's.

2. The Law of God (13:8–10)

The Christian governs his behavior according to the commandments of God's moral law. Here, the apostle restates five of the ten commandments, but he lifts our keeping of those commandments to a higher plane—we keep God's moral law, not because of *law* but because of *love*—"Love worketh no ill to his neighbor: therefore love is the fulfilling of the law" (v. 10).

C. The Christian and His Lord (13:11–14)

The Christian governs his behavior on the principle that the Lord is coming soon. "The night is far spent, the day is at hand: let us therefore cast off the works of darkness" (v. 12).

D. The Christian and His Light (14:1–15:7)

The Christian also governs his behavior on the principle that others may not have as much light as he does. He is to consider his weaker brother and not to do anything that would cause him to stumble. This settles, once and for all, such questions as whether or not a Christian should smoke or drink, dance or play cards, go to see certain movies, or indulge in other kinds of questionable amusements. Paul doesn't deal with these specifics. He deals instead with the hottest issue of his day among Christians—the issue of whether or not a believer could eat certain kinds of meat—and he refrains from giving us a list of dos and don'ts. He tells us not to cause our weaker brother to stumble.

By the same token, the weaker brother is not to hold the stronger brother ransom to his scruples.

E. The Christian and the Lost (15:8–33)

The Christian must govern his behavior on the principle that he has a solemn duty, before God, to be actively engaged in reaching lost people for Christ. Paul not only gave exhortation along this line, he cited himself as an example. He was going to Jerusalem, but he is coming to Rome, and then he is going on to Spain. His *policy* was to "preach the gospel, not where Christ was named, lest I should build upon another man's foundation" (v. 20). His *passion* was for the regions beyond, and that should be the passion of every member of heaven's family.

F. The Christian and His Love (16:1–16)

The Christian is called upon to love all the people of God and should be actively involved in making friends of those of like precious faith. He should know many by name, they should be in his prayer book, their names should come readily to his mind. He should take a positive and friendly interest in the whole family.

Paul's remarkable example of his own involvement with the Lord's people is seen in the list of names he introduces into his letter. He mentions about thirty people and several groups, one right after another! Most of these people were in Rome—a city he had not yet visited.

That is Christian love. That is the wonderful fellowship of the family of God.

G. The Christian and the Lie (16:17–20)

So far as the lie is concerned—the active work of Satan in seeking to subvert and destroy the family of God—the Christian governs his behavior on the principle that those who teach false doctrine are to be marked and avoided. Christian love does not mean that you receive false teachers into your home, have fellowship with them, and help them on their way. "They that are such," says Paul, "serve not our Lord Jesus Christ" (v. 18). They have a Christ in the cults, but he is not *our* Lord Jesus Christ.

H. The Christian and His Lot (16:21–27)

The Christian has a marvelous lot in life—he is in touch with the most wonderful *family* on earth. The brotherhood into which he has been introduced by means of the new birth is without peer or parallel in the world. All God's children are his brothers and sisters.

Moreover, he is in touch with the most marvelous *facts* ever taught among men. Bible in hand, he has the key to all the issues of time and to the great issues of eternity. The humblest believer, versed in the Scriptures, taught of the Holy Spirit, knows more truth than the most learned scholar in the most prestigious university in the world who is not a believer in the Lord Jesus Christ. What a lot in life!

Such is the book of Romans. It finds us lost and condemned, and leaves us pressing boldly up the straight and narrow way in company with the very aristocracy of heaven.

CHAPTER 10

1 Corinthians

Order in the Church

Corinth was a wealthy city of the Roman Empire. It was situated on a narrow neck of land that joined the southern part of Greece to the northern part. It had two harbors—one facing eastward toward the Aegean Sea and the other facing westward toward the Adriatic. Situated thus, Corinth became the marketplace of the rich trade that flowed between the eastern and western parts of the empire. On a clear day one could see the Acropolis of Athens, some forty-five miles away to the east. To the north could be seen the mountains of Greece, which towered above Delphi, the home of the oracle. The Corinth known to Paul had risen from the ashes of an overthrow at the hands of Rome. Julius Caesar, with his keen sense of military and mercantile importance of a place, rebuilt the city and colonized it with Italians, mostly freedmen.

Naturally, with ships from every sea dropping anchor in her harbors, Neptune was her god. Famous athletic games were held here every two years. The wealth, luxury, and profligacy of Corinth were a byword in the ancient world. Like most seaports, Corinth was very wicked; it was the Vanity Fair of the Roman Empire, so famous for its debauchery and drunkenness that the very name *Corinthian* became a synonym for vice.

On his second missionary journey Paul stayed eighteen months at Corinth to establish the church there. From Corinth he wrote his two letters to the Thessalonians. On his third missionary journey he visited Corinth again and, on that occasion, wrote his letter to the Romans. He wrote this letter to the Corinthians on his third missionary journey, while at Ephesus. We place it in the book of Acts in chapter 19 between verses 20 and 21.

This, the longest of Paul's letters, deals with the quarrels and questions of this church—a very gifted church but one that was carnal, worldly, and childish. The chief theological note is *the cross*—Paul refers to Calvary numerous times, bringing the cross of Christ to bear on Corinthian conceit, carnality, and corruption.

   I. Introduction (1:1–9)
  II. Divisions in the Church (1:10–4:21)
      A. The True Narrowness of Sectarianism (1:10–2:16)
         1. Its Clannishness Is a Mistake (1:10–17)
         2. Its Cleverness Is a Mistake (1:18–2:16)
      B. The True Nature of Sectarianism (chaps. 3–4)
         1. Sectarianism Is Not Spiritual (3:1–17)
         2. Sectarianism Is Not Sensible (3:18–4:21)
 III. Discipline in the Church (chaps. 5–6)
      A. A Moral Problem (chap. 5)
      B. A Material Problem (chap. 6)
  IV. Difficulties in the Church (chaps. 7–14)
      A. The Matter of One's Personal Walk (chaps. 7–10)
         1. Paul's Exhortation (chaps. 7–8)
            a. Regarding Marriage (chap. 7)
            b. Regarding Meats (chap. 8)
         2. Paul's Example (chap. 9)
         3. Paul's Explanation (chap. 10)
      B. The Matter of One's Public Worship (chaps. 11–14)
         1. The Gift of the Lord's Supper (chap. 11)
         2. The Gifts of the Lord's Servants (chaps. 12–14)
   V. Disbelief in the Church (chap. 15)
      A. The Resurrection of Christ (15:1–19)
      B. The Resurrection of Christians (15:20–58)
  VI. Conclusion (chap. 16)
      A. The Church and Its Finances (16:1–9)
      B. The Church and Its Fellowship (16:10–24)

The key to 1 Corinthians is found in 1:30, where we read, "But of him are ye in Christ Jesus, who of God is made unto us wisdom, and righteousness, and sanctification, and redemption." The four divisions of the epistle form a commentary on this verse.

I. INTRODUCTION (1:1–9)

In his introduction Paul underlines his apostleship and his consequent authority. He makes it clear from the start that, even though he is dealing in this letter with local issues, the letter itself is for "all that in every place call upon the name of Jesus Christ our Lord, both theirs and ours" (1:2). Moreover, he acknowledges that the Corinthian church is exceedingly gifted but that this only added to its responsibility.

II. DIVISIONS IN THE CHURCH (1:10–4:21)

Because of the disorders in this church, this letter is preeminently the epistle of church order. By dealing with what was wrong at Corinth, Paul shows us how to do what is right in our own local church.

The divisions in the church then were based on the same thing as divisions in the church now—personality and pride. "Our man is the best man," was the concept. Thus today we have churches that follow Calvin and churches that follow Luther, churches that follow Wesley and churches that follow John Knox.

In Paul's day, this sectarian, denominational spirit had raised its head at Corinth. Only there some were saying, "I am of Paul," others were saying, "I am of Apollos," while another faction was saying, "Peter's our man." One super-pious group was saying, "We are of Christ."

There were those who were saying, "We are of Paul. Paul is a *scholar*. He is a graduate of the Tarsus University. Paul has a degree from the Jerusalem University. Paul is the only intellectual there among the apostles. We like Paul. There is nothing narrow-minded about Paul. Besides, Paul founded this church."

Some were saying, "We are of Apollos. Apollos is the *speaker*. He's an eloquent man. We always get something when he speaks." Apollos was from Alexandria, and he had brought with him to Corinth a blend of Jewishness and a dash of Hellenist sophistication. Moreover, he was an orator. He could preach people right out of their seats, get them shouting "Amen!" So there were plenty in Corinth who wanted Apollos. Never mind that his theology was not always right. Apollos was their man.

Others were boasting, "We are of Peter [Cephas]. Peter is *solid*. He's the rock on which the church is founded. He comes before either Paul or Apollos; he is the one who took the lead at Pentecost. Besides, Peter inclines toward the old paths. He's a safe man, is Peter, and he has the confidence of the mother church."

Worst of all, some were saying, "We are of Christ. After all, Christ is the *Savior*. We are gathered to the Lord's name alone; we are not a denomination, we *are* the church. We understand church truth and the headship of Christ. We have gone forth to Him outside the camp. We are of Christ."

Such were the divisions in the Corinthian church. Paul lumps them all together and throws out all such party spirit. "Is Christ divided? was Paul crucified for you? . . . I have planted, Apollos watered; but God gave the increase" (1:13; 3:6).

Paul utterly repudiated such a spirit and refused to have his name linked with a religious party in the church. Then, knowing the Greek love for intellectualism, Paul denounced all worldly wisdom as being out of place in the believer's thinking. At the heart of divine wisdom is the cross, which is a source of stumbling to the Jews, and foolishness to the Greeks. Returning to his theme of sectarianism, Paul showed that only carnal Christians have a party spirit and warned that in view of the judgment seat of Christ, Christians would be wise to cease glorying in men and begin living lives acceptable to God.

III. DISCIPLINE IN THE CHURCH (CHAPS. 5–6)

There were two serious social problems in the church at Corinth.

A. A Moral Problem (chap. 5)

"It is reported commonly that there is fornication among you, and such fornication as is not so much as named among the Gentiles" (v. 1). It sometimes happens that a believer falls into sin. When he does, it sometimes is the case that he goes deeper into sin than even his unsaved neighbors. Satan makes a special effort to drag believers down and, through them, bring disgrace on the entire Christian community. Such was the case of David, to whom it may truly have been said, "Thou hast given great occasion to the enemies of the LORD to blaspheme" (2 Sam. 12:14).

Paul does not hesitate in a case like this. "Excommunicate the man at once," he demanded. "Hand him over to Satan for the destruction of the flesh" (see v. 5). Paul diagnosed the case as one calling for instant expulsion from the fellowship of the church. The local church is not to be defiled by the presence in its midst and at the Lord's Table of those who are morally impure. The demand for instant judgment and excommunication was not intended, however, to be the end of the matter. The aim was repentance and restoration, though this might not come until some terrible thing from Satan had overtaken the guilty individual. God *never* condones immorality in the believer.

There was not only a moral problem at Corinth.

B. A Material Problem (chap. 6)

"Dare any of you, having a matter against another, go to law before the un[saved], and not before the saints?" (v. 1). It is bad enough when believers squabble. It is worse when they squabble before the unsaved. It is worse still when they squabble over the matter of money. It is worst of all when there is deliberate fraud involved.

Paul says that the believer has two recourses in such a matter. First, he should bring the accused before a meeting of the church—not necessarily the whole church, but chosen men in the church known for their fairness and wisdom. If that fails to produce results, the spiritual thing is to defer the case to the court of heaven and leave the matter in God's hands, even if it means being defrauded. In no case should a believer take another believer to court. Whether or not the man practicing the fraud is a believer, however, is not determined in this letter. It is hard to see how a person who habitually defrauds others can be a believer. Perhaps this was a case of just a single incident of temptation overtaking a man.

IV. DIFFICULTIES IN THE CHURCH (CHAPS. 7–14)

Four basic difficulties surfaced, which Paul had to resolve for the believers at Corinth—four difficulties of two kinds. There were those connected with our *personal walk* as believers, and those dealing with our *public worship* as Christians.

A. The Matter of One's Personal Walk (chaps. 7–10)

1. Paul's Exhortation (chaps. 7–8)

a. Regarding Marriage (chap. 7)

This is Paul's great chapter on the relationship of husband and wife, single and married, and it is a chapter of much sanctified common sense. Paul views various possible domestic situations.

There is the question of husband and wife giving each other their marital rights; there is the question of whether a person should remain single or get married, and the companion question of whether it is fair for a man to lead a woman on in this area and not make good her hopes; there is the question of one partner being a saved person and the other an unsaved person. Presumably, this kind of unequal yoke arose either out of a forced marriage or because one of the partners became a Christian after marriage. The Bible does not countenance the willful marriage of a believer to an unbeliever, although, if ignorance of God's Word is at the bottom of such a marriage, there might be some excuse. Where an unequal yoke exists, the saved one should be such a reflection of Christ as will make the gospel attractive to the unsaved one.

Paul also discusses in this important section of his letter the question of the children of a mixed marriage; the question of celibacy deliberately chosen in order to further the cause of Christ; the question of the separation of the two marriage partners. Paul explores all these questions and puts each one in its proper perspective.

b. Regarding Meats (chap. 8)

A vexing problem in Paul's day revolved around the question of whether a believer should eat meat that was sacrificed to idols. The church was split on the issue. Some said it made no difference how meat was killed, or if it was offered to an idol, since idols were nothing. A Christian had freedom of conscience to eat what he liked. He was not under law since the Mosaic ceremonial law was obsolete. On the other hand were those who said that a believer should not eat such meat. It was a serious form of compromise. Some would go further and say there were all kinds of things about which a believer should have scruples. This is really the point of this whole passage.

The whole question of meat is totally irrelevant in our day, but the issue of questionable amusements and doubtful practices is as relevant as ever it was. In our culture the question for a Christian would not be so much a matter of what he should *eat* as whether he should *drink*. Should he take a social glass of wine? Or should he go to movies? Should he read certain books? Should he play cards for money? Should he go to a dance? Should he have a cable channel on his TV that shows dirty movies? These are all questions that have to do with our conscience.

The principle that covered the question of meats in Paul's day covers all such matters in our day. The rule was simple: "For if any man see thee which hast knowledge sit at meat in the idol's temple, shall not the conscience of him which is weak be emboldened to eat those things which are offered to idols; And through thy knowledge shall the weak brother perish, for whom Christ died? But when ye sin so against the brethren, and wound their weak conscience, ye sin against Christ. Wherefore, if meat [if what I do, what I permit in my life] make my brother to [stumble], I will eat no flesh while the world standeth, lest I make my brother to [stumble]" (vv. 10–13).

Paul sidesteps the issue of meat—an issue that was of only passing relevance and deals instead with the broader issue. I may see nothing wrong with a certain line of behavior. Indeed, I may be strong enough that I can read that book or do that thing without it doing me any harm at all. *But what about my brother?* He may see me doing this thing, think he can do it, too—and become a drunkard, become a slave to the thing, fall into overpowering temptation. He may be ruined, and I would be responsible. I have become guilty of a sin against Christ.

In all *questionable* matters, the law of Christ is that we refrain from doing things that will cause our brethren to stumble. That simple principle will rule out of our lives all kinds of questionable amusements and practices.

2. Paul's Example (chap. 9)

This is one of those great autobiographical passages that occur from time to time in Paul's writings and that give us such fascinating glimpses of the man himself. Here, Paul shows how he could have claimed his rights as an apostle and as a man, he could have asserted his rights in the matter of marriage and joined Peter in the ranks of married men, he could have insisted on monetary support for his ministry. But he set aside his rights for the sake of the gospel.

3. Paul's Explanation (chap. 10)

At this point Paul develops some of the remarkable typology of the Old Testament and draws pertinent lessons from it for the benefit of the believers who were making such an issue of "meats." He follows it up with some practical exhortation before finally moving on to other problems at Corinth.

B. The Matter of One's Public Worship (chaps. 11–14)

1. The Gift of the Lord's Supper (chap. 11)

The institution of the Lord's Table is one of the great provisions made for us by the Lord. Its great function is to remind us of His person, His passion, and His position. He said, "This do in remembrance of me. . . . Ye do show the Lord's death till he come" (vv. 24, 26). The word translated "show" is literally "proclaim." The Lord's Table is a proclamation to the world and to the spirit watchers in the unseen world of the victory of the Lord's death.

In Corinth, this feast was preceded by a love feast—a communal meal where all the believers joined to eat together. The trouble was that it had degenerated into a society parade. The rich and wealthy feasted with abandon; the poor made do with almost nothing. Paul tells them to get this deplorable situation put right at once—and anything else he sees wrong he will deal with when he comes.

All this is preceded by a controversial passage on headship, hair, and head coverings. The underlying principle in these verses (vv. 1–16) is clear enough, however. In the church, God has vested headship and leadership in the man, not the woman (not a popular teaching in this age of feminist movements), and the man is directly responsible to Christ, who owns the headship of the Godhead itself. We accept this kind of teaching, regardless of social and political challenge, because believers are to be ruled by the Spirit of God, not by the spirit of this world.

2. The Gifts of the Lord's Servants (chaps. 12–14)

The disorder in the church over the question of gifts—what these gifts are, how permanent they are, who should have such gifts, who could exercise their gifts, and the outright abuse of gifts—was extensive.

Paul points out that *no one man* has *all* the gifts; and *no one gift* is given to any one man. Spiritual gifts are sovereignly bestowed by the Holy Spirit—some to this believer, some to that one. We cannot demand a gift of God. The Holy Spirit distributes them as He sees fit. Nor can we work up a gift by some of the psychological conditioning that goes on in so-called "charismatic" circles.

Some gifts were of a temporary, transitional nature because they were sign-gifts, especially given to convince unbelieving Jews of the divine calling of the Christian church or because they were necessary for the instruction of scattered believers until such time as the New Testament was completed and in general circulation. Once the Jewish nation was destroyed by the Romans and the canon of Scripture was completed by the Holy Spirit, these transitional gifts ceased.

Then, too, one man should not covet another man's gift. As every member of a body is essential, has its own place in the body and its own particular function, and as each member of the body functions for the good of the whole, so with the mystical body of Christ. The Holy Spirit has sovereignly distributed the gifts so that the whole church can benefit and grow.

The biggest problem in Corinth had to do with the gift of tongues. Paul dealt severely with those who claimed to have this gift. They seemed to think they were heaven's favorites. He first of all silenced the women (that in itself would put an end to much of the so-called charismatic movement in our day), and then he said that, when the gift of tongues was exercised, it had to be in order. At the most only three people could indulge the gift at a given service, they were to exercise their gift one at a time, and they had to have an interpreter present.

Moreover, "tongues" was one of the transitional gifts. It would come to an automatic end in the church when it had served its purpose (13:8). It was a *sign*, it was a *Jewish* sign—its purpose was to convince the unbelieving Jew (14:21–22) with special attention to be paid to Paul's Old Testament quotation from Isaiah 28:11–12. And it was a *judgment* sign on the nation of Israel. Added to all that, it was the least important of the gifts. Far better to speak a few words everyone could understand than babble in an unknown tongue for hours.

Later on, the apostle John would add even more stringent warnings because of the possibility of believers being deceived by lying spirits (1 John 4:1–4).

More important than gift is grace. In that matchless thirteenth chapter, Paul eulogizes love as being supreme in the life of a believer.

V. Disbelief in the Church (chap. 15)

The great cardinal doctrine of the church was the doctrine of resurrection. This doctrine had come under attack at Corinth, and Paul therefore dealt with it under two specific heads.

A. The Resurrection of Christ (15:1–19)

He makes it abundantly clear that Christ's resurrection was a solid fact of history, attested to by all kinds of credible witnesses. A denial of the doctrine of resurrection was a denial of the doctrine of salvation: "If Christ be not raised, your faith is vain; ye are yet in your sins" (v. 17). Let no Christ-denying liberal think he is a Christian, and let no one who denies the resurrection of Christ think he will be in heaven. To deny the resurrection is to deny the faith.

B. The Resurrection of Christians (15:20–58)

Christ arose and so shall we! His resurrection is the unconditional guarantee of ours, and we shall have a body "like unto his glorious body" (Phil. 3:21). Paul spells out seven ways in which our bodies will be changed in the resurrection, to enable us to live in a new dimension. He draws his teaching on this subject to a close with a composite quotation from the Old Testament (Isa. 25:8; Hos. 13:14): "O death, where is thy sting? O grave, where is thy victory?" (v. 55). When the day of the rapture dawns, this will be sung as a duet—those who are alive and remain at the Lord's coming will cleave the skies with the triumphant shout, "O death, where is thy sting?" Those who, down through the ages, have died before the Lord's return will leap from their tombs shouting, "O grave, where is thy victory?"

VI. Conclusion (chap. 16)

A. The Church and Its Finances (16:1–9)

Paul was most concerned that money matters in the church be above suspicion. He says that we should give *periodically*, on the first day of the week; that we should give *proportionately*, "as God hath prospered," in direct proportion to our income; that giving should be done *purposefully*, "that there be no [collections] when I come" (v. 2). Paul wanted no high-pressure appeals. He did not want people to give on impulse, just because he was there. Giving should be done in a much more deliberate and dispassionate way than as a result of pressure.

B. The Church and Its Fellowship (16:10–24)

Paul mentions his own continuing interest in his friends at Corinth and expresses his desire to come and fellowship with them when it is God's time. He mentions the coming of Timothy and Apollos, and recalls this one and that one by name in the fellowship of the church there at Corinth. "My love be with you all in Christ Jesus" (v. 24), he says as his parting word. No divisions, difficulties, or doubts on their part could ever stop him from loving them.

CHAPTER 11

2 CORINTHIANS

One More Warning

When Paul wrote 2 Corinthians he was disappointed, apprehensive, and physically ill. Troubles seemed to be brewing at a number of churches. Many at Corinth appeared to be in full revolt against him. Galatia was falling away to what Paul stigmatizes as "another gospel." He had himself narrowly escaped from the enraged mob at Ephesus. Stress and strain had left their mark. "We were pressed out of measure, above strength, insomuch that we despaired even of life," he writes (1:8).

Between the writing of 1 and 2 Corinthians, Paul had intended to visit Corinth but matters were taken out of his hands by the riot at Ephesus. Instead, Paul fled north, making his way to Troas and to Macedonia. Titus had gone to Corinth instead and was supposed to meet Paul at Troas with a report. Paul was very anxious to know how his first letter had been received. But Titus failed to show up, and Paul's concern for his beloved Corinthian converts deepened. He found it hard to sit still. Restless, like a caged lion, he went on to Macedonia, probably to Philippi. And there, at last, Titus showed up with news from Corinth, good news mixed with bad.

Paul's letter to the Corinthians had produced a good effect, on the whole. The immoral brother, for example, had been expelled from the fellowship and had shown deep repentance. A vocal minority in the church, however, was stirring up trouble against Paul, challenging his apostleship and attacking him in a slanderous way. They accused Paul of fickleness and cowardice. Paul, they hinted, was afraid to come and meet them face to face. "I call God for a record upon my soul," wrote the indignant apostle, "that to spare you I came not as yet unto Corinth" (1:23).

Their attacks on Paul continued. They accused him of pride and boasting and of preaching in riddles. "If our gospel be hid, it is hid to them that are lost," was Paul's stinging rejoinder to that (4:3). They accused him of weakness and of crudeness of speech. "Perhaps I am not a polished speaker," retorts Paul, "but I do know what I am talking about" (11:6 PHILLIPS). They accused him of unkempt appearance. Is that so! Well, well! "We have this treasure in earthen vessels," flashes out Paul, "that the excellency of the power may be of God, and not of us" (4:7). They accused him of dishonesty, even of near insanity. "If we have been 'mad,'" says Paul, "it was for God's glory" (5:13 PHILLIPS). Many a totally dedicated believer, consumed with a master-passion for Christ, has been accused of insanity. Worst of all they accused him of a spurious, false apostleship. "I was not a whit behind the very chiefest apostles," is Paul's answer to that (11:5)—a fact to which Luke bears ample evidence in the book of Acts.

So then, like molten lava from an erupting volcano, Paul pours out his heart in this second letter in a passionate answer to his critics. It is the most personal of all Paul's epistles. He gives us insights into his great heart, insights found nowhere else in all his writings. It had become a duty and a necessity for Paul, for the sake of his ministry and his apostleship, to defend himself. He was driven by his enemies to meet them on their own ground. (The word forms for *boast*, for example, appear numerous times in the book.)

From chapter 10 on, where Paul comes to final grips with his adversaries, we see a man, inspired of God, not only to tell things about himself that hitherto he had never told a soul, but able, with consummate skill, to expose those fine-feathered birds, who formed the minority party at Corinth, for what they really were—birds of prey.

What, though, were they after? They were out for money, for high office in the church at a cheap price. But what price had they ever paid for the cause of Christ? They were said to have had visions and revelations, but Paul had been to heaven itself and, with all his vast gifts of eloquence notwithstanding, he could not, would not dare to tell what he heard and saw there.

These opponents aimed at nothing less than to discredit an apostle and to enslave the Gentile churches to the direction and control of Jerusalem. They were not ambassadors for Christ. Theirs was another Jesus . . . another spirit . . . another gospel. Truly it was a bold man or a foolhardy one to ever get into the ring with Paul!

For all their malice toward the great apostle, we can thank these old-time detractors of his for one thing: they stung Paul to the point where he had to defend himself for the sake of the gospel he preached. In so doing, he left us with a letter that gives us our best glimpse of the personality of the great apostle.

The two Corinthian letters of Paul can be contrasted thus:

COMPARISON OF 1 AND 2 CORINTHIANS	
1 Corinthians	**2 Corinthians**
• Insight into the life, character, and conditions of the church	• Insight into the life, character, and conditions of the apostle Paul
• Objective and practical	• Subjective and personal
• Deliberate	• Impassioned
• Warns against pagan influences	• Warns against Judaistic influences

   I. Introduction (1:1–2)
  II. Paul and His Commission (1:3–5:21)
    A. He Defends His Motives (1:3–2:17)
      1. By Describing His Tribulations (1:3–11)
      2. By Declaring His Truthfulness (1:12–2:2)
      3. By Depicting His Triumphs (2:3–17)
        a. The Triumph of His Letter (2:3–11)
        b. The Triumph of His Leading (2:12–13)
        c. The Triumph of His Life (2:14–17)
    B. He Defends His Message (chaps. 3–5)
      1. The Commendation of His Message (3:1–5)
      2. The Comprehension of His Message (3:6–18)
      3. The Completeness of His Message (4:1–5:10)
        a. Its Power to Give Light (4:1–6)
        b. Its Power to Give Life (4:7–5:10)
      4. The Compulsion of His Message (5:11–21)
 III. Paul and His Converts (chaps. 6–9)
    A. Their Faithful Partnership in the Gospel (chaps. 6–7)
    The cost in terms of:
      1. Sacrifice (6:1–10)
      2. Separation (6:11–18)
      3. Sanctity (7:1)
      4. Sincerity (7:2–16)
    B. Their Financial Partnership in the Gospel (chaps. 8–9)
    Giving is an act of:

I. INTRODUCTION (1:1–2)

We begin our survey of this book with a glimpse of Paul's credentials.

II. PAUL AND HIS COMMISSION (1:3–5:21)

Paul begins his letter by restating his apostolic commission, which some were calling into question.

A. He Defends His Motives (1:3–2:17)

Paul was the most honest and transparent of men, detesting any kind of double dealing. It pained him deeply that any should question his integrity. So he defended the motives of his ministry.

1. By Describing His Tribulations (1:3–11)

"We should like you, our brothers, to know something of what we went through in Asia," he says (1:8 PHILLIPS). "At that time we were completely overwhelmed; the burden was more than we could bear; in fact we told ourselves that this was the end." He faced imminent death for the cause of Christ.

A person's motives, to say the least, have to be above suspicion when he is prepared to lay his life on the line for the cause he promotes.

Nor was there only the matter of his tribulations.

2. By Declaring His Truthfulness (1:12–2:2)

"Our dealings with you," he says, "have been absolutely aboveboard and sincere before God" (see 1:12). Just because circumstances above and beyond his control had forced a change of plans, so that it had been impossible for him to come to Corinth as promised, this did not mean he was fickle and two-faced. Paul's personal integrity, which the Corinthians themselves had experienced, was the guarantee that his motives were pure.

3. By Depicting His Triumphs (2:3–17)

Look, he says in effect, how God has triumphed through my ministry. Let that be the measure of my motives. Look, for example, at the way He blessed my *letter*. That sinful brother was not only disciplined as I demanded but he has repented and can now be restored.

Look at the way He has blessed my *leading*. Sure, I was going to come to Corinth. Sure, I was hounded out of Ephesus. But instead God led me to Troas where "a door was opened unto me of the Lord" (2:12). Look at the way He has blessed my *life*. "Thanks be to God who leads us, wherever we are, on his own triumphant way and makes our knowledge of him spread throughout the world like a lovely perfume" (2:14 PHILLIPS).

Here is one proof of the sincerity of our motives. The very triumphs of the gospel prove that God's hand is upon us. So then, Paul defended his motives.

B. He Defends His Message (chaps. 3–5)

It was not only *why* he preached but *what* he preached that was being called into question by his enemies. So Paul puts up a fourfold defense of his message.

1. The Commendation of His Message (3:1–5)

"Do we begin again to commend ourselves? or need we, as some others, epistles of commendation to you, or letters of commendation from you? Ye are our epistle" (vv. 1–2). Paul is saying, "Now let's not be silly, brethren. What about our message? You yourselves are an open letter about Christ, which we ourselves have written. Why, the fact that you are saved and in the church is living proof of the purity, the power, and the productiveness of our preaching!"

2. The Comprehension of His Message (3:6–18)

It was a glorious message, far more glorious than the Old Testament law, so much admired by Paul's Judaizing foes. It was true that the Old Testament law had a glory, but it was a fading glory. But the gospel! Instead of waning, like the glow on Moses' face, the glory of the gospel waxes and waxes with the passing of time. "But we all, with open face beholding as in a glass the glory of the Lord, are changed into the same image from glory to glory, even as by the Spirit of the Lord" (v. 18). Moses had to veil his face so that Israel would not see the glory dim and fade, which had been imprinted on it by his meeting with God on the mount. But as we look into the face of Jesus our own face glows. We have all met Christians who simply seem to radiate the beauty and sunshine of Christ. And it never fades.

3. The Completeness of His Message (4:1–5:10)

There are two things about my message, says Paul, that you must never forget. It has power to give *light*—"If our gospel be hid, it is hid to them that are lost: In whom the god of this world hath blinded the minds of them which believe not, lest the light of the glorious gospel of Christ, who is the image of God, should shine unto them. . . . For God, who commanded the light to shine out of darkness, hath shined in our hearts, to give the light of the knowledge of the glory of God in the face of Jesus Christ" (4:3–4, 6). Yes, the gospel has power to give light. Satan may seize upon the minds. But God goes deeper—He shines His light into the heart.

Moreover, Paul says, my gospel not only has power to give light, it has power to give *life*—"This priceless treasure we hold, so to speak, in a common earthenware jar—to show that the splendid power of it belongs to God and not to us. We are handicapped on all sides, but we are never frustrated; we are puzzled, but never in despair. We are persecuted, but we never have to stand it alone: we may be knocked down but we are never knocked out! Every day we experience something of the death of the Lord Jesus, so that we may also know the power of the life of Jesus in these bodies of ours" (4:7–10 PHILLIPS).

Not just victorious life, but everlasting life. What had happened at Ephesus seems to have left a deep impression on Paul. He felt it likely that he might, one day, actually be killed in the pursuit of his mission. At first he shrank from this thought of dying—"We do not want to be unclothed," he says (see 5:4). But then he remembered that to be "absent from the body" is to be "present with the Lord" (5:8). The message he proclaims is complete. It has power to impart light and life!

4. The Compulsion of His Message (5:11–21)

"Knowing therefore," he says, "the terror of the Lord, we persuade men . . ." (v. 11). "Now then," he concludes, "we are ambassadors for Christ, as though God did beseech you by us: we pray you in Christ's stead, be ye reconciled to God" (v. 20).

This, then, was Paul's commission. He was, when all is said and done, an ambassador for Christ. He represented the court of heaven at the court of the human heart. His motives were pure; his message was powerful. He was unafraid of his foes. They had nothing on him.

III. PAUL AND HIS CONVERTS (CHAPS. 6–9)

Paul had by no means finished with his foes but before he opened up his really heavy guns on them, he had a few words to say to his friends. He wished to speak to his friends about their partnerships.

A. Their Faithful Partnership in the Gospel (chaps. 6–7)

"We then," he begins, "as workers together . . ." He must discuss with these friends of his the cost involved in out-and-out service for God. There is cost in several terms.

1. The Cost in Terms of Sacrifice (6:1–10)

This, says Paul, is what partnership in the gospel costs: "We want to prove ourselves genuine ministers of God whatever we have to go through—patient endurance of troubles or even disasters, being flogged or imprisoned; being mobbed, having to work like slaves, having to go without food or sleep. . . . Never far from death, yet here we are alive, always 'going through it' yet never 'going under.' We know sorrow, yet our joy is inextinguishable. We have 'nothing to bless ourselves with,' yet we bless many others with true riches. We are penniless, and yet in reality we have everything worth having" (6:4–5, 10 PHILLIPS). What is our Christian service costing us?

2. The Cost in Terms of Separation (6:11–18)

"Don't link up with unbelievers and try to work with them. What common interest can there be between goodness and evil? How can light and darkness share life together? How can there be harmony between Christ and the devil? What business can a believer have with an unbeliever? What common ground can idols hold with the temple of God? . . . Wherefore come ye out from among them and be ye separate, saith the Lord" (6:14–17 PHILLIPS). It's not the man who stands inside the barrel who can lift it—it's the man who stands outside. Archimedes said, "Give me a place to stand and with a lever I will move the whole world."[1]

3. The Cost in Terms of Sanctity (7:1)

"Having therefore these promises, dearly beloved, let us cleanse ourselves from all filthiness of the flesh and spirit, perfecting holiness in the fear of God." Faithful partnership in the gospel calls for cleanliness of life. God does not need a golden or a silver vessel. He can use an old clay pot. But He must have a clean one.

4. The Cost in Terms of Sincerity (7:2–16)

"To your face," says Paul, "I talk to you with utter frankness; behind your back I talk about you with deepest pride" (7:4 PHILLIPS).

So then Paul talks about their faithful partnership in the gospel and all that such partnership costs.

B. Their Financial Partnership in the Gospel (chaps. 8–9)

On the subject of giving, these two chapters are among the greatest chapters in the New Testament. Briefly we should note what the act of giving means.

1. Giving Is an Act of Grace (8:1–12)

Paul cites the example of the Macedonians who, as he puts it, "being down to their last penny themselves, produced a magnificent concern for other people. I can guarantee that they were willing to give to the limit of their means, yes and beyond their means, without the slightest urging from me or anyone else. In fact they simply begged us to accept their gifts and so let them share the honor of supporting their brothers in Christ" (8:2–4 PHILLIPS).

What an example of giving that is! But more! What an example of giving this is—"Ye know the grace of our Lord Jesus Christ, that, though he was rich, yet for your sakes he became poor, that ye through his poverty might be rich" (v. 9). Giving is an act of grace.

2. Giving Is an Act of Gratitude (8:13–9:5)

Giving is a matter of share and share alike. "At present your plenty should supply their need, and then at some future date their plenty may supply your need" (8:14 PHILLIPS).

Giving is not only an act of grace and an act of gratitude. It is more.

3. Giving Is an Act of Getting (9:6)

The more you give, the more you get. "But this I say, He which soweth sparingly shall reap also sparingly; and he which soweth bountifully shall reap also bountifully." What could make more sense than that? But, while this is true, we must beware of any attempt to manipulate God, of using even a biblical principle for wrong motives. This was the essence of Balaam's sin. In hope of financial gain, he taught Balak, King of Moab, how to use a biblical principle (the holiness of God and His governmental dealings with His people) to bring about an end he coveted—the discomfiture of Israel. Balaam got his money—and God's judgment. Nothing is more reprehensible in our day than the pleas of certain high-powered radio and TV personalities who assure people that God will make them rich if they give money to the "ministries" of these personalities.

4. Giving Is an Act of Gladness (9:7–14)

"Every man according as he purposeth in his heart, so let him give; not grudgingly, or of necessity: for God loveth a cheerful giver" (v. 7). Or, as one might literally translate the Greek, "God loves a hilarious giver!"

But, above all, giving is an act from above.

5. Giving Is an Act of God (9:15)

Paul winds up this whole magnificent passage with the statement: "Thanks be unto God for his unspeakable gift." What higher motive could we have than that?

Thus, Paul speaks to his converts and talks with them about their faithful partnership in the gospel and about their financial partnership in the gospel. Now he turns his attention once more to his foes.

IV. Paul and His Critics (10:1–13:10)

These last four chapters deal with three great issues.

A. His Personal Appearance (chap. 10)

"His letters," Paul's critics were saying, "are weighty and powerful; but his bodily presence is weak, and his speech contemptible" (v. 10). But Paul has something better to boast about than splendid physique, good looks, handsome mien, and eloquent words. He has spiritual strength, spiritual stateliness, and spiritual stature.

B. His Proven Apostleship (11:1–12:13)

Paul bases his apostleship on the fourfold argument: the greatness of his exercise, his example, his experience, and his exaltation. The New Testament church has few who can compare with him in these things.

It is in this section of the epistle we have that famous list of Paul's sufferings for the sake of the gospel. In this section, too, Paul tells of that mysterious experience he had when he was caught up into the third heaven and saw things "that cannot, and indeed must not, be translated into human speech." It is in this section also he tells of that equally mysterious "messenger of Satan" (12:7) sent to buffet him lest he be exalted out of measure.

C. His Passionate Appeal (12:14–13:10)

He tells his friends that he still plans to come to Corinth. In view of this third coming, he prepares them.

1. In View of His Third Coming He Woos Them (12:14–18)

"It is you I want," he says, "not your money. . . . I will most gladly spend and be spent for your good, even though it means that the more I love you, the less you love me" (12:15 PHILLIPS).

2. In View of His Third Coming He Warns Them (12:19–13:10)

Paul was now ready to visit the Corinthians for the third time. "My coming will *not* mean leniency for those who had sinned. . . . It will in fact be a proof that I speak by the power of Christ. . . . You should be looking at yourselves to make sure that you are really Christ's. It is yourselves you should be testing, not me" (13:2–3, 5 PHILLIPS, emphasis in original).

And woven into all this is a passionate appeal that those at Corinth, friend and foe alike, might indeed go on to true Christian maturity.

V. CONCLUSION (13:11–14)

"Greet one another with an holy kiss," says Paul (13:12), or as J. B. Phillips renders it, "A handshake all round, please!" Yes, a hearty handshake even to those who have been waving a hostile fist in his face. "Here, brother," says Paul, extending his hand. "Put it there! I don't want to fight you; I want to fellowship with you." There speaks a man of God!

CHAPTER 12

GALATIANS

Magna Carta of Christian Liberty

Paul's epistle to the Galatians has been likened to "the sketch for the finished picture [of] Romans,"[1] and certainly the two letters have much in common. Both emphasize salvation, the believer's emancipation from the law, and the removal before God of any difference between Jew and Gentile. Paul's Galatian letter also has common ground with 2 Corinthians, for both letters emphasize the fact of his apostleship.

The geographic area covered by Galatia varied from time to time. Originally it was a country in northwestern Asia Minor settled by the Gauls, who gave the area its name. Later, Galatia was taken over by the Romans, who enlarged the territory southward and incorporated it into the empire as a province. It is a disputed point as to whether or not Paul addressed his Galatian epistle to churches located in the southern part of the province, founded on his first missionary journey, or whether he addressed churches located in the northern part of the province, founded on his second missionary journey.

The following sequence is suggested:

1. Paul was converted on the Damascus road and stayed for a short time in that city, at which time he testified in the synagogue.
2. Paul left Damascus for Arabia, where he stayed for some three years, thinking through the scope and implications of the gospel in the light of Old Testament revelation and the advent of the Christ, whom he had recently met on the Damascus road.
3. Paul returned from Arabia to Damascus and witnessed in the city. At this time his enemies sought to kill him, and he escaped down over the wall in a basket.

4. Paul came to Jerusalem (three years after his conversion) and was introduced to the apostles by Barnabas. At this time he received a vision telling him to leave Jerusalem and go to the Gentiles.

5. Paul left Jerusalem for Caesarea and thence to Tarsus, where he probably not only labored for the Lord but was disinherited by his family.

6. Barnabas sought him out at Tarsus and brought him to Antioch to help evangelize that important city.

7. Paul paid a second visit to Jerusalem, carrying with him relief money from the young Antioch assembly, probably some time after the death of Herod Agrippa I. It was most likely at this time he had his interview with the apostles to make sure they recognized his status as an apostle.

8. Paul and Barnabas returned to Antioch with John Mark.

9. Paul undertook his first missionary journey, which took him into south Galatia. He then returned to Antioch.

10. Peter visited Antioch and had free intercourse with the Gentiles until certain men from Judea came to the city "from James." Peter then retreated back into strict Judaistic separation from Gentiles, to the consternation and confusion of the Gentile converts in Antioch. Paul at this time rebuked Peter to his face. This was followed by a growing dispute over the law.

11. It was probably at this point that Paul wrote the epistle to the Galatian church, founded by him just a short while before, to warn them against the Judaizers, who were sowing discord and division far and wide among his converts (if so, Galatians is the first of Paul's New Testament epistles).

12. Paul and Barnabas decided, with the backing of the Antioch church, to take the whole matter of Judaistic Christianity to Jerusalem and have it out with the other apostles. This was Paul's third visit to Jerusalem.

13. After the law-keeping issue had been decided on a sound, scriptural basis, Paul and Barnabas returned to Antioch.

14. There, Paul had his dispute with Barnabas over John Mark and parted company with him. Next he selected Silas (a member of the Jerusalem church, who was entrusted with the important circular letter to Gentile churches from Jerusalem) to be his future companion.

15. Paul began his second missionary journey going first to Syria and Cilicia, where Paul had labored in comparative seclusion after his first visit to Jerusalem. Then he went on into Galatia, penetrating to old Galatia in the north before setting out for Europe and the west.

Paul's Galatian letter reveals much about the people who occupied so large and warm a place in his heart. They had received Paul "as an angel of God" (4:14). They would have plucked out their eyes and given them to him, so warmly did they love him. Then they were "so soon removed" by new teachers from Him that called them and embraced "another gospel" (1:6). They had "run well" (5:7) but then were "hinder[ed]" (5:7) and "bewitched" (3:1). They were as ready in their party spirit to "bite and devour one another" (5:15) as they were willing to change teachers and gospels. It is significant that eight out of fifteen "works of the flesh" in Galatians 5:19–21 are sins of strife. They were generous, but inconsistent, impulsive, vehement, treacherous in their dealings, easily discouraged, and quarrelsome.

    I. Introduction (1:1–2)
   II. Paul's Explanation (1:3–2:21)
      A. The Declaration of the Gospel (1:3–5)
         1. Sovereign Grace (1:3)
         2. Saving Grace (1:4a)
         3. Sustaining Grace (1:4b–5)
      B. The Distortion of the Gospel (1:6–10)
      C. The Dynamic of the Gospel (1:11–24)
         1. Paul's Reception of the Gospel (1:11–17)
         2. Paul's Reputation in the Gospel (1:18–24)
      D. The Defense of the Gospel (chap. 2)
         1. How Paul Challenged the Church at Jerusalem (2:1–10)
         2. How Paul Challenged the Church at Antioch (2:11–21)
  III. Paul's Exposition (chaps. 3–4)
      A. How Paul Interrogated the Galatians (3:1–5)
         1. Their Seducers (3:1)
         2. Their Salvation (3:2)
         3. Their Stupidity (3:3a)
         4. Their Sanctification (3:3b)
         5. Their Sufferings (3:4)
         6. Their Successes (3:5)
      B. How Paul Instructed the Galatians (3:6–4:31)
         1. Believers Are the Seed of Abraham (3:6–29)
            a. The Priority of Grace (3:6–18)
            b. The Purpose of Law (3:19–29)
               (1) To Probe the Soul for Sin (3:19–22)
               (2) To Prepare the Soul for Salvation (3:23–29)
         2. Believers Are the Sons of God (chap. 4)
            a. Their Birthright (4:1–7)
            b. Their Betrayal (4:8–20)
               (1) Their Liberty Surrendered (4:8–11)
               (2) Their Love Suppressed (4:12–16)

I. INTRODUCTION (1:1–2)

Paul's introduction is brusque, brief, and bristling with apostolic authority. It has none of the tender overtones that appear in so many of his other letters. He comes straight to the point. He is "Paul, an apostle, (not of men . . . but by Jesus Christ) . . ." (v. 1).

In all his other epistles Paul adds some words of commendation such as "beloved of God" or "saints." The deliberate omission of any such commendation here shows what a serious view he took of the error that the Galatians had embraced.

Also, this is the only epistle addressed to a group of churches. Although some of his other letters appear to be circular letters (notably Ephesians), Galatians stands alone in being formally addressed to "the churches of Galatia" (v. 2).

II. PAUL'S EXPLANATION (1:3–2:21)

Paul devotes the first two chapters to explaining some basic facts about the gospel.

A. The Declaration of the Gospel (1:3–5)

1. Sovereign Grace (1:3)

"Grace be to you and peace from God the Father, and from our Lord Jesus Christ." All the initiative is with God. We have no merit, no claim upon God, no assets. We are poor, wretched, blind, miserable, and naked. Yet God loved us and turned toward us in sovereign, condescending, matchless grace.

2. Saving Grace (1:4a)

"Who gave himself for our sins." This is something we cannot fathom now and shall fathom still less when we see Him as He is, and have the full realization of what that gift of Himself involved.

3. Sustaining Grace (1:4b–5)

"That he might deliver us from this present evil world." The grace of God will see us safely home. God does nothing by halves. He has no intention of being thwarted in His plans and purposes for those who are the objects of His grace.

B. The Distortion of the Gospel (1:6–10)

We are living in an age when toleration is the thing. If one were to speak on a radio broadcast about the Seventh Day Adventists the way Paul speaks here about their counterpart in Galatia, the program would be cut off the air and the station deluged with phone calls and letters. It is not considered good taste to uphold the truth with conviction. Paul declares that those who are distorting the gospel are accursed. And curse them he does more than once in this epistle. This is very solemn and should indicate our attitude toward all false gospels: "But though we, or an angel from heaven, preach any other gospel unto you than that which we have preached unto you, let him be accursed. As we said before, so say I now again, If any man preach any other gospel unto you than that ye have received, let him be accursed" (vv. 8–9).

C. The Dynamic of the Gospel (1:11–24)

At this point Paul gives some background on his own experiences in connection with the gospel. He tells of his *reception* of the gospel (vv. 11–17), and his *reputation* in the gospel (vv. 18–24).

He emphatically claims that his message was not learned at the feet of Peter, James, or John. It was learned at the feet of Jesus. After his conversion he had gone into Arabia to think through the implications of that momentous meeting with the risen Christ on the Damascus road. He took with him "Moses and the prophets" (see Acts 26:22) and returned three years later with all his epistles in his heart. "I certify you, brethren, that the gospel which was preached of me is not after man. For I neither received it of man, neither was I taught it, but by the revelation of Jesus Christ" (1:11–12).

After his wilderness retreat, he went up to see Peter and the apostles—but not as a disciple, as an apostle himself. He tells us of his *acceptance* in Jerusalem, his *activity* among the Gentiles, and of his *acknowledgment* throughout Judea.

Galatians 2 continues Paul's explanation of the gospel.

D. The Defense of the Gospel (chap. 2)

This is an absorbingly interesting chapter because it gives us a great glimpse of Paul's *undiluted convictions* and Paul's *undying courage*. In verses 1 through 10 we are at Jerusalem, the center of Jewish Christianity; in verses 11 through 21 we are at Antioch, the center of Gentile Christianity. In verses 1 through 10 we have a picture of Paul's courage; in verses 11 through 21 we have a picture of Peter's cowardice.

The first ten verses tell of Paul's second visit to Jerusalem. This visit took place after Paul's ministry at Antioch but before his first missionary journey. At this time his convictions on the relationship of Judaism to Christianity had already reached maturity. At this time also he had a private interview with all the apostles to make sure that his status as an apostle was recognized. Typical of Paul, he took Titus along with him—a Gentile convert—and forced the other apostles to take a stand on the matter of the reception of this full-blooded Gentile into their fellowship. At this time the apostles all gave Paul the right hand of fellowship and privately endorsed his stand on the emancipation of believers from the law.

The second part of the chapter tells of Peter's visit to Antioch and how he behaved on that occasion. At first he consorted freely with the Gentiles, but when some brethren from Judea came, close friends of the rather narrow and ascetic James, Peter was alarmed. Because he wanted to keep in with James and the exclusive party in Jerusalem, he withdrew from the Gentile fellowship. The result was an uproar in the Antioch church. Then Paul stepped in and boldly told Peter exactly what he thought of his conduct.

At this point Paul tells the Galatians what in essence he said to Peter. It is interesting because it exposes the fallacy of any type of legalism in the church. Paul argues that *the law cannot bring us up to redemption ground* (see vv. 15–18). "A man is not justified by the works of the law, but by the faith of Jesus Christ, even we have believed in Jesus Christ, that we might be justified by the faith of Christ, and not by the works of the law: for by the works of the law shall no flesh be justified" (v. 16). He argues further that *the law cannot bring us down from resurrection ground* (see vv. 19–21). "For I . . . am dead to the law, that I might live unto God. I am crucified with Christ: nevertheless I live; yet not I, but Christ liveth in me" (vv. 19–20). The believer has a standing before God on the resurrection side of Calvary. Since the law is on the other side of the cross it cannot arrest us now. We are beyond its power, we have died, we are risen again.

So much then for Paul's explanation of the gospel. Now we must observe how he expands on that explanation.

III. PAUL'S EXPOSITION (CHAPS. 3–4)

In these two chapters, Paul expounds his gospel in the light of the Old Testament and ruthlessly exposes those who would seduce the believer into bondage. The section is in two parts.

A. How Paul Interrogated the Galatians (3:1–5)
He begins his exposition by hurling a series of searching questions at them.

1. Their Seducers (3:1)
"O foolish Galatians, who hath bewitched you . . . ?" Come on, he says, let me meet these new-fangled teachers of yours. Who are they? Where did they come from? What are their names? What are their qualifications? Let me have a look at these unsavory characters!

2. Their Salvation (3:2)
"This only would I learn of you, Received ye the Spirit by the works of the law, or by the hearing of faith?" Let us get down to basic issues. How were you saved? By trying or by trusting?

3. Their Stupidity (3:3a)
Paul uses some strong language at times. He says, "Are ye so foolish?"—literally, "Are you so senseless?" Can you possibly be so unintelligent? It is remarkable how gullible some Christians can be.

4. Their Sanctification (3:3b)
"Having begun in the Spirit, are ye now made perfect by the flesh?" Do you mean to say, he demands, that you are saved by grace and sanctified by works? Do you mean to say that you are saved by trusting and sanctified by trying? Do you mean to say God only makes half a job of saving you and means for you to complete it on your own?

5. Their Sufferings (3:4)
"Have ye suffered so many things in vain?" During Paul's first missionary journey into Galatia he had been persecuted without mercy from place to place. On one occasion he was actually stoned and left for dead. The Galatians had become partakers of his sufferings. Do you mean to say, says Paul, that you cannot remember how the Jews treated you for your faith in Christ? Are you going to abandon your glorious position in Christ now that you have already paid such a price for it in sufferings for His name?

6. Their Successes (3:5)
"He therefore that ministereth to you the Spirit, and worketh miracles among you, doeth he it by the works of the law, or by the hearing of faith?" Who is the fruitful man among you? Who is the man who is winning souls and seeing miracles

wrought in the lives of men? Is it the Spirit-filled man or is it the man who is forever harping on the law?

Thus Paul interrogated the Galatians, and this interrogation has its application to some of our own churches today.

B. How Paul Instructed the Galatians (3:6–4:31)

He shows that believers have a twofold relationship. They are the seed of Abraham, and they are the sons of God.

1. Believers Are the Seed of Abraham (3:6–29)

"Abraham," he said, "believed God, and it was accounted to him for righteousness. Know ye therefore that they which are of faith, the same are the children of Abraham" (vv. 6–7).

Paul's whole point in this important section is that Abraham was converted 430 years before the giving of the law. The purpose of the law (which was added to a redeemed people long after the principle of salvation by faith had been firmly established) was to convict, not to convert. Its twofold function was to (a) probe the soul for sin (vv. 19–22), and (b) prepare the soul for Christ (3:22–29). "The law was our schoolmaster to bring us unto Christ" (3:24).

2. Believers Are the Sons of God (chap. 4)

Paul discusses the implications of their adoption.

a. Their Birthright (4:1–7)

"God sent forth his Son, made of a woman, made under the law, to redeem them that were under the law, that we might receive the adoption of sons. And because ye are sons, God hath sent forth the Spirit of his Son into your hearts, crying, Abba, Father"(vv. 4–6). Believers are put into the family of God. We can actually address God as Father in the same words Jesus did in Gethsemane.

b. Their Betrayal (4:8–20)

"How turn ye again to the weak and beggarly elements? . . . Ye observe days, and months, and times, and years. I am afraid [for] you. . . . Am I therefore become your enemy, because I tell you the truth? They zealously affect you, but not well" (vv. 9, 10–11, 16–17). "Oh, I know how keen these men are to win you over, but can't you see that it is for their own ends? They would like to see you and me separated altogether, and have you all to themselves" (v. 17 PHILLIPS).

c. Their Bondage (4:21–31)

Now comes the famous passage about Sarah and Hagar, Isaac and Ishmael, in which Paul converts the historical incident recorded in Genesis 21:1–21 into an allegory. The point that Paul was after may perhaps best be understood by retelling the allegory in different words.

Abraham had two sons, one by a slave and the other by a free woman. The son of the slave was born in the usual way, but the son of the free woman was born as a result of God's promise. This can be viewed allegorically. The two women represent two covenants: the Mount Sinai covenant bears children into slavery, for Hagar typifies Mount Sinai in Arabia, and she typifies Jerusalem of the present day—for the Jews are still in spiritual bondage. But Sarah, the free woman, symbolizes the heavenly Jerusalem, the mother of all of us who are spiritually free.

Now we, brethren, like Isaac, are children born by promise. But just as in Isaac's day, the natural son persecuted the son born after the Spirit, so it is today. But what did the Scripture say? "Cast out the bondwoman and her son: for the son of the bondwoman shall not be an heir with the son of the freewoman" (v. 30). So, brethren, we are not to look upon ourselves as sons of the bondwoman, but of the free.

In other words, we are not sons of bondage under the law, but sons of freedom, under grace. So much then for Paul's explanation and exposition. Now he intends to force the Galatians to face the issues.

IV. Paul's Exhortation (5:1–6:10)

In this closing section, Paul spells out four great laws.

A. The Law of Liberty in Christ (5:1–15)

"Stand fast therefore in the liberty wherewith Christ hath made us free, and be not entangled again with the yoke of bondage" (5:1). Then Paul tackles head-on the question of circumcising believers—forcing upon them a religious rite that was contrary to the whole spirit of Christianity. He also speaks plainly about those who were troubling the Galatians. "I would," he says, "they were cut off."

B. The Law of Likeness to Christ (5:16–26)

He spells out two contrasting ways of life—the self-life with its unhallowed "works of the flesh" (v. 19) and the Spirit-life with its "fruit of the Spirit" (v. 22). The fruit selfward is love, joy, peace; the fruit manward is longsuffering, gentleness, goodness; the fruit godward is faith, meekness, temperance. "They that are Christ's have crucified the flesh with the affections and lusts. If we live in the Spirit, let us also walk in the Spirit" (vv. 24–25).

C. The Law of Love for Christ (6:1–6)

It is love that *woos sympathetically*: "Brethren, if a man be overtaken in a fault, ye which are spiritual, restore such an one in the spirit of meekness; considering thyself, lest thou also be tempted" (v. 1). It is love that *walks softly*: "If a man think himself to be something, when he is nothing, he deceiveth himself" (v. 3). It is love that *works sincerely*: "Let him that is taught in the word communicate unto him that teacheth in all good things" (v. 6).

D. The Law of Life in Christ (6:7–10)

Ten times in Genesis 1 we have the expression "after its kind," separating species from species.[2] Here we have its equivalent in the spiritual realm: "Whatsoever a man soweth, that shall he also reap" (v. 7). This is just as much a law of the *soul* as it is a law of the *soil*. Paul adds, "Let us not be weary in well doing: for in due season we shall reap, if we faint not. As we have therefore opportunity, let us do good unto all men, especially unto them who are of the household of faith" (vv. 9–10).

V. CONCLUSION (6:11–18)

Paul's conclusion sums up and emphasizes in a fourfold way the truths he has been hammering home in this great magna carta of Christian liberty. He reemphasizes the truth.

A. The Truth Stated Positively (6:11)

"Ye see how large a letter I have written unto you in mine own hand." "Look at these huge letters I am making in writing these words with my own hand" (PHILLIPS). Or, as used in the ancient East, the words could say, "Note how heavily I have pressed upon the pen in writing this," or, "Notice how heavily I underline these words to you."

B. The Truth Stated Persuasively (6:12–16)

Paul points out that the motives of the false teachers will not bear scrutiny. They want to glory in your flesh, he says, they want to boast about your submission to their ruling. In contrast, his own motives were absolutely transparent: "God forbid that I should glory, save in the cross of our Lord Jesus Christ" (v. 14).

C. The Truth Stated Personally (6:17)

"From henceforth let no man trouble me: for I bear in my body the marks of the Lord Jesus." They want to mark your bodies with a religious rite, he says, but look how my body has been marked! If you want a body marked by man, make sure they are the honorable scars of persecution, not the cutting done by a cult.

D. The Truth Stated Pastorally (6:18)

"Brethren, the grace of our Lord Jesus Christ be with your spirit. Amen."

Thus Paul concludes this important epistle. What a priceless document it is. How thankful we need to be for such an exposition of the Lord's statement, "If the Son therefore shall make you free, ye shall be free indeed" (John 8:36).

No wonder Martin Luther loved this epistle. "The epistle to the Galatians is my epistle," he said. "I have betrothed myself to it. It is my wife."[3]

CHAPTER 13

EPHESIANS

Higher Ground

Ephesians is a letter from jail. The epistles of Paul to the Ephesians, Colossians, Philippians, and to Philemon are known as prison epistles because they were written during his first captivity at Rome. The book of Acts records Paul's arrival under armed escort at Rome and his two-year detention in his own hired house. Paul turned his imprisonment to good account, making important contacts in the very household of Caesar (Philem. vv. 13, 22), and writing four of the greatest and most Christ exalting books of the New Testament. It is helpful to see the relationship the prison epistles have to Paul's other letters in the table below.

Paul's epistle to the Ephesians was probably a circular letter intended for the Ephesian church and also for the other churches of Asia mentioned in Revelation

IMPRISONMENT AND PAUL'S EPISTLES		
Written Before Imprisonment	**Written During Imprisonment**	**Written After Imprisonment**
Galatians 1 Thessalonians 2 Thessalonians 1 Corinthians 2 Corinthians Romans	Colossians Ephesians Philippians Philemon	1 Timothy Titus 2 Timothy (Paul was back in prison when he wrote this.)

2 and 3. The church at Ephesus was located in one of the great cities of the Roman Empire. At the close of Paul's second missionary journey he spent a weekend at Ephesus with Aquilla and Priscilla, promising to return as soon as his planned visit to Jerusalem was over. On his third missionary journey, he came back to Ephesus, remained for about three years, and established one of the greatest of all his churches. Tradition has it that the apostle John spent the last years of his life at Ephesus and that he died there.

    I. Introduction (1:1–2)
   II. Considering the Heights (1:3–14)
      A. The Mercies of God the Father (1:3–6)
      B. The Mediation of God the Son (1:7–12)
      C. The Ministry of God the Spirit (1:13–14)
        1. The Fact of Our Salvation (1:13)
        2. The Fullness of Our Salvation (1:14)
  III. Climbing the Heights (1:15–23)
      A. Our Spiritual Enlightenment (1:15–18)
      B. Our Spiritual Enablement (1:19–23)
        1. Christ Raised from the Tomb (1:19–20a)
        2. Christ Raised to the Throne (1:20b–23)
  IV. Comprehending the Heights (2:1–3:21)
      A. Redemption (2:1–10)
        1. The Terrible Pit of Man's Ruin (2:1–3)
        2. The Towering Pinnacle of Man's Redemption (2:4–10)
      B. Relationship (2:11–14)
        1. By Nature We Were Outside the Promises of God (2:11–12)
        2. But Now We Are Inside the Purposes of God (2:13–14)
      C. Reconciliation (2:15–18)
        1. The Hostility of the Old Commandment Removed (2:15a)
        2. The Harmony of the New Creation Revealed (2:15b–18)
      D. Reconstruction (2:19–22)
      E. Revelation (3:1–6)
      F. Responsibility (3:7–13)
        1. To Proclaim the Gospel (3:7–9)
        2. To Ponder the Gospel (3:10–11)
        3. To Prize the Gospel (3:12–13)
      G. Resources (3:14–21)
   V. Claiming the Heights (4:1–6:9)
      A. The Vitality of the Body of Christ (4:1–16)
        1. The Greatness of the Church (4:1–6)

In Romans, the first great doctrinal epistle, we have the mystery of Christ's cross; in Ephesians, the second great doctrinal epistle, we have the mystery of Christ's church. In Romans we learn the truth of our identification with Christ in His death, burial, and resurrection; that when Christ died, we died; when He was buried, we were buried; when He arose, we arose. In Ephesians we are carried still further. We learn our identification with Christ in His ascension and enthronement at God's right hand.

I. INTRODUCTION (1:1–2)

Colossians and Ephesians are twin epistles centered around Christ and the church. In Colossians, Christ is set forth as the Head of the body (the church), and in Ephesians the church is set forth as the body of Christ, the Head. Thus, in Ephesians, Paul was at pains to promote more unity between Jews and Gentiles in the church, since there were not two churches, a Jewish church and a Gentile church, only one.

This idea of oneness, in fact, runs through the epistle. There is "one body, and

one Spirit . . . one hope . . . one Lord, one faith, one baptism, one God and Father"
(4:4–6). While the church is depicted as a building (2:20–22), a body (4:4–13),
and a bride (5:23–33), there is nonetheless only one church. Further, in two great
prayers (1:15–23; 3:14–21), Paul sets before us the wealth, the walk, and the warfare of all Christians.

In his introduction Paul strikes one of the great notes that occurs twelve times
in the epistle—grace![1] In Galatians it was all law, law, law; in Ephesians it is all
grace, grace, grace. The keynote, however, is struck in verse 3: "Blessed be the God
and Father of our Lord Jesus Christ, who hath blessed us with all spiritual blessings
in heavenly places in Christ." In this book, then, we climb the Alpine heights of
Scripture. The theme is,

> A higher plane than I have found,
> Lord, plant my feet on higher ground.
> —Johnson Oatman Jr.,
> "Higher Ground"

II. CONSIDERING THE HEIGHTS (1:3–14)

The opening verses of Ephesians introduce us to the heights. The apostle's very
language illustrates the magnificence of his theme. We are "blessed" (v. 3), "chosen"
(v. 4), "predestinated" (v. 5), and "accepted" (v. 6). We have "redemption through
his blood," we have "forgiveness of sins" (v. 7), and we have "obtained an inheritance." We are faced with "the [mystery] of his will" (v. 11) and with "the praise of
his glory" (v. 12).

Verses 3 through 14 of Ephesians 1 form one long sentence and encompass
three great themes.

A. The Mercies of God the Father (1:3–6)

The epistle begins with one of the most profound problems of theology—pre-
destination. "According as he hath chosen us in him before the foundation of the
world, that we should be holy and without blame before him in love" (v. 4).

This verse tells us two things—first, *when* He chose us: "Before the foundation of the world." The question in this controversial matter of election can
be put like this: "Did I choose Him because He chose me, or did He choose
me because I chose Him?" For, unless we are *puppets*, not morally accountable
people, possessed of volitional powers, some kind of choice must be ours. Sin
entered the world as a result of human choice. That a choice is inherent in God's
offer of salvation is evident from scores of passages of Scripture. But who chose
whom first?

In most discussions of God's sovereign election and man's volitional choice, the forgotten factor is the time factor. Paul says we were chosen in Christ "before the foundation of the world" (v. 4). That is true, but essentially it is true from *our* point of view because we are creatures of time. We live our lives in three tenses of time and express our mode of being by saying, I was, I am, I will be. God transcends time and lives in the eternal present. In His omniscience He gathers all the ages and moments of time into one eternal present. He has revealed Himself as the I AM. God does not express His mode of being in three tenses of time as we do. He would express His relationship to time by saying, "I am, I am, I am." Jesus did not say to the Pharisees, "Before Abraham was, I was"—though that would have been a startling statement and absolutely true; instead He said, "Before Abraham was, *I am*" (John 8:58), thus claiming to be partaker of the divine nature and possessing eternity of being, transcending all time. Since God transcends time, from His perspective His decision to choose me and my decision to accept Christ were simultaneous acts. They took place at the same moment.

This verse, however, also tells us *why* God chose us—"that we should be holy and without blame before him in love." There is that about the doctrine of election that *bewilders the mind*, but there is also something about it that *blesses the heart*. The next verse goes on to say that God has "predestinated us unto the adoption of children by Jesus Christ to Himself." A story is told about a child named Freddie. The news leaked out at school that Freddie was adopted and, with the cynical cruelty of childhood, some of the boys teased him about it. One day Freddie turned on his chief tormenter: "All right, Frankie," he said, "your parents *had* to take you; mine *chose* me!"

As to why God chose us, He did so for His eternal glory and for our eternal good. "Now we see through a glass darkly," Paul wrote to the Corinthians, in a different context but something that is certainly true about the doctrine of election. We'll understand it better when our traveling days on earth are done.

B. The Mediation of God the Son (1:7–12)

"In whom we have redemption through his blood, the forgiveness of sins, according to the riches of his grace" (v. 7). Christ's vast resources in redemption are *shown* to us and they are *shared* with us. Of these resources, Paul says, "In [Christ] also we have obtained an inheritance" (v. 11).

At a Trade Fair in Chicago some years ago, one of the banks had one million dollars in bank notes on display. Half a dozen guards were highly visible to ensure against theft. This wealth was shown to us but it wasn't shared with us.

In another instance, a man once said to his friend as they passed a certain bank, "They put half a million dollars in that bank yesterday!" The friend was interested—but only mildly so. If his companion had added two more words it would have made all the difference. Suppose he had said, "They put half a million dollars in that bank yesterday *for you!*" Thank God His resources are not only shown to us but shared with us.

C. The Ministry of God the Spirit (1:13–14)
He makes certain guarantees.

1. The Fact of Our Salvation (1:13)
There is a twofold witness—the *Scripture* ("the word of truth, the gospel of your salvation") and the *seal* ("ye were sealed with that holy Spirit of promise"). When the seal is affixed to a legal document it becomes binding. The contract of salvation is drawn up, executed, and signed by God; the moment we sign, by personally accepting Christ as Savior, God puts on the seal. It now cannot be revoked but becomes a binding contract.

2. The Fullness of Our Salvation (1:14)
"Which is the earnest of our inheritance until the redemption of the purchased possession, unto the praise of His glory." The "earnest" carries the idea of a down payment. When one makes an offer on a home in the real estate market, he is expected to accompany it with what realtors call "earnest money." It is a cash deposit to prove that one is in earnest about the offer being made. The Holy Spirit is God's "Earnest"—the guarantee that God means business and intends to fully complete the transaction of salvation. That includes the redemption of the body as well as the redemption of the soul.

III. CLIMBING THE HEIGHTS (1:15–23)
On May 29, 1953, two men stood for the first time on the top of Mount Everest. Sir Edmund Hillary and his Shirpa companion planted the British flag on the summit of the world. In this section of Ephesians, Paul tells us how to climb the heights, how to scale God's Everest, how to show the flag of Christ on the highest summit of the faith.

These verses tell us how, recording the first of two great prayers in Ephesians. The first prayer closes chapter one, the second prayer closes chapter three; the first tells us *what we are to know*, the second tells us *what we are to be*.

Paul's first prayer is in two parts.

A. Our Spiritual Enlightenment (1:15–18)
"That the God of our Lord Jesus Christ, the Father of glory [the all-glorious Father], may give unto you the spirit of wisdom and revelation in the knowledge of him . . ." (v. 17). Get to know your Father, says Paul, that He "will give you

spiritual wisdom and the insight to know more of him" (PHILLIPS). We can picture the prodigal in the far country with a pig pail in his hand, sitting in his filth and rags, scraping out the pig-swill from the pail for something to eat. He gets up at last with a new look in his eye and goes up to the house on the hill. He says to the citizen of that country, "Here's your pig pail. I'm going back home." We can imagine what the response was: "*You! Home! Like that?* After spending your father's money and disgracing his name? After all your cursing and carousing? After the riotous, ribald life you've lived? After all your wild ways with wine, women, and song? You! Going home? After living with the harlots and the hogs? Going home—with the stench of the swine trough on your clothes? *Your father will turn his dogs on you! I would!*" And we can imagine the prodigal's reply: "You don't know my father. He'll make me as one of his hired servants and give me bread enough and to spare." Later that restored prodigal had "wisdom and insight to know" that he was not going to be treated like a servant at all; he was going to be treated like a *son*. Later he would look at the shoes on his feet, at the best robe on his back, and at the ring on his finger; he would recall the warm, wondrous, welcoming smile on his father's face, the loaded table and the fatted calf. He would have "wisdom and insight to know" more of his father than he had ever known before. Ah, says Paul, get to know your Father! I'm praying for this. I'm praying for your spiritual enlightenment.

He prays, too, for something else.

B. Our Spiritual Enablement (1:19–23)

He speaks of "the exceeding greatness of his power to us-ward who believe, according to the working of his mighty power" (v. 19). Paul prays that we might enter fully into the mighty victory of Calvary. The power that Christ puts at our disposal is based on a twofold fact—*Christ raised from the tomb*: "[T]his mighty power, which he wrought in Christ when he raised him from the dead . . ." The second fact is *Christ raised to the throne*: "[T]his mighty power, which he wrought in Christ, when he raised him from the dead, and set him at his own right hand in the heavenly places, Far above all principality, and power, and might, and dominion, and every name that is named, not only in this world, but also in that which is to come . . ." (vv. 19b–21).

Think of it, says Paul. All the mighty power of God in Christ is to be unleashed through the church. Men think of the church as weak and ineffective. They see it broken into a thousand fragments, see warring factions, hear a babel of conflicting voices. But God sees the church as the body of Christ—the instrument through which the risen, ascended Lord perpetuates His power and presence on earth. "The church," says Paul, "Which is his body, the fullness of him that filleth all in all" (v. 23). "In that body lives fully the one who fills the whole wide universe" (PHILLIPS). Talk about climbing the heights! Who can climb any higher than that?

IV. COMPREHENDING THE HEIGHTS (2:1–3:21)

In this great central section of the epistle, Paul spells out seven cardinal truths of Christianity, pointing out seven massive peaks of truth that form the Rocky Mountains of New Testament truth. We can do little more in this survey than look from one to another and promise ourselves that we will come back, respond to their challenge, and scale them for ourselves.[2]

Look then at the towering truth.

A. Redemption (2:1–10)

Paul wants us to appreciate what it means for us to be on "redemption ground" so he indicates first the nature of our nature.

1. The Terrible Pit of Man's Ruin (2:1–3)

He would have us consider "the hole of the pit from whence we have been digged" (see Isa. 51:1). We were "dead in trespasses and sins" (v. 1). We were Satan's captives, filled with vile lusts, "children of wrath" (v. 3). Like the prophet David of old we can say, "He brought me up also out of an horrible pit" (Ps. 40:2).

2. The Towering Pinnacle of Man's Redemption (2:4–10)

"But God, who is rich in mercy . . . hath raised us up together, and made us sit together in heavenly places in Christ Jesus: That in the ages to come he might show the exceeding riches of his grace in his kindness toward us through Christ Jesus" (vv. 4, 6–7). Quickened together! Raised together! Seated together! When a young man loves a young woman and a young woman loves a young man, they like to do everything *together*. That is the way it is between us and Him. God has joined us together! We are to be the showpiece of His grace.

A sculptor once saw a beautiful piece of marble on a rubbish heap in a stone-mason's yard. It had been ruined by amateur attempts to turn it into a statue. He pointed it out to a friend: "What do you see in that block of marble?" he asked. His friend replied, "Nothing! It's been ruined." Said the sculptor, "I can see an angel in it." He bought it, took it to his shop, and transformed it into a thing of beauty.

God has done that with us. He has taken ruined clay and transformed us into sons of God. We are the work of His hands, trophies of His grace, destined to be displayed for all eternity to an admiring universe as the triumph of His redemptive work.

B. Relationship (2:11–14)

Paul shows us another aspect of our nature.

1. By Nature We Were Outside the Promises of God (2:11–12)

That is, as Gentiles we were outside the Hebrew *family* ("in time past Gentiles in the flesh . . ." [v. 11]). We were outside the Hebrew *fold* ("without Christ, being aliens from the commonwealth of Israel, and strangers from the covenants of promise" [v. 12]). We were outside the Hebrew *faith* ("having no hope, and without God in the world" [v. 12]).

2. But Now We Are Inside the Purposes of God (2:13–14)

"But now in Christ Jesus ye who sometimes were far off are made nigh by the blood of Christ" (v. 13). We have a new, indeed a near relationship—a blood relationship to the Son of God. Moreover, God has broken down the "middle wall of partition" that separated Jews and Gentiles. The reference is to the palisade about three and a half feet high, which separated the Court of the Gentiles from that of the Jews in the Jerusalem temple. A large warning was posted there, telling Gentiles that it was death for them to pass that palisade. Spiritually, and historically, that spiritual "middle wall" was broken down in Acts 10.

C. Reconciliation (2:15–18)

Next, Paul discusses the hostility provoked by a broken law.

1. The Hostility of the Old Commandment Removed (2:15a)

"Having abolished in his flesh the enmity, even the law of commandments contained in ordinances." By His sacrifice, Christ has removed the hostility of the law with all its dos and don'ts. It is important to keep in mind that the hostility and enmity was all on our side. We are invited to be reconciled to God, to accept the fact that the cross has made such reconciliation possible. Not once is God said to be reconciled to us. God is not our enemy! He has never stopped loving us.

2. The Harmony of the New Creation Revealed (2:15b–18)

"To make in himself of twain one new man, so making peace; and that he might reconcile both unto God in one body." Paul is still emphasizing that Gentiles and Jews in Christ are now one.

D. Reconstruction (2:19–22)

The Jewish temple was obsolete! God is now building something new—a building not made with hands. We are "built upon the foundation of the apostles and prophets, Jesus Christ himself being the chief corner stone; . . . an habitation of God through the Spirit" (vv. 20, 22). As the hymn writer puts it,

> In Him it is ordained to raise
> A temple to Father's praise,

Composed of all His saints who own
No Savior but the "Living Stone."

View the vast building, see it rise,
The work how great, the plan how wise.
O wondrous fabric, power unknown,
That rests it on the "Living Stone."

—P. Ritter,
"On Christ Salvation Rests Secure"

God is building a spiritual structure that will call forth the wonder and admiration of those who behold it for all eternity. That structure is His church. He has drawn materials from every nation under heaven, from the refuse, the debris, the rubble heaps of earth. He has quarried deep in nature's dark and ruined mine, and is now creating the architectural wonder of the ages—a church that rests upon Christ Himself.

The work of the apostles and prophets is associated with the foundation of the building. Once that foundation was well laid, the gifts of the apostle and the prophet were withdrawn. Pretensions in some quarters to have "apostles" and "the gift of prophecy" must be viewed with skepticism.

E. Revelation (3:1–6)

Paul now speaks of "the mystery . . . [of Christ], which in other ages was not made known unto the sons of men, as it is now revealed unto his holy apostles and prophets by the Spirit; That the Gentiles should be fellowheirs, and of the same body, and partakers of his promise in Christ by the gospel" (vv. 3–6). Paul was entrusted with truth concerning the mystery of the church, the body of Christ. That the Gentiles would be saved was no mystery; but that God would make of Jew and Gentile something new—the church, the body of Christ—this was something not revealed in Old Testament times. Paul will develop this mystery of the church in fuller detail later on in the letter. No wonder the exclusive, Judaistic, Jewish believers could not understand Paul, and looked upon him as a radical and a rebel! It went against the grain with them to think that in God's sight they were no better than Gentiles.

Paul points out next the towering truth.

F. Responsibility (3:7–13)

To know our blessings in Christ is not only a great privilege, it is also a responsibility. Paul goes on to show in what way we are responsible.

1. To Proclaim the Gospel (3:7–9)

We are to "make all men see what is the fellowship of the mystery" (v. 9). We are to "preach among the Gentiles the unsearchable riches of Christ" (v. 8). We need not be apologetic about the gospel. No mere religion can compare with it. We are to *preach Christ clearly*: "Make all men see," that is, "make the message clear and plain." We are to *preach Christ completely*, proclaiming "the fellowship of the mystery." This involves far more than quoting John 3:16—it means expounding the entire New Testament!

2. To Ponder the Gospel (3:10–11)

The angels do! The truths unveiled in the gospel are truths the angels desire to look into. There are depths in the gospel that call for years of careful and patient meditation.

3. To Prize the Gospel (3:12–13)

It should be prized because it gives us confidence in our approach to God. "In whom we have boldness and access with confidence" (v. 12). As a British-born individual and a Canadian citizen, I have *acceptance* as a subject of the Queen of England, but I do not have *access* to her majesty. Similarly, as a properly registered alien in the United States, I have acceptance with the United States Government, but that does not give me ready access to the White House. In Christ, I have not only acceptance as a subject, I have access as a son. That gives confidence in appealing to men. A proper appreciation of the gospel will make us scornful of human opposition to the message. We will prize the gospel above all earthly considerations.

Then Paul points out to us the tremendous nature of what is available to us in achieving what we are to be.

G. Resources (3:14–21)

This section, the second of Paul's prayers in this epistle, sums up for us the tremendous resources available to us as we live on the heights. Talk about comprehending the heights! Listen to the man: "That he would grant you, according to the riches of his glory, to be strengthened with might by his Spirit in the inner man, . . . that ye . . . May be able to comprehend with all saints what is the breadth, and length, and depth, and height; And to know the love of Christ, which passeth knowledge, that ye might be filled with all the fulness of God. Now unto him that is able to do exceeding abundantly above all that we ask or think, according to the power that worketh in us . . ." (vv. 16–20). My word! We'd need a whole volume to do justice to words like that! These are our resources. These great truths of redemption, relationship, reconciliation, reconstruction, revelation, responsibility, and resources are all ours to enjoy on the Alpine heights of Christian experience.

In chapter 4, Paul brings us abruptly back down to earth! "I therefore, the prisoner of the Lord, beseech you that ye walk worthy of the vocation wherewith ye are called" (v. 1). It is all very well to enjoy "truth" in the abstract (I suppose that is why conferences are so popular!), but we have to translate truth into daily living. Paul therefore brings us down to the hard fact of daily living.

V. CLAIMING THE HEIGHTS (4:1–6:9)

In these chapters he discusses practical truths connected with the church and the Christian.

A. The Vitality of the Body of Christ (4:1–16)

1. The Greatness of the Church (4:1–6)

"There is one body, and one Spirit, . . . one hope . . . one Lord, one faith, one baptism, One God and Father of all" (vv. 4–6). What a clear and comprehensive statement of the absolute unity of the true church! Men see it torn and divided; God sees it in its perfect oneness. He sees it as supernatural in its *creation*, in its *career*, and in its *capacity*.

2. The Gifts of the Church (4:7–16)

The gifts with which Christ has endowed the church, His body, are in keeping with the lofty relationship the church bears to Him. Hence they are *magnificent* gifts—the whole discussion is introduced by one of the loftiest passages in Scripture, showing that all realms are under Christ's control and command—things below, things all around, and things above. Hence the gifts of the church assume a universal and eternal significance.

They are *multiplied* gifts—there are apostles and prophets gifted to deal with *situations*, able to guide the infant church in its proper direction and to ground the infant church in its proper doctrine; there are evangelists gifted to deal with *sinners*; pastors and teachers gifted to deal with *saints*. Moreover, they are *meaningful* gifts—they are for "the perfecting of the saints, for the work of the ministry, for the edifying of the body of Christ" (v. 12).

Thus Paul discusses the vitality of the body of Christ. Next he brings the truth of Ephesians to bear on every area of Christian life.

B. The Victory of the Believer in Christ (4:17–6:9)

1. The Believer and Self (4:17–24)

We are to "put off" (v. 22) the old man and "put on" (v. 24) the new. The old man is utterly depraved, degraded, deceived. He not only wants to sin, he wallows in sin. He likes to "work all uncleanness with greediness" (v. 19) or, as J. B. Phillips puts it, he likes to practice "any form of impurity which lust can suggest." The believer is to deliberately "put off" this kind of thing.

2. The Believer and Satan (4:25–27)

"Neither give place to the devil" (v. 27), says Paul. In the larger context, this command refers to all kinds of falsehood. Untruth is Satan's specialty, and the believer is to be victorious over it and not to give in to it.

3. The Believer and Sin (4:28–5:4)

Paul shows that sin *debases our conduct*; there are those who would prefer to steal than to work, and there are those who despise manual labor as a means of earning a living. "Work with your hands" (see 4:28), says Paul. Sin *defiles our conversation*, so we are to let no corrupt communication proceed out of our mouths. Sin *degrades our character*, so instead of bitterness we must exhibit tenderness; instead of wrath, anger, and clamor, we must manifest a forgiving spirit. Sin *determines our course*, so we are to be followers of God and walk in love. Sin *deadens our conscience*, so we are to have no part in impurity and uncleanness. Sin *dishonors our calling*—the whoremonger or covetous man cannot possibly be identified with the kingdom of Christ.

4. The Believer and Salvation (5:5–14)

Paul next gives a graphic picture of the standards by which the world governs its behavior, and sums up the world's way as "darkness" (v. 11). The Christian has been saved from all that. He is the citizen of another realm, lives in the light, and stands on resurrection ground. Light and darkness cannot coexist.

5. The Believer and Service (5:15–21)

We are to "redeem the time" (see v. 16) and understand "what the will of the Lord is" (v. 17). Put these two things together, and we have a life of service. Paul gives us the key for living the Christian life: "Be filled with the Spirit" (v. 18), he says. This important statement is the key to all the dimensions of Christian living set forth in the New Testament. We need to study Paul's analogy. He likens being filled with the Spirit to being drunk with wine. Both are deliberate acts, and neither alcoholic intoxication or a Holy Spirit filling are permanent conditions. We need continual filling.

6. The Believer and Society (5:22–6:9)

In this important section, Paul deals with our two major points of contact with other people.

a. The Marital Obligations of the Christian (5:22–6:4)

Husband, wife, and children are all brought into focus and shown the way to victory. Submission and Christ-centered, Spirit-filled living are the keys to a happy and holy home life.

b. The Moral Obligations of the Christian (6:5–9)

The relationship between master and men is next reviewed. The two words that cover all social relationships, as set forth in Ephesians, are the words "love" (5:25, 28, 33) and "obedience" (see 6:5). We should never have heard of Trade Unions or Communism if the principles Paul discusses in these verses had been applied in business.

Thus we are to claim the heights and live in victory. The *church* is to be victorious in its testimony; the *Christian* is to be victorious in his testimony. We are to claim the heights and make them our own.

There is one problem, however—an enemy is encamped in these "heavenly places" (3:10). For the heavenly places of Ephesians, while *the seat of all our blessings*, are also *the scene of all our battles*. Before closing his letter, then, Paul must talk about winning the battles.

VI. Conquering the Heights (6:10–20)

Neither the church nor the Christian can live victoriously in the earthlies if they are not living victoriously in the heavenlies.

A. The Adversary (6:10–12)

The Enemy is *carefully described*: "We wrestle not against flesh and blood, but against principalities, against powers, against the rulers of the darkness of this world, against spiritual wickedness in high places" (v. 12). We must remember that the enemy is *completely defeated*. We are to "be strong in the Lord, and in the power of his might" (v. 10). Satan cannot stand against that kind of might.

B. The Armor (6:13–17)

We are not to be presumptuous, however, when we engage the enemy. God has provided full protection for us, and we are foolish indeed to attempt spiritual warfare without being properly arrayed. Fleshly weapons are of no avail. Intellectual brilliance, surcharged emotions, iron-willed resolve will not do. "I cannot go with these," said David as he laid aside the armor of Saul (1 Sam. 17:39). The weapons of our warfare are not carnal, they are spiritual weapons. We must know them, put them on, and become proficient in their use. To invade Satan's realm presumptuously, without putting on the gospel armor, is almost as bad a mistake as going to the king's feast without a wedding garment. Acts 19 tells how the seven sons of Sceva tried to imitate Paul's power over evil spirits and in consequence suffered terrible violence at the hands of the evil spirits. They did not have Paul's armor.

God has made ample provision for our protection but He does not guarantee protection against presumption. And every time we pray we invade Satan's realm, as Paul goes on to show.

C. The Attack (6:18–20)
We take the heights by prayer. Paul tells us what we are to do.

1. Pray Frequently (6:18a)
"Praying always," he says. Prayer should be as natural to the soul as breathing is to the body. Prayer does not always need to be a formal kneeling by the bedside; prayer can be an upward glancing of the eye. In Nehemiah 1 we are told of a formal prayer of this great man; in the next chapter we are told of a flash prayer—"So I prayed to the God of heaven. And I said unto the king . . ." (Neh. 2:4–5). We can be quite sure, on the second occasion, that Nehemiah did not fall on his knees and begin a long, involved petition to God.

2. Pray Fully (6:18b)
Paul says we are to pray "with all prayer and supplication." Prayer includes confession, worship, intercession, petition, and thanksgiving. That is "all prayer."

3. Pray Fervently (6:18c)
We are to pray "in the Spirit." There is a great deal of difference between praying and saying prayers. We can only pray aright with the Holy Spirit's enlightenment, energy, and endurance.

4. Pray Faithfully (6:18d)
Paul adds, "Watching thereunto with all perseverance and supplication for all saints." To pray properly calls for perseverance. Most of us skimp our prayers. As the hymn writer enjoins us, we should

> Take time to be holy,
> The world rushes on;
> Spend much time in secret
> With Jesus alone.
> —William D. Longstaff,
> "Take Time to Be Holy"

5. Pray Factually (6:19–20)

"And for me," says Paul, and then tells them exactly what they were to pray for. He wanted them to pray that he might speak for Christ courageously—"that I may open my mouth boldly"; speak clearly—"to make known the mystery of the gospel" (v. 19); speak conscientiously—"that therein I may speak boldly, as I ought to speak" (v. 20).

VII. CONCLUSION (6:21–24)

Paul ends this monumental letter, noting that his friend Tychicus will bring up-to-date news of him to the churches in and around Ephesus. Tychicus, named a number of times in the New Testament (Acts 20:4; Col. 4:7; 2 Tim. 4:12; Titus 3:12), was one of Paul's faithful helpers. His association with Trophimus (Acts 20:4; 21:29) suggests that he was himself an Ephesian.

So, there are the heights! All that remains now is to live on them!

CHAPTER 14

PHILIPPIANS

Continual Rejoicing

Paul's letter to the Philippians was sent to the first Christian church he planted in Europe. His original visit to Philippi was on his second missionary journey, and he was accompanied by Silas, Timothy, and Luke (Acts 16). The city of Philippi was a Roman military colony in Macedonia, and probably had very few Jews in its population. Persecution of the missionaries at Philippi arose from Gentile sources. Only twice in the book of Acts do we see Gentiles persecuting Christians, and on each of these occasions it was because the gospel threatened vested financial interests.

The Philippian believers had retained their first love for Paul and had helped him more than once with his financial needs. The apostle's gratitude is shown repeatedly in the epistle. The church at Philippi was also quite free from the many errors that called forth most of Paul's other letters. Rather, Paul's reasons for writing were twofold. He wished to acknowledge the receipt of the financial gift delivered by Epaphroditus, and he wished to urge some of the members of the church to lay aside animosity and live in peace one with another.

Although this letter was written in prison by a man chained day and night to a soldier, by a man with few friends in Rome, and a man with numerous vocal enemies, it nevertheless resounds with a note of joy. The word "rejoice" and its synonyms occur sixteen times in four short chapters.

This epistle, then, tells the Christian how to live in conscious victory over the irritations, annoyances, inconveniences, and hardships of life. We put our hand upon its pulse and feel at once how it throbs throughout with the radiant fruit of the Spirit— joy! "Happiness" depends on what happens; joy is independent of the changing circumstances of life. Happiness comes to us from without; joy wells up from within. Even beneath the very shadow of the cross, the Lord Jesus could speak of joy.

We can readily envision that little circle of believers at Philippi when Paul's precious letter was opened and read. There was Lydia, the seller of purple, whose home had been flung open to the missionary party when her heart was conquered by Paul's beloved Christ. There were the members of her household, too, faithfully won to the Lord by the apostle while sojourning beneath this gracious businesswoman's roof. There, perhaps, was that slave girl, set free forever from the shackles of sin by the ministry of Christ in Paul. There was the jailer, his wife, and his household. There was Epaphroditus, the bearer of the letter and Paul's dear friend. There were Euodias and Syntyche, sitting across from one another and, from all accounts, not on the best of terms one with another. There also were Clement and all the others, called by Paul "my fellowlabourers" (4:3), whose names are in the Book of Life.

The great moment comes and the precious scroll is unrolled: "Paul and Timotheus, the servants of Jesus Christ, to all the saints in Christ Jesus which are at Philippi, with the bishops and deacons. . . . I thank my God upon every remembrance of you, always in every prayer of mine for you all making request with joy" (vv. 1, 3–4). And there, right in the prologue, is the keynote.

"Joy?" echoes one, perhaps. "Joy? As a prisoner of Nero?" "Amen," says the jailer. "I know how Paul can sing in prison!" And, for the thousandth time, the jailer gives his testimony!

  I. Paul's Triumphant Experiences (1:1–30)
      A. Paul and His Pen (1:1–8)
          1. Paul Was Thinking of His Friends (1:1–2)
              a. Ecclesiastically (1:1)
              b. Evangelically (1:2)
          2. Paul Was Thankful for His Friends (1:3–8)
      B. Paul and His Prayers (1:9–11)
          He prayed they would remain:
          1. Superlative in Their Doctrine of Christ (1:9)
          2. Sound in Their Devotion to Christ (1:10a)
          3. Sincere in Their Demonstration of Christ (1:10b–11)
      C. Paul and His Purpose (1:12–18)
          1. He Relates How the Gospel Is Going Forth (1:12–17)
              a. By His Bonds (1:12–13)
              b. By His Brethren (1:14)
              c. By His Betrayers (1:15–17)
          2. He Rejoices That the Gospel Is Going Forth (1:18)
      D. Paul and His Prospects (1:19–26)
          He faced them:
          1. Prayerfully (1:19)

2. Positively (1:20–21)
3. Preparedly (1:22–23)
4. Practically (1:24–26)
 E. Paul and His Pulpit (1:27–30)
  1. The Believer's Convictions (1:27–28)
  2. The Believer's Conflicts (1:29–30)
II. Paul's Tremendous Examples (2:1–30)
 A. Christ: Triumph in Sacrifice (2:1–18)
  1. Paul's Approach to This Example (2:1–4)
  2. Paul's Appeal to This Example (2:5–11)
  3. Paul's Application of This Example (2:12–18)
   a. One's Conduct Transformed (2:12–13)
   b. One's Character Transformed (2:14–16)
   c. One's Concepts Transformed (2:17–18)
 B. Timothy: Triumph in Service (2:19–24)
  1. An Example of True Service (2:19–20)
  2. An Example of Total Service (2:21)
  3. An Example of Tested Service (2:22–24)
 C. Epaphroditus: Triumph in Sickness (2:25–30)
  1. How Paul Regarded Him (2:25)
  2. Why Paul Returned Him (2:26–29)
   a. His Malady (2:26–27a)
    (1) The Selflessness of the Sufferer (2:26)
    (2) The Seriousness of the Sickness (2:27a)
   b. God's Mercy (2:27b)
   c. Paul's Maturity (2:28–29)
  3. Why Paul Regretted Him (2:30)
   He missed him for:
   a. The Loyalty He Showed (2:30a)
   b. The Lack He Supplied (2:30b)
III. Paul's Typical Exhortations (3:1–4:19)
 A. The Power of Proper Theology (3:1–21)
  1. Some Spiritual Guarantees (3:1–3)
  2. Some Spiritual Goals (3:4–14)
   a. Salvation (3:4–9)
   b. Sanctification (3:10–11)
   c. Service (3:12–14)
  3. Some Spiritual Glimpses (3:15–21)
   a. Our Path (3:15–17)
   b. Our Perils (3:18–19)

    c. Our Position (3:20)
    d. Our Prospects (3:21)
  B. The Power of Positive Thinking (4:1–9)
    1. In Our Social Life (4:1–2)
    2. In Our Spiritual Life (4:3–5)
    3. In Our Secular Life (4:6)
    4. In Our Secret Life (4:7–9)
  C. The Power of Perpetual Thanksgiving (4:10–19)
    Thanking them for their gift, Paul underlines:
    1. The Experiences Connected with It (4:10–13)
      a. Of Being Made to Wait (4:10)
      b. Of Being Made to Want (4:11–12)
      c. Of Being Made to Win (4:13)
    2. The Exercises Connected with It (4:14–19)
      a. On His Part (4:14–17)
      b. On Their Part (4:18)
      c. On God's Part (4:19)
IV. Conclusion (4:20–23)

I. Paul's Triumphant Experiences (1:1–30)

Glancing down chapter 1 and the opening verses of chapter 2, we discover that Paul is simply irrepressible. What can Satan do with a man like Paul? Behead him, and you usher him into the immediate presence of Christ—an event for which he longs with all his heart—and into the bargain you earn him a martyr's crown. Lock him up in prison, and you give him much-needed leisure to pray and write Scripture and do irreparable damage to the powers of the pit. Turn him loose, and he'll evangelize cities, countries, and continents. Bruise him and beat him, and you add to his reward in heaven. These verses show us just how much Paul himself was "more than conqueror" through Christ.

Paul has not forgotten his bonds. How could he? Indeed, in chapter 1 he makes four distinct references to them (vv. 7, 13, 14, 16). He has not forgotten them; he has conquered them. The four walls of the house where he was imprisoned did not constitute a *cell* but a *center* from which he could continue to evangelize the world.

A. Paul and His Pen (1:1–8)

1. Paul Was Thinking of His Friends (1:1–2)

He was thinking of them *ecclesiastically*. He mentions three classes of believer—saints, deacons, bishops. *Saints*—these are the *sinews* of the church. The word is defined in 1 Corinthians 1:2—"them that are sanctified in Christ Jesus, called to be saints." The true church is not an admixture of saint and sinner. *Deacons*—these are the *servants* of the church. The first deacons were appointed in the days of Stephen to be entrusted with the more secular aspects of the church's administration, but they had to be Spirit-filled. *Bishops*—these are the *shepherds* of the church. The word *episkopos* is used of the Lord Himself in 1 Peter 2:25 to describe His care for the flock.

Moreover Paul was thinking of them *evangelistically*. As so often in his opening remarks, he mentions "grace" and "peace" (v. 2) the two great words of the gospel as well as of greeting.

2. Paul Was Thankful for His Friends (1:3–8)

He was thankful for their *fellowship* in the gospel (1:3–5). Here he strikes the dominant note of "joy," which peals out again and again from this letter as Paul rings joy's bells (1:18, 25; 2:2, 17–18, 28–29; 3:1; 4:1, 4, 10). More than once the Philippians had taken care of his financial needs, and Paul was full of joy for that. He was thankful, too, for their *faithfulness* in the gospel (1:6).

They were going on for God, a fact that called forth Paul's important comment: "He which hath begun a good work in you will perform it until the day of Jesus Christ" (v. 6). God never leaves a work half finished. Moreover he was thankful for their *fearlessness* in the gospel, saying, "Both in my bonds, and in the defense and confirmation of the gospel, ye all are partakers of my grace" (v. 7). Paul had set before them from the start an example of holy boldness in the faith. Encouraged from the start by Paul's disregard of danger, they, too, had become fearless in their witness. Also, Paul was thankful for their *friendship* in the gospel: "Greatly I long after you all," he says (v. 8). The only other object of his longing mentioned by Paul in his epistles is for his glorified body (2 Cor. 5:2).

B. Paul and His Prayers (1:9–11)

If prison could not keep Paul from his pen, it certainly could not keep him from his prayers. Paul's prayers are second only to the prayers of Jesus. They are not only masterpieces of intercession, they are also magnificent statements of doctrine. There are no vague generalities in Paul's prayers. Through them, he sharpens his intellect and makes specific demands upon the throne. Paul prayed, for instance, that the Philippians might be *superlative in their devotion to Christ* (v. 9). The ever-rising tides of Christian love must not overflow, however, in mere sentiment, they must flow between well-defined banks. On the one bank is written "knowledge" and on the other "all judgment." He prayed, too, that they might be *sound in their doctrine of Christ* (1:10a). Love to Christ produces loyalty to Christ, and the Christian's approval will be given only to those things that are pleasing to God. Moreover, Paul prayed that they would continue *sincere in their demonstration of Christ* (1:10b):

"That ye may be sincere and without offence." Much is said about sincerity in the Scriptures. Hypocrisy was the one sin that brought forth terrible woes from the lips of the Lord. To aid us in maintaining a genuine faith, Paul mentioned the Lord's second coming, and prays that our lives will produce the fruit of righteousness.

C. Paul and His Purpose (1:12–18)

Paul's one great purpose and passion in life was to tell all men of Christ. Even his bonds could not keep Paul from this purpose.

1. He Relates How the Gospel Is Going Forth (1:12–17)

Paul's presence in Rome (even though it was as a prisoner) contributed in three ways to the outreach of the gospel. His *bonds* (1:12–13) were a means of getting the gospel to people. The whole imperial guard had been brought under the sound of the gospel since he had come to Rome as a prisoner. Then, too, his *brethren*, inspired by Paul's example (v. 14), were taking courage and were throwing caution to the winds in a new zeal for soul winning. Even his *betrayers* (vv. 15–17) were preaching with greater zeal, with motives that were deplorable, it is true, but, so what? The message was getting out! All they were able to get out of Paul was a resounding "Hallelujah!"

2. He Rejoices That the Gospel Is Going Forth (1:18)

"Christ is preached," says Paul, "and I therein do rejoice, yea, and will rejoice." Paul was too big a man to let some mean-spirited believer's spite sour his own soul.

D. Paul and His Prospects (1:19–26)

Outwardly the future was anything but certain for Paul. Yet it held for him one glorious certainty that nothing could dim. In life or in death his whole horizon was dominated by the presence of that glorious Man he had met back yonder on the Damascus road.

Paul faced his prospect *prayerfully* (1:19). "I know that what is happening will be for the good of my own soul, thanks to your prayers and the resources of the Spirit of Jesus Christ" (PHILLIPS). There was no doubt about it that Paul was on the victory side. His Father was too wise to make any mistakes, too loving to be unkind, and too strong to be defeated. When we pray, God may not always remove our difficulties but He will remove our doubts.

Moreover, he faced his prospects *positively* (1:20–21). Paul wanted his body to be the stage upon which Christ would be glorified. His great passion was that Christ might be magnified in his body. "Lord," he could pray, "let it be that as men and women come into physical contact with me and my life, Christ will loom so large—shining through my eyes, thrilling through my voice, manifest in my very gestures and movements—that, in some mystical yet manifest way, they might know they have come into actual contact with Him."

"Christ," says Paul, "shall be magnified in my body . . . by life . . . for to me to live is Christ." And like his glorious Master, Paul drew back from no legitimate experience of life, seeking as wide a sympathy and as broad a contact as could possibly be attained in order to win men and women for Christ. To the Jew he became a Jew; to the Greek he became a Greek; to the Roman he became a Roman; to the outcast he became an outcast. He could quote with equal ease from Amos or from Aratus; from Chronicles or from Cleanthes.

Paul was not afraid of life; neither was he affrighted by death. "For to me to live is Christ and to die is gain," he wrote. Paul could snap his fingers at death. To him it was a welcome friend who would usher him into the immediate gain of glory. And this was no morbid, unhealthy obsession of a man disillusioned with life, but the happy, holy, healthy anticipation of a man who knew what it was to live!

To die is to be absent from the body and present with the Lord. It is to see Him face to face; hear the actual sound of His voice; feel the warm pressure of His hand; stand spellbound by a personality and an appearance more wonderful, more thrilling, more utterly, gloriously enslaving than anything dreamed of on earth.

But Paul was not merely a visionary. If he had his head in the clouds, he also had his feet planted firmly on earth. So he faced his prospects *preparedly* (1:22–23). He says, "I realize, of course, that the work which I have started may make it necessary for me to go on living in this world" (PHILLIPS). He comes immediately down to earth with the practical observation that the work he had begun was far from finished, and so he would probably be released from prison. If so, then he was going after more fruit. No retirement for him!

Indeed, Paul found himself torn between two desires—a desire "to depart, and to be with Christ; which is far better" (v. 23), and the willingness to remain here to win souls, to support and strengthen the church and the Christians in their many and varied needs.

He was prepared, too, to face his prospect *practically* (1:24–26). Weighty matters evidently now coming to a head at court, it seemed to Paul that there was a very good chance he would be released from prison. "And having this confidence, I know that I shall abide and continue with you all for your furtherance and joy of faith; That your rejoicing may be more abundant in Jesus Christ for me by my coming to you again" (vv. 25–26). Paul could almost see the happy smiles on their faces as he walked, a free man, into their meeting place.

E. Paul and His Pulpit (1:27–30)
Paul was living a triumphant life for Christ in that Roman prison. He wanted all to share his victory. So, iron chain and all, he transformed his prison into a

pulpit and proclaimed his message of victory to all within the sphere of his influence. Far from watering down his message, this bold apostle proclaimed emphatically the *beliefs*, *battles*, and *behavior* of the people of God.

1. The Believer's Convictions (1:27–28)

Paul challenges the believers to be *unyielding*: "Let your conversation [manner of life] be as it becometh the gospel of Christ: that whether I come and see you, or else be absent, I may hear of your affairs, that ye stand fast" (v. 27). He challenges them, further, to be *undivided*: "Striving together for the faith of the gospel" (v. 27). It is Satan's strategy to turn believers one against another. He urges them to be *unafraid*: "And in nothing terrified by your adversaries: which is to them an evident token of perdition, but to you of salvation, and that of God" (v. 28).

It was the triumphant end of the martyr Stephen that first smote conviction into the heart of fanatical Saul of Tarsus in his unconverted days. It was a lesson Paul never forgot. He learned from that experience never to shrink from danger and never to cringe from the worst abuses of the ungodly. In the answers, the attitude, and the actions of Stephen, Paul knew full well what fires of perdition, hot with conviction, had been lit in his own unconverted soul, when that bold man had turned his trial into a testimony and his murder into a martyrdom.

2. The Believer's Conflicts (1:29–30)

Never once did either Jesus or Paul paint the Christian path as one of leisure, prosperity, and guaranteed good health. It was to be a bitter battle against fearful odds from the moment of conversion to the moment of coronation. Paul reminded the Philippians of *the factual aspect* of suffering for Christ: "For unto you it is given in the behalf of Christ, not only to believe on him, but also to suffer for his sake" (v. 29). Paul does not hesitate to underline that the Christian can expect to suffer for the Savior. To step into the ranks of the redeemed is to take sides with God against the world, the flesh, and the Devil, and to run the risk of certain reprisals from all three. Tribulation is not something foreign to the church, it is its natural climate— a truth endorsed by all of history.

Paul reminds them, too, of *the fellowship aspect* of suffering for Christ. It is not only "for His sake" but it is also in fellowship with other believers. "Having the same conflict which ye saw in me, and now hear to be in me" (v. 30). Paul is here pointedly reminding them of the unjust thrashing and the harsh imprisonment they had witnessed in him at Philippi. He reminds them that they can expect the same treatment and can look upon it as being part of the same conflict.

II. PAUL'S TREMENDOUS EXAMPLES (2:1–30)

The background of Philippians 2 is a petty squabble going on at Philippi between two of the sisters in the church, a squabble that was souring the whole life of the fellowship. Paul does not actually come out and name the culprits until chapter 4, but he evidently has them in mind here. Strife and vainglory! Perhaps the believers were already beginning to take sides in the issue. Paul takes as his theme "the mind of Christ," and shows that such a mind spells death to squabbling, party spirit, and conceit. Strife and vainglory! These two words spoiled the whole picture of the Philippian church. D. L. Moody used to say, "Strife is knocking somebody else down; vainglory is setting oneself up."

A. Christ: Triumph in Sacrifice (2:1–18)
Paul begins carefully.

1. Paul's Approach to This Example (2:1–4)
"Fulfill ye my joy," he pleads (v. 2), or "fill my cup of joy full!" He had, as it were, a golden goblet in his hand. It was nearly full. The soul-intoxicating drink in that cup was joy, "joy unspeakable and full of glory!" Paul had drunk again and again of the joy there is in Christ. It was meat and drink to him; it was man and wife to him; it was body and soul to him. "Friends," he says to the Philippians, "if there be any consolation in Christ, if any comfort of love, if any fellowship of the Spirit, if any heart of compassion . . . fill up my cup, it's not quite full. I want it full and running over [see v. 1]. Fulfill ye my joy, that ye be likeminded, having the same love, being of one accord, of one mind. Let nothing be done through strife or vainglory [vv. 2–3]."

He piled up argument upon argument. "Fill up my cup," he says—"if there be any compulsion in Christ, if Christ is an advocate at all; if there be any comfort in love, if love is worth anything, if love can persuade; if there be any communion in the Holy Spirit, if fellowship in the Spirit is a reality; if there be any compassion in your hearts—then fill up my cup. Stop this bickering and fighting. If, like Christ, you would just take the humble place, my joy would be complete."

2. Paul's Appeal to This Example (2:5–11)
We now have before us one of the most magnificent Christological statements in the New Testament. In its relation to the context, this passage is really a practical application of Christ's incarnation. Paul uses it to teach the great lesson of humility, which underlies all unity. Christ was humble; we should be humble. Looked at separately, as a separate jewel in the expositional crown, the passage traces seven downward steps in Christ's self-emptying and seven upward steps in His subsequent exaltation.

The Lord Jesus did not empty Himself of His deity in His incarnation; not for a moment did He cease to be God. The incarnation was an addition of humanity, not a subtraction of deity. He emptied Himself of His glory, and voluntarily limited Himself to accomplishing the will of the Father (John 17:4). Thus He spoke only those words the Father gave Him (John 3:34; 7:16; 8:28) and obeyed His Father in all things, did only those things His Father appointed Him to do (Heb. 10:5–7), subjected His own will to the Father's will, and became obedient unto death, even the death of the cross. Once that was accomplished, He was exalted on high and given a name above every name. Every knee shall bow to Him one day and every tongue will confess Him as Lord. The greatest human folly is for a person to reject Jesus as *Savior* and wake up in a lost eternity, compelled to own Him eternally as *Sovereign*.

3. Paul's Application of This Example (2:12–18)

Christ's yieldedness, humility, and obedience point the way for us. As Christ was triumphant—"trod all [His] foes beneath His feet by being trodden down"—so we can be triumphant.[1] The application of Christ's example to our life will bring about transformation in our *conduct*. This will manifest itself in a life of full surrender: "Wherefore, my beloved, as ye have always obeyed, not as in my presence only, but now much more in my absence" (v. 12). You might say to a child, "Leave that cookie jar alone." As long as you are around, he will leave the cookie jar alone. He has learned that much, anyway. But the real test of obedience is whether or not the child will leave the cookie jar alone when you are not there! Paul wanted that kind of submission to God—the kind that did not need to be supervised, that was not merely trying to impress.

It will also bring about a life of faithful service. Paul says, "Work out your own salvation with fear and trembling. For it is God which worketh in you both to will and to do of his good pleasure" (vv. 12–13). Salvation is a gift, there is no doubt about that, but it can be likened to the gift of a gold mine—it is a very valuable thing in itself but its value can only be realized as we work away at it.

There will be not only transformation of our conduct, but transformation of our *character* (2:14–16). The believer's life is to be startlingly different from the life of the unbeliever. This contrast is, first of all, evident in a *Christ-exemplifying temperament*: "That ye may be blameless and harmless, the sons of God, without rebuke, in the midst of a crooked and perverse nation, among whom ye shine as lights in the world" (v. 15).

It will also result in a *Christ-exalting testimony*: "Holding forth the word of life; that I may rejoice in the day of Christ, that I have not run in vain, neither labored in vain" (v. 16). The gospel testimony, backed by a Christlike life, will be rewarded at the rapture. Paul was anticipating that day. He wanted to rejoice in that day when the saints from Philippi passed in review and received their reward.

Furthermore, there will be a transformation in our *concepts*: "Yea, and if I be offered upon the sacrifice and service of your faith, I joy, and rejoice with you all. For the same cause also do ye joy, and rejoice with me" (vv. 17–18). Here Paul views the Philippians as consecrated believers who have presented themselves to God as a living sacrifice; they are a "holocaust" to God, being burned up for the Lord upon the altar of surrender, sacrifice, and service. Upon that sacrifice is the drink offering, the outpoured wine of his own blood, his martyrdom for the gospel he has preached to them.

B. Timothy: Triumph in Service (2:19–24)

The Philippians knew Timothy, for he had been with Paul and Silas when the church was founded at Philippi. He was also with Paul at Thessalonica, Corinth, and Ephesus. He was with Paul after his release from his first Roman imprisonment. At the end of Paul's second Roman imprisonment, when he was expecting to be martyred, he sent for Timothy. Paul, in his epistles, says more about Timothy than any of his other associates in the ministry.

Here he tells the Philippians that he was planning to send Timothy to them soon. He praised Timothy's dedication to the service of the Lord Jesus: "I have no man likeminded, who will naturally care for your state" (v. 20). Timothy had learned to think and act like Paul. As soon as Paul had word as to how his case had been decided at court, he would send Timothy. Timothy would bring them news of him. It is a sad comment Paul has to make about the rank and file of Christians: "All seek their own, not the things which are Jesus Christ's" (v. 21). Timothy was an inspiring exception.

C. Epaphroditus: Triumph in Sickness (2:25–30)

Epaphroditus had been sent by the Philippians to bring a gift of money to Paul, to stay with him, and to minister to him on their behalf. While Paul gives him the highest commendation, he felt obliged to send him back home because he had been seriously ill. We can learn much about sickness in the believer's experience from this man. First, Epaphroditus was uncomplaining, concerned only that the Philippians, learning about the desperate nature of his illness, might be overly concerned. Secondly, Paul, who had the gift of healing, did not miraculously heal him, suggesting that already the sign-gifts were waning. Epaphroditus did get better, however, something Paul regarded as a mercy—both to the sufferer and to himself, who already had so much to bear.

As for Epaphroditus, he was utterly reckless in ignoring his sickness in order to minister to Paul. Indeed, it seems his overexertion had brought on his sickness and that it was aggravated by his determination to make light of it in order to minister to Paul.

III. PAUL'S TYPICAL EXHORTATIONS (3:1–4:19)

A. The Power of Proper Theology (3:1–21)

There seems to be an interruption in Paul's letter at this point. He resumes again on quite a different note with a warning against Judaizing and antinomian tendencies springing up in the church.

1. Some Spiritual Guarantees (3:1–3)

"Beware!" he says, there are wolves abroad. But to be well grounded in the Word of God means that we shall be able to *sight* the attacks of the enemy (vv. 1–2) and *fight* the attacks of the enemy (v. 3).

2. Some Spiritual Goals (3:4–14)

The first goal, of course, is *salvation* (vv. 4–9). In this famous passage of Scripture, Paul looks back at his unconverted days, back to the day when he had discovered that all he had been trusting in for salvation was not only worthless but wicked. He had been trusting in the things he lists here and had not only been an unsaved man but also an active enemy of God and a committed foe of Jesus Christ. He lists the typical false hopes of religious men, false hopes that the power of a proper theology explodes.

Paul shows the appalling nature of his former *blindness*—it was all "confidence in the flesh" (v. 4); the appalling nature of his *boasting*—if anyone had anything religiously to boast about in the flesh, he had more; the appalling nature of his *bankruptcy*—all the things he was trusting in were liabilities, not assets. He had to write them all off to "win" (literally "gain") Christ.

The second goal is *sanctification* (vv. 10–11). "That I may know him," Paul writes (v. 10). To know Christ is the key to everything. We must know Him in His *resurrection power*, in all the vitality of His endless life; know Him in His *rejected position*, having fellowship with His sufferings; know Him in His *redemptive passion*, being made conformable unto His death. Few have known Christ like this. Paul did. He knew that no intellectual error or moral lapse could take root in the soul of a man who knew the power of this kind of Christ-centered theology.

The third goal is *service* (vv. 12–14). "Not as though I had already attained," said Paul (v. 12)—he had already evangelized a considerable segment of the Roman Empire! "But this one thing I do, forgetting those things which are behind, and reaching forth unto those things which are before" (v. 13). Our service never rests on its laurels, never considers the task finished, never goes into retirement, never takes a vacation. Paul had touched two continents for Christ, but there were three more untouched as yet. He had reached Rome, but he wanted to reach Spain, the outposts of the empire, and lands where Roman eagles had never flown. The task was unfinished! Unfinished! There was only one thing to do—cut adrift from all memories and begin each day as if nothing had been accomplished at all.

"There remaineth yet very much land to be possessed," was Joshua's challenge to Israel (Josh. 13:1). "I press toward the mark for the prize of the high calling of God in Christ Jesus," is Paul's challenge to the church (v. 14). What really motivated Paul was not the map but the Master; he did not want merely continents, he wanted Christ; the vision of the Lord lay behind the vision of the lands. Paul was looking forward to "the high calling" (i.e., "the calling above"), to the rapture. "O Lord, that I could lay at Your feet trophies from every nation and kindred and people and tongue," was his prayer (see Rev. 5:9).

All this stems, then, from the power of a proper theology—a theology of salvation, sanctification, and service, which is centered not in a precept but in a person, not in a dead creed but in a living Christ.

3. Some Spiritual Glimpses (3:15–21)

"Be followers together of me," writes Paul (v. 17), indicating the Christian *path*. How many of us could say that? There are *perils*. Some in whom Paul had reposed confidence and whom he had held up as examples to others had since turned out to be enemies of the gospel (vv. 18–19). Paul wept tears over them. But our *position* is secure if we are saved, for our citizenship is in heaven (v. 20). And as for our *prospects*, well, Paul points again to the return of Christ and the coming transformation of our bodies into one just like His (v. 21).

B. The Power of Positive Thinking (4:1–9)

Only certain people can really think positively. They are the children of God, in touch with heaven, indwelt by the Holy Spirit, with God's Word to fashion and direct their thoughts, and with their eyes on Christ.

Paul shows the need for Spirit-directed thinking as he now, for the first time, comes out and names Euodias and Syntyche, and pleads with them to put an end to their squabbles.

The passage ends with that important challenge: "Finally, brethren, whatsoever things are true, whatsoever things are honest, whatsoever things are just, whatsoever things are pure, whatsoever things are lovely, whatsoever things are of good report; if there be any virtue, and if there be any praise, think on these things" (v. 8). Behind that statement lies the easily proven fact that we can really think of only one thing at a time. If we are thinking of *these* things, we cannot be thinking of other things. When tempted to dwell on wrongful, lustful, evil things, we should make a deliberate, conscious effort to think about *these* things.

C. The Power of Perpetual Thanksgiving (4:10–19)

This last section of the letter is woven around Paul's thanksgiving to the Philippian believers for a gift made to him in prison.

1. Thanking Them for Their Gift, Paul Underlines the Experiences Connected with It (4:10–13)

Paul experienced being made to *wait*: "But I rejoiced in the Lord greatly, that now at the last your care of me hath flourished again" (v. 10). That sigh "at last" shows that Paul had been going through some real financial testings.

Paul experienced being made to *want*: "I know both how to be abased, and I know how to abound: every where and in all things I am instructed both to be full and to be hungry, both to abound and to suffer need" (v. 12). The Lord Jesus began His public ministry by being hungry, and He ended it by being thirsty. The servant is not greater than His Lord. Paul knew the pinch of poverty as well as the pleasure of plenty.

Paul experienced being made to *win*: "I can do all things through Christ which strengtheneth me" (v. 13). The believer can be victorious in any situation. No man can overthrow the believer who knows the power of perpetual thanksgiving.

2. Thanking Them for Their Gift, Paul Underlines the Exercises Connected with It (4:14–19)

On *Paul's* part the gift stimulated happy memories of the Philippians' past generosity. It is not so much the money, he says, it's the thought that God has credited your generosity to your account in that book of remembrance He is writing over yonder. On *their* part they had abundantly provided for Paul's present temporal needs. "I am full," was Paul's acknowledgment (v. 18). And, on *God's* part—for He, too, was actively involved in the giving of this gift—the rewarding of it. "But my God shall supply all your need according to his riches in glory by Christ Jesus" (v. 19). God is no man's debtor. The Philippians had given of their substance to God. God would see to it that they lacked nothing on account of this exercise.

IV. CONCLUSION (4:20–23)

Paul's letter to the Philippians, then, is about triumph. This is a book in the Bible that, above all others, shows us how to live above our circumstances.

CHAPTER 15

Colossians

Christect Supreme

C olossians stands in the same relation to Ephesians as Galatians does to Romans. Like Galatians, Colossians is polemic, written to combat error. The error against which Paul warned in Colossians later became known as Gnosticism. Besides the Gnostic teachings, Jewish ideas were being entertained in the church at Colossae. Paul's answer to this subtle mixture was the supremacy of Christ.

The Gnostic heresy, a philosophy based on the notion that matter is evil, concerned itself with the origin of the universe and the nature of evil. The great goal of the Gnostics was for knowledge, and they watered down the gospel to a mere philosophy. They put their emphasis on this rather than on faith.

The Gnostics assumed that, since God is good and evil exists, and since (according to their assumption) evil is inherent in matter, God could not have created matter. Between God and matter they placed a series of emanations, spirits, and angels.

According to Gnosticism, the first of these spirits emanated from God, then from this one came another, and so on until finally there was one far enough away from God to still have the power to create, and who created evil matter, but, because he was so far removed from God, the evil matter he had created did not contaminate God. This bottom aeon or spirit was called the Demiurge. The god of the Gnostics was not the God of the Bible, who was only one of the emanations.

Confronted with the person of Christ, the Gnostics placed Him either at the bottom of the list of spirits or somewhere in the center. In other words, they interpreted Christ in the light of their pagan philosophy. Some denied the humanity of Jesus. Others took an opposite view and claimed that Jesus was an ordinary man until His baptism, at which time the aeon Christ came upon Him and remained with Him until just prior to His death on the cross.

The Gnostic view that matter was essentially evil caused these heretics to take divergent views of ethical problems. Some argued that, since the body was evil, it should be subdued, and the result was asceticism; the Essenes, and to some extent the Stoics, followed this line. Others took the view that the only way to overcome sensuality was to indulge bodily cravings to the full, even to excess, exhaustion, and satiety; the Epicureans were examples of this.

Grafted onto this pagan philosophy at Colossae was a form of Pharisaical Judaism. The narrowest view of Jewish ritualism (insisting on circumcision, dietary laws, observance of feasts and fasts, and the whole cumbersome apparatus of ceremonial religion) was wedded to Gnostic heresy, and the resulting conglomerate of error was presented as truth to the Colossian Christians. This special form of knowledge was presented as a "mystery," a secret available only to the initiated, one to be received by revelation and not by logical deduction. Much of this type of "teaching" has been revived in present-day cults. In Colossians, Paul wrote an inspired "nonsense" across the whole thing.

    I. Introduction (1:1–14)
        A. Paul's Passion for People (1:1–2)
        B. Paul's Passion for Prayer (1:3)
        C. Paul's Passion for Principle (1:4–5)
        D. Paul's Passion for Progress (1:6)
        E. Paul's Passion for Preachers (1:7–8)
        F. Paul's Passion for Perspective (1:9–14)
            1. His Petition (1:9–11)
            2. His Praise (1:12–14)
    II. The Truth About the Christ (1:15–29)
        A. The Deity of Christ (1:15–19)
            1. The Person of God Revealed (1:15)
            2. The Power of God Revealed (1:16–17)
            3. The Purposes of God Revealed (1:18–19)
        B. The Death of Christ (1:20–22)
        C. The Demands of Christ (1:23–29)
            1. We Are to Be Loyal to Him (1:23)
            2. We Are to Be Living for Him (1:24–29)
   III. The Truth About the Cult (2:1–23)
        A. Experiencing the Truth (2:1–7)
        B. Exposing the Lie (2:8–23)
            1. Secular Reasoning (2:8–10)

I. INTRODUCTION (1:1–14)

Paul's introduction is somewhat lengthy. This is so probably because he was not the actual founder of the church at Colossae and because he had to take immediate and uncompromising issue with the false teachers who had arisen in the church. Thus, Paul lays his foundation and introduction with special care.

We observe at once *Paul's passion for people* (vv. 1–2). This is evident from his addressing people who, for the most part, were strangers to him, yet he greets them with the same easy cordiality he does old friends. He calls them "saints and faithful brethren" (v. 2). In the New Testament, the word "saints" is one of those universal terms for depicting the Lord's people. People were not Baptists or Lutherans or Mennonites or Presbyterians; they were saints, brethren, believers, disciples, Christians. Denominational labels were unknown. All belonged to the same great commonwealth of faith. Paul felt as much at home, addressing these unknown members of the body of Christ, as he did those in churches he had founded himself. People were Paul's priority.

We note, too, *Paul's passion for prayer* (v. 3). In almost every epistle, he hardly puts pen to paper before he is off to the throne of grace to lay his rejoicing and his requests before God. Paul tells these Colossian believers that he was always in prayer for them. One wonders how Paul could ever keep up with the enormous prayer lists he compiled. Certainly he could never have wasted a minute.

Then, too, we have *Paul's passion for principle* (vv. 4–5). The Christian faith revolves, without apology, around certain great truths. Our message revolves around faith, hope, and love. Paul now strikes all three notes. The Colossians had saving faith, sustaining hope, and supernatural love. Perhaps he hammers on this dominant chord because the truth as it is in Christ Jesus was under special attack at Colossae.

We note also *Paul's passion for progress* (v. 6). He assures the Colossians that already the gospel is taking root far and wide. Immobilized by his imprisonment, unable to open up new frontiers for the faith himself, he nevertheless maintained an active interest in world evangelism. And, so far as he was able and with all the means in his power, he was encouraging and supporting the gospel outreach. He rejoiced that the world was being reached.

Then there is *Paul's passion for preachers* (vv. 7–8). This comes out in his warm commendation of Epaphras. Paul had nothing but respect and praise for a man who would pioneer a new mission field. Epaphras was their own minister, perhaps the very man who had planted the Colossian church. Paul threw all the weight of his apostolic authority behind him. He scorned that professional jealousy all too common among preachers, which manifests itself in attempts to depreciate the ministry of others.

We have also *Paul's passion for perspective* (vv. 9–14). At this point he lifts the Colossian Christians to God's throne and prays that they might have spiritual vision, spiritual vitality to walk worthy of the Lord, and spiritual victory drawing on the boundless resources of God. This prayer concludes with praise to God for remaking us, for rescuing us, and for redeeming us, and it prepares the way for Paul's coming attack on the cult that was undermining these truths.

II. THE TRUTH ABOUT THE CHRIST (1:15–29)

A. The Deity of Christ (1:15–19)

This passage is one of the great dogmatic statements in the New Testament and centers on the absolute Godhead of the Lord Jesus. Paul begins by declaring that in Christ the *person of God is revealed*: He is "the image of the invisible God, the firstborn of every creature" (v. 15). He is "the visible expression of the invisible God" (PHILLIPS). In the person of the Lord Jesus, God has shown us exactly what He is like. There is no particle of difference between all that the Father is in His person, nature, and personality and what the Lord Jesus is in His person, nature, and personality.

And, though He condescended to enter into human life, He was the Firstborn, the Head of all creation. That is, He took priority over creation. We learn why in the next verse. He created all things.

In Christ the *power of God is revealed* (vv. 16–17). Paul tells us that Jesus Christ created, claims, and controls the entire universe. Every star in space, every atom in the universe, every drop of water, every blade of grass are His—He made them all. Astronomers tell us there are a hundred billion stars in our galaxy, a hundred million galaxies in known space, and that known space is only one billionth of theoretical space. According to Sir James Jeans, "the total number of stars in the universe is probably something like the total number of grains of sand on all the seashores of the world."[1] And Jesus made them all! He controls all the factors of time and space. He takes countless stars and their satellites, throws them into prodigious orbits, and keeps them whirling and moving at inconceivable velocities with such mathematical precision we can foretell years in advance the visit of a comet or the occasion of an eclipse.

Then, too, in Him the *purposes of God are revealed*: He is "the head of the body, the church: who is the beginning, the firstborn from the dead; that in all things he might have the preeminence. For it pleased the Father that in him should all fulness dwell" (vv. 18–19). God has no plan, no purpose that does not find its center in the Lord Jesus Christ.

B. The Death of Christ (1:20–22)

Paul swings the spotlight with startling suddenness from Christ the Creator to Christ the crucified, from the blaze of glory to the brow of Golgotha, from the scenes of His power to the scenes of His passion. "And he made peace," he says, "through the blood of his cross, to reconcile all things to himself" (see v. 20).

Here we touch the very heart of the mystery of God's grace. He made peace through the blood of that *cross!* Think of it! That holy, lovely, peerless, perfect, compassionate, gentle Son of His was spit upon, beaten, bruised, blindfolded, scourged, crowned with thorns, derided, and crucified—and all for human sin.

Men murdered their Maker. They killed Him on an instrument of torture designed to ensure an excruciatingly slow and painful death. They murdered their Maker and mocked Him as He died, while twelve legions of angels with drawn swords strained over the battlements of heaven waiting for one single word that would have sent them hurtling down to earth to execute summary vengeance on the human race. We could have understood God's making *war* over the blood of that cross; instead we read He has "made *peace* through the blood of the cross." All we can do is wonder and worship at such matchless grace.

C. The Demands of Christ (1:23–29)

Paul shows that all this was suffered that we might have a means of being reconciled with God. The Lord Jesus takes the hand of a holy, loving God in His and holds out to each one of us His other nail-scarred hand. He wishes to put our hand into the hand of God so that, through Himself, we can be pardoned, forgiven, reconciled, made holy, unblameable, and unreprovable!

But He will make demands upon us. He will insist that, once reconciled, we begin to live a life that is pleasing to God, that we be loyal to Him, and that we live for Him (vv. 24–29). He will demand that we "continue in the faith grounded and settled, and be not moved away from the hope of the gospel" (v. 23). When we consider that His Holy Spirit comes into our lives to make it possible, that is not too much to ask. All He is saying is that He will be looking for evidence in our lives that our faith in Him is real and that our reconciliation is true.

It seems incredible that those who have been *thus* reconciled should become interested in the vagaries, the uncertainties, the falsehoods, fables, follies, fantasies, and fetters of a cult!

III. THE TRUTH ABOUT THE CULT (2:1–23)

A. Experiencing the Truth (2:1–7)
Paul emphasizes the positive before he deals with the negative. He shows us how to experience the truth before he exposes the lie. The best way to expose a forged one-hundred dollar bill is to set it alongside a genuine one. An FBI agent was once asked how he could recognize all the different kinds of forged bills there were in circulation. He said, "We just study the genuine so thoroughly that we instinctively recognize the forgery, no matter how deceptive it is."

So Paul simply goes over genuine Christianity one more time and urges God's people to recognize the truth about *Christians* (vv. 1–2a), about *Christ* (vv. 2b–4), about *Christianity* (vv. 5–7). He is drawing near his main subject, however. He tells the Colossians, for instance, that in Christ "are hid all the treasures of wisdom and knowledge" (v. 3). That was an opening blow at the Gnostic heretics, who were parading themselves as initiates of secret knowledge. "If it is not centered in Christ," Paul is saying, "it is not worth anything at all, and if it is to be found in Him then it is freely available to all."

The Lord Jesus was forever opening that treasure chest of His when He lived on earth, to give glimpses of the inexhaustible treasure of His wisdom. Where in all of this world's philosophies can we find anything to compare with the Sermon on the Mount? What venerated sage could ever handle a trap so sublime as the question, "Is it right to pay tribute to Caesar?" What laureled magistrate ever handled the question of sin and law, judgment and mercy so magnificently as Jesus when He was confronted by the law's custodians, who hated Him and the woman taken in adultery? No! There is none like Him! They said, "Whence hath this man wisdom, never having learned?" (see John 7:15). They said, "Never man spake like this man" (John 7:46). He Himself declared, "A greater than Solomon is here" (Matt. 12:42).

B. Exposing the Lie (2:8–23)
The cults that plague Christendom today are all freshly articulated versions of the cults that assailed the church in the apostolic era. In Colossians, Paul defends

the simplicity of the Christian faith against a fourfold perversion. He exposes the lie that Christianity can borrow anything from *secular reasoning* (vv. 8–10). "Beware lest any man spoil you through philosophy and vain deceit" (v. 8). ("Intellectualism or high-sounding nonsense" is J. B. Phillips's famous rendering of that.) The Greek philosophers had all had their day. They had been given centuries to make it clear that human philosophies do not have the answer to life's mysteries. And philosophy that disregards Christ is empty and vain. "In Him dwelleth all the fullness of the Godhead bodily," says Paul, seizing the word for fullness (*plērōma*) back from the Gnostics.

He exposes the lie that *sundry rituals* can add anything to Christianity (2:11–17). The only two ordinances Christ left with the church are baptism and the Lord's Supper—both are Christ-centered and cross-related. "In *baptism* I set forth my death with Him; at the *Lord's Table* I set forth His death for me" (see vv. 12, 16). Paul pours scorn upon the Judaistic tendencies of the cultists who were demanding that Christians submit to circumcision as an obligatory rite. "The handwriting of ordinances that was against us," Paul says (v. 14). The law simply exposed human failure. Indeed the ritual law ("the ordinances") was given only because of Israel's failure to keep the moral law. The very existence of the ritual law was a testimony to Israel's sin—and ours. The cross has written "paid in full" across all the failure that the "ordinances" exposed. Moreover, all the ranks of the unseen powers have been completely shattered by the cross. The only kind of aeons the cultists were likely to encounter were "principalities and powers"—Satan's rulers of this world's darkness. But in the cross, Christ has triumphed over all such spirit beings.

Paul next exposed the lie that *special revelations* can add anything to Christianity (2:18–19). Christianity *is* involved in the supernatural, everything about it is supernatural. It is based on a supernatural book we call the Bible; it is concerned with a supernatural Godhead; it tells of One, who had a supernatural birth, lived a supernatural life, died a supernatural death, and experienced a supernatural resurrection and ascension; it tells of the coming of another supernatural Being, the Holy Spirit, who brought the church into existence in a supernatural way. We can only become Christians by means of a supernatural experience called the new birth; we become members of the church by the supernatural baptism of the Holy Spirit; we can live the Christian life only in the power of the supernatural indwelling, filling, and anointing of the Holy Spirit. We anticipate another supernatural event we call the rapture, when the believing dead will be supernaturally raised to be joined in the air by the supernaturally ascending living believers, all of us supernaturally changed to have a supernatural body "like unto His glorious body."

There is nothing natural about Christianity at all. The moment it descends to the natural it becomes just another world religion.

But, because Christianity is essentially supernatural in nature, we must beware of all counterfeit supernaturalism. We are up against supernatural foes and deceivers in the spirit world. We must beware of dreams, visions, voices, rappings, trances, spirit manifestations, ecstatic utterances, tongues, mass healings, angel worship. At Colossae, false teachers were claiming to have had special revelations, insisting upon angel worship. They were cultivating a false humility through careful training, the idea of abasing oneself for a "false idol," and missing altogether the true humility of a redeemed sinner at the feet of Jesus. "Nor let any man cheat you of your joy in Christ by persuading you to make yourselves 'humble' and fall down and worship angels. Such a man, inflated by an unspiritual imagination, is pushing his way into matters he knows nothing about, and in his cleverness forgetting the head [Christ]" (PHILLIPS).

Finally Paul exposes the lie that *stricter rules* can enhance Christianity (2:20–23). Christianity has always been plagued by legalists, those who think that simple faith in Christ is not sufficient and who think it can be improved by whole lists of rules and regulations added to the principles of holy living given in the New Testament. Paul declares that these ideas are worldly and not spiritual. How man loves to multiply his lists of rules and regulations! He loves to encourage asceticism, loves to ban books, loves to encourage this and that or forbid the other. It all sounds so wise and clever, but in the end it does honor to human pride, not God.

All these things, attacked here by Paul, are still with us in Christendom. The cults are peddling them, and many in our great Protestant churches have endorsed them, but they have nothing to do with New Testament Christianity at all. They are part and parcel of Romanism and cultism, the trappings of religion. Christianity is not an organized system or religion, but Christ!

IV. The Truth About the Christian (3:1–4:6)

As usual, Paul turned his attention to practical issues. In the closing chapters of Colossians he discussed the outworking of proper belief in proper behavior. The Christian truly is "risen with Christ" (3:1) and is to set his affections on things above, manifesting the life of Christ in every situation as he lives in an evil world. His *personal life* is to be characterized by purity and love (vv. 5–14). The Word of God, ruling in his *spiritual life*, will issue in songs that ring out from the heart (vv. 15–17), and everything he does will be governed by the name of the Lord Jesus. In his *domestic life*, the Christian will quietly take the place of wife or husband, child or parent, and radiate Christ (vv. 18–21). In his *business relationships*, he will be considerate of the rights of others, be he employer or employee, master or slave (3:22–4:1). In all the *secular aspects* of life the Christian will so live that others will wish to become Christians, too (4:2–6). His prayers will be pointed, his time properly invested, and his conversation will be pungent.

These practical applications of divine truth are designed to bring Christianity back down to earth. After all, Christian testimony is much more a matter of the kitchen and the workshop than it is the cloister and the monastery. Christianity wears working clothes. That housewife radiating Christ in her domain, singing at the sink, making every meal a sacrament, dusting and tidying up with a hallelujah in her heart is what Christianity is all about. That employee determined to be the most diligent, conscientious, and efficient man on the job; that employer dedicated to the welfare of every person on his payroll and using his means to further the cause of Christ—that is what Christianity is all about. The Christian employer should not have to deal with a labor relations board before taking care of the interests of his workers. The union will never need to organize his employees. They will be the best paid, the best treated workers in the trade, for the Christian employer will never lose sight that he, too, has a Master to whom he must answer. Paul lifts all employment for the Christian right out of the sphere of the secular into the sphere of the sacred, just as he does everything else.

V. Conclusion (4:7–18)

Paul closed this letter by referring by name to believers dear to him and known to the Colossians. These believers—Tychicus, Onesimus, Aristarchus, Marcus, Justus, Epaphras, Luke, Demas, Nymphas, and Archippus—are well worth getting to know with the aid of a concordance and a Bible dictionary. May our names shine as gloriously in the Book of God as do the names of some of these. Here were people who exemplified the great truths Paul has been emphasizing. They are a galaxy of God's great, though the world knows nothing of them at all.

There is another lesson to be learned from these names. Says Alexander Maclaren, "There is something very solemn and pathetic in these shadowy names which appear for a moment on the page of Scripture, and are swallowed up of black night, like stars that suddenly blaze out for a week or two, and then dwindle and at last disappear altogether. They, too, lived and loved and strove and suffered and enjoyed; and now—all is gone, gone; the hot fire burned down to such a little handful of white ashes. Tychicus! Onesimus! Two shadows that once were men! And as they are, so we shall be."[2]

Paul's final word is significant, too. "Remember my bonds," he says (v. 18). Salvation is free—but the cost of being a Christian is great. It may mean imprisonment, beatings, ridicule, loss of worldly goods, and even death. But the cost of *not* being a Christian is far greater. It will certainly mean banishment from God and an eternity in hell.

CHAPTER 16

1 THESSALONIANS

Jesus Is Coming Again

The church at Thessalonica was founded by Paul on his second missionary journey (Acts 17:1–9). Although some Jews believed, the majority of the Christians were Gentiles, and these were mostly slaves and members of the working class (1 Thess. 4:11–12). Paul's brief but amazingly fruitful ministry at Thessalonica was abruptly terminated by unbelieving Jews who incited a riot, obliging Paul to move on.

The Thessalonians had enthusiastically received the Word of God, and the work done among them was the beginning of vigorous missionary activity in Achaia and Macedonia, an area about the same size as the British Isles or the state of Oregon. In their zeal for missionary work, the Macedonians were an ideal church. The Word of God sounded out from them, as they became examples to other believers.

Paul and his companions then journeyed on to Berea where, after an initial good reception, he was again driven out by persecution. Paul went on to Athens, leaving Timothy and Silas behind. At Athens Paul sent word for his companions to follow him speedily. From 1 Thessalonians 3:1–2 we learn he sent Timothy back to Thessalonica to inquire after the welfare of the infant church. In time, Timothy returned to Paul (now at Corinth), bringing a glowing account of the Thessalonian church (3:6). This prompted Paul to write his first letter to them.

The letter was intended to do a number of things for the Thessalonians: it was intended to encourage them in the midst of persecution (2:14); to defend against certain slanderous charges regarding his own conduct while with them (2:1–10); to assure them of his love for them, of his desire to see them, and his delight in Timothy's report; to rebuke indolence on the part of some; to give instruction regarding the Lord's return; to encourage spiritual unity.

It is of interest that there is not a single Old Testament quotation in the epistle. The letter is characterized more than any other of Paul's letters by simplicity, gentleness, and affection. The keynote is eschatology—each of the five chapters ends on the note of the Lord's return. The chief difference between 1 Thessalonians and 2 Thessalonians is that 1 Thessalonians gives us information on the Lord's return as it will affect believers; 2 Thessalonians deals with the Lord's return as it affects unbelievers.

   I. Introduction (1:1–2)
  II. The Coming of Christ Is a Saving Truth (1:3–10)
     A. Their Continuance in Christ Is Recorded (1:3–4)
     B. Their Coming to Christ Is Recalled (1:5–10)
       Paul recalls:
       1. The Tremendous Power of the Gospel (1:5–8)
         The power with which it was:
         a. Preached (1:5)
         b. Practiced (1:6–7)
           (1) How They Saw the Example of Paul (1:6)
           (2) How They Set an Example for All (1:7)
         c. Proclaimed (1:8)
       2. The Transforming Power of the Gospel (1:9–10)
         a. Its Impact (1:9a)
         b. Its Import (1:9b–10)
           (1) The Revolution in Character (1:9b)
           (2) The Revelation of Christ (1:10)
 III. The Coming of Christ Is a Stimulating Truth (2:1–20)
     A. The Totality of Paul's Committal (2:1–2)
       Note how boldly he:
       1. Seized Opportunity (2:1)
       2. Scorned Opposition (2:2)
     B. The Transparency of Paul's Conduct (2:3–12)
       He reminds them that:
       1. His Life Was Compellingly True (2:3–6)
       2. His Love Was Compassionately Tender (2:7–8)
       3. His Labor Was Completely Tireless (2:9–12)
     C. The Triumph of Paul's Converts (2:13–14)
       1. Trusting Nobly in the Word (2:13a)
       2. Transformed Notably by the Word (2:13b–14b)
         a. Its Effectual Working Declared (2:13b)
         b. Its Effectual Working Described (2:14a–b)

D. The Tragedy of Paul's Countrymen (2:15–16)
   1. Their Impenitent Deeds (2:15–16a)
     Rejecting:
     a. The Message of the Prophets
     b. The Messiahship of the Lord
     c. The Ministry of the Apostles
   2. Their Impending Doom (2:16b)
E. The Tangibility of Paul's Crown (2:17–20)
   1. His Great Exercise Now (2:17–18)
   2. His Great Expectations Then (2:19–20)
IV. The Coming of Christ Is a Stabilizing Truth (3:1–13)
   A. Paul's Concern (3:1–5)
     1. How It Was Experienced (3:1a)
     2. How It Was Expressed (3:1b–3)
     3. How It Was Explained (3:4–5)
   B. Paul's Comfort (3:6–11)
     The good news:
     1. Cheered Paul
     2. Challenged Paul
   C. Paul's Call (3:12–13)
     1. A Call to Greater Love (3:12)
     Based on the Pattern of Paul
     2. A Call to Greater Loyalty (3:13)
     Based on the Coming of Christ
V. The Coming of Christ Is a Strengthening Truth (4:1–18)
   The Christian life is one of:
   A. Mighty Potential (4:1–2)
     1. Teaching the Goals (4:1)
     2. Reaching the Goals (4:2)
   B. Moral Purity (4:3–8)
     1. Purity Expected of Us (4:3)
     a. Positively
     b. Negatively
     2. Purity Experienced by Us (4:4–5)
     In terms of:
     a. Self Control (4:4)
     b. Simple Contrast (4:5)
     3. Purity Explained to Us (4:6–8)
     a. The Severity of God Makes Purity a Priority (4:6)
     b. The Spirit of God Makes Purity a Possibility (4:7–8)

C. Measured Progress (4:9–10)
  1. A Word of Praise (4:9–10a)
  2. A Word of Precaution (4:10b)
D. Manifest Purpose (4:11–12)
  Don't be:
  1. A Busybody (4:11a)
  2. A Lazybones (4:11b–12)
E. Magnificent Prospects (4:13–18)
  1. The Promise of the Rapture (4:13–15)
    a. The Word of Comfort Given (4:13)
    b. The Word of Comfort Guaranteed (4:14–15)
      (1) By the Resurrection of Christ (4:14)
      (2) By the Revelation of God (4:15)
  2. The Prospect of the Rapture (4:16–18)
    a. For Those Who Are Sound Asleep When He Comes (4:16)
      (1) The Shout of the Lord
         To Summon the Saints to Glory
      (2) The Voice of the Archangel
         To Send the Angels to War
      (3) The Trump of God
         To Sound the Alarm for Israel
    b. For Those Who Are Still Alive When He Comes (4:17–18)
    The blessing of:
      (1) Home in Heaven (4:17)
      (2) Hope on Earth (4:18)
VI. The Coming of Christ Is a Sanctifying Truth (5:1–24)
  A. By Way of Explanation (5:1–13)
    1. For the Sons of Men: No Escape from the Impact of the Day of the Lord (5:1–3)
      a. Its Coming Is Decreed (5:1–2)
      b. Its Coming Is Described (5:3)
    2. For the Saints of God: No Escape from the Import of the Day of the Lord (5:4–13)
      a. A Call to Watch (5:4–6)
      b. A Call to War (5:7–8)
      c. A Call to Wait (5:9–11)
      d. A Call to Work (5:12–13)
  B. By Way of Exhortation (5:14–24)
    1. To Walk Virtuously (5:14–15)
    The need for:

The epistle begins on a note of warmth.

I. Introduction (1:1–2)

"Paul, and Silvanus, and Timotheus, unto the church of the Thessalonians . . . Grace be unto you, and peace" (v. 1). Except for his Thessalonians letters, his epistle to the Philippians, and his brief note to Philemon, Paul always adds "an apostle" after his signature. But at Philippi and Thessalonica, Paul was held in such tender regard and esteem that there was no need for him to assert his authority. Thus, he salutes the saints with the utmost cordiality. Both Timothy and Silas, associated with him in this letter, were fellowlaborers of Paul. Silas was with Paul when he evangelized Thessalonica, and Timothy had been their teacher and Paul's personal representative, sent to them from Athens not long after he had left them.

II. The Coming of Christ Is a Saving Truth (1:3–10)

Paul devotes the first chapter of this epistle to discussing the basic truth of salvation and to showing how the Lord's coming is an integral part of the doctrine of salvation. Preachers are quite right in using eschatology to give a sense of urgency to the gospel message. Paul did. We would think it rather out of place, however, to start by teaching new converts prophetic truth. Paul, though, with only a very limited time at his disposal in his stay at Thessalonica, apparently placed heavy emphasis on the truth of the Lord's return and its practical implications for saint and sinner alike.

A. Their Continuance in Christ Is Recorded (1:3–4)

Paul mentions their work of faith, their labor of love, and their patience of hope. In contrast, the Ephesian church had left its first love, as indicated in Revelation 3, seen in the fact that while they were commended by the Lord for their works, their labor, and their patience, the more important dimensions—faith, love, and hope—were missing.

Paul rejoiced at the news, brought by Timothy, that this infant Thessalonian church was thriving in its spiritual up-reach as well as in its gospel outreach. It is so easy for us to go on with a spiritual work by force of habit, out of sheer momentum from the initial exercise, and to be merely going through the motions. To illustrate, for all we know, the Andromeda Galaxy may have become extinct a million years ago, and yet its light would still be reaching us for another million and a half light years. It could be shining solely by the light of a brilliant past. Similarly, it is possible to have a name that one lives by and yet be completely out of touch with God. Paul praised God for his Thessalonian converts and for their continuance in Christ. Any soul winner knows that the saved ones who go on in Christ are the ones who bring real joy to the heart. The thrill experienced in the hour of decision is always modified by anxiety lest the work be only superficial in the soul.

B. Their Coming to Christ Is Recalled (1:5–10)

Paul had happy memories of his three Sabbath days in the synagogue at Thessalonica before the unbelieving Jews incited the riot. He recalls with pleasure how some Jews believed and how a great multitude of Greeks came to Christ, including a large number of society women.

1. Paul Recalls the Tremendous Power of the Gospel (1:5–8)

He recalls the power with which the gospel was *preached*: "For our gospel came not unto you in word only, but also in power, and in the Holy Ghost, and in much assurance" (v. 5). That is the kind of preaching we lack in the church today! He recalls, too, the power with which it was *practiced*: "Ye were examples to all that believe in Macedonia and Achaia" (v. 7). The Thessalonian Christians had become model believers. The eyes of the whole of Greece were focused on them to see how Christians ought to behave—what they should be in character, conduct, and conversation.

He recalls, as well, the power with which the gospel was *proclaimed*. "For from you sounded out the word of the Lord not only in Macedonia and Achaia, but also in every place your faith to God-ward is spread abroad; so that we need not speak any thing" (v. 8). Paul is saying, "We don't have to tell people about our work in Thessalonica. They come and tell us about it!" The Thessalonians had become a transmitter, booming out the truth and the triumph of the cross at home and abroad.

2. Paul Recalls the Transforming Power of the Gospel (1:9–10)

"Ye turned to God from idols" (the past: their conversion), "to serve the living and true God" (v. 9, the present: their commitment), "And to wait for his Son from heaven" (v. 10, the prospect: their consummation). Emphasis on prophecy is of little value if it does not result in the salvation of sinners and the sanctification of believers. The truth of the Lord's return was a powerful stimulus to both salvation and sanctification at Thessalonica. Only about two decades had passed since Christ's death and burial, resurrection and ascension when Paul wrote this letter and first taught these truths at Thessalonica. The hope of His soon return still burned very brightly indeed.

III. THE COMING OF CHRIST IS A STIMULATING TRUTH (2:1–20)

In this chapter Paul takes up five distinct topics.

A. The Totality of Paul's Committal (2:1–2)

When Paul had come to Thessalonica with Silas, they were likely still black and blue from the thrashing they had received at Philippi. Their legs were probably stiff and sore from the stocks, and their wrists red and inflamed from the chafing chains of the inner prison. But we can listen to them as they walk into Thessalonica, and we can be sure they were singing and making melody in their hearts unto the Lord. The songs that had shaken a prison will soon shake a city!

"For yourselves, brethren, know our entrance in unto you, that it was not in vain. But even after that we had suffered before, and were shamefully entreated, as ye know, at Philippi, we were bold in our God to speak unto you the gospel of God with much contention." Paul evidently did not expect his message to be popular, but preached it anyway.

B. The Transparency of Paul's Conduct (2:3–12)

Here, Paul summarizes his behavior as an evangelist at Thessalonica. He is saying, "We were under a sense of solemn obligation to God to discharge our responsibilities to men; we did not aim to please men; we made no attempt to use flattering words to conceal greedy motives; we were absolutely honest; we sought no honor from anybody—not even our converts; our attitude toward you was one of tenderness; we worked day and night so that our evangelistic efforts should not cost you a penny; our lives were above criticism in every respect; our sole object was your salvation and your growth in Christ."

In these days of slick evangelism that uses high pressure methods, psychological formats, and well-oiled appeals for large sums of money, these rules could well be noted afresh.

C. The Triumph of Paul's Converts (2:13–14)

"For this cause also we thank God without ceasing, because, when ye received the word of God which ye heard of us, ye received it not as the word of men, but as

it is in truth, the word of God, which effectively worketh also in you that believe."
Any evangelist knows what a joy that kind of thing is—to open God's Word to men
and women and have them respond to it at once and bow to its authority. This
verse, incidentally, is one of the places in the New Testament where Paul places his
word on a par with Scripture.

D. The Tragedy of Paul's Countrymen (2:15–16)

Paul suffered much from the Jews. At Thessalonica it was the Jews who hounded
him out of the city. When he went on to Berea, it was Jews from Thessalonica who
came and stirred up more trouble. The Jews in Asia Minor detested him, the Jews
in Europe detested him, the Jews in Jerusalem detested him. Yet Paul loved them,
longed to win them to Christ, lived for the day when the veil would be lifted and
Christ would be honored among them. Paul reminds the Thessalonians that the
Jews were guilty of *rejecting the message of the prophets*—"[They] killed . . . their own
prophets" (v. 15); of *rejecting the messiahship of the Lord Jesus*—"[They] killed the
Lord Jesus" (v. 15); and of *rejecting the ministry of the apostles*—"[They] . . . have
persecuted us; and they please not God, and are contrary to all men: Forbidding us
to speak to the Gentiles" (vv. 15–16).

Now the Thessalonians were suffering persecution at the hands of their own
countrymen. Paul makes no apology for that! He does not say he is sorry! He simply
reminds them that this is to be counted as part of the price of being a Christian.

E. The Tangibility of Paul's Crown (2:17–20)

And what was Paul's word of encouragement to these embattled but not em-
bittered saints? The judgment seat of Christ, and the second coming of the Lord
Jesus! He says in effect, "I'm thinking of the Lord's return, my brothers! I'm going
to get a crown by-and-by—I'm going to stand before the Lord full of joy and pride.
Now then, who do you think, of all my converts, will be my real pride and joy at
the Lord's coming? You, brethren, you! Oh," he says, "I am going to be so proud of
you when Jesus comes. I'm proud of you now, but what will it be on that day to see
you receiving your reward!"

Thus the Lord's coming is a stimulating truth. It challenges the Thessalonians
and cheers the apostle.

IV. THE COMING OF CHRIST IS A STABILIZING TRUTH (3:1–13)

In this chapter, Paul recounts again the experiences that were his after he had been
forced to leave Thessalonica in such haste. The riot at Thessalonica had resulted
in the arrest of Jason. (There is a Jason mentioned in Romans 16:21 as a kinsman
of Paul. It is likely the same man.) Jason had been entertaining Paul at his home
when the riot had broken out. The mob had assaulted his house and, not finding

the apostle, had dragged Jason before the rulers, who eventually released him on bail. It would seem Jason and the other believers sent the apostle to Beroea for their own safety.

Paul's hands had been tied by this action, so he had left sooner than he had intended. Timothy came into the picture at this point. He had been with Paul at Berea, remaining behind there with Silas when Paul went on to Athens, and from Athens Paul had sent Timothy back to Thessalonica to help build up the new converts. Later Timothy rejoined Paul at Corinth, bringing good news of the Thessalonian church.

It is to this that Paul refers here. Paul was greatly cheered and challenged by the news Timothy brought. "As cold waters to a thirsty soul, so is good news from a far country" (Prov. 25:25). "But now when Timotheus came from you unto us, and brought us good tidings of your faith and charity . . . we were comforted" (vv. 6–7). Then Paul pours out his soul in prayer and shows what a stabilizing truth the Lord's coming is: "May he establish you, holy and blameless in heart and soul, before himself, the Father of us all, when our Lord Jesus Christ comes with all who belong to him" (v. 13 PHILLIPS).

V. The Coming of Christ Is a Strengthening Truth (4:1–18)

In this chapter, with its thrilling climax on the Lord's coming for the living and the dead, Paul points out the experience of the Christian life.

A. Mighty Potential (4:1–2)

"To sum up, my brothers, we beg and pray you by the Lord Jesus, that you continue to learn more and more of the life that pleases God." This is *the* life! It is a life of mighty potential, learning that opens up for us that which pleases God. And what is it that pleases God? We have His own Word on that. He once opened heaven to say of Jesus, "This is my beloved Son, in whom I am well pleased" (Matt. 3:17). So the life that pleases God is the life that is rooted and grounded in Christ and that grows more and more to be like Christ. Since there are no boundaries to that kind of life, it is a life of mighty potentiality indeed. Jesus said, "Learn of Me" (Matt. 11:29). Who can ever say they have learned all that can be learned of Him?

B. Moral Purity (4:3–8)

"God's plan is to make you holy, and that entails first of all a complete cut with immorality." We can sing,

> Search all my thoughts, the secret springs
> The motives that control;

Those chambers where polluted things
Hold empire o'er the soul.
—Francis Bottome,
"Search Me, O God! My Actions Try"

As it was for Paul, we, too, are living in a day and age when moral standards have been abandoned. The Bible insists on absolute purity as the only rule for life.

C. Measured Progress (4:9–10)
"But as touching brotherly love ye need not that I write unto you: for ye yourselves are taught of God to love one another. And indeed ye do it toward all the brethren which are in Macedonia: but we beseech you, brethren, that ye increase more and more."

D. Manifest Purpose (4:11–12)
Paul makes two demands in these verses. He says: Don't be a *busybody*: "Study to be quiet, and to do your own business" (v. 11). Don't be a *lazybones*: "Work with your own hands, as we commanded you; that ye may walk honestly toward them that are without, and that ye may have lack of nothing" (vv. 11–12). God will not do for us what we can do for ourselves.

E. Magnificent Prospects (4:13–18)
"But I would not have you to be ignorant, brethren, concerning them which are asleep, that ye sorrow not, even as others which have no hope" (v. 13). Looking into the calm, cold face of a dead person somehow brings home to us the seeming finality of death. Paul is saying, "Cheer up! All is well if that loved one died in Christ."

In this magnificent passage, Paul sets before us a threefold action on the resurrection morning when the dead in Christ shall rise. There is, first, the *shout of the Lord—to summon the saints to glory*. What a mighty shout that will be! Three times in the New Testament the Lord is said to speak with a loud voice or with a shout, and each time the gates of death are opened. The first time was at the tomb of Lazarus, the second time was on the cross, and the third time will be at the rapture. And what will He say when He descends the sky to call us home with this mighty shout? The *Song of Solomon* gives us a clue: "Rise up, my love, my fair one, and come away. For, lo, the winter is past, the rain is over and gone; The flowers appear on the earth; the time of the singing of birds is come, and the voice of the turtle is heard in the land; . . . Arise, my love, my fair one, and come away" (Song 2:10–13).

The shout of the Lord is accompanied by the *voice of the archangel—to speed the angels to war*. The rapture of the church will signify that God has broken off diplomatic relations with earth by calling home the nationals of heaven. Michael is then introduced. He is the field marshal of the armies of heaven. Thus it is that the book of Revelation is filled with the noise of war and with the activity of God's angel hosts.

Then, too, there is the *trump of God—to sound the alarm for Israel.* Trumpets were prominent at the giving of the law at Sinai; throughout the wilderness journey of Israel in connection with their worship, walk, and warfare; at the fall of Jericho; in connection with Gideon's victory; and, particularly, at the annual Feast of Trumpets.

The annual feasts of Israel were grouped by the calendar into two series, corresponding to the two comings of Christ. The ritual connected with feasts of the Passover, unleavened bread, firstfruits, and Pentecost has all been fulfilled. What was symbolized by these four feasts was all fulfilled at Christ's first coming—literally and historically. The ritual had to do with Christ's death, resurrection, the putting away of sin, and the coming of the Holy Spirit. Then came the gap of several months in the Jewish religious calendar, a gap that depicted the present age between the two comings. Three more feasts (trumpets, atonement, and tabernacles) then were kept, and these await their literal fulfillment at Christ's second coming. The first of these remaining feasts was the Feast of Trumpets. It heralds Israel's final return to the Land. The fact that the State of Israel has been reborn and that several million Jews have already gone back to the Promised Land is a clear indication that the rapture of the church, to be accompanied by a trumpet blast for Israel, must be very near now.

What magnificent prospects await us. The dead in Christ shall arise first, and we who are alive and remain shall be caught up together with them. The pull of glory will conquer the pull of gravity; the forces of *that* world will overcome the forces of *this* world; the magnetism of Jesus will draw all saved ones to Him.

The coming of Christ is a strengthening truth. We sorrow not as others who have no hope. As the hymn says,

> Hope's anchor, holding in the stormy strife,
> Is stronger as the days go by;
> We feel the throbbings of immortal life
> Grow stronger as the days go by.
> —Eliza E. Hewitt,
> "Sweeter as the Days Go By"

VI. The Coming of Christ Is a Sanctifying Truth (5:1–24)

A. By Way of Explanation (5:1–13)

Paul's explanation has to do with "the day of the Lord" (v. 2). The day of the Lord is not the same as the day of Christ, as many Scriptures prove and the following chart shows:

The Day of the Lord	The Day of Christ
A time of judgment	A time of jubilation
Has to do with the world	Has to do with the church
A day of wrath	A day of rapture
An Old Testament revelation	A New Testament revelation

The Thessalonians knew all about the day of the Lord, for it is referred to directly sixteen times in the Old Testament (twenty times altogether in the Bible).[1] Isaiah, Ezekiel, Joel, Amos, Obadiah, Zephaniah, Zechariah, and Malachi all mention it. Paul says, "You yourselves know perfectly that the day of the Lord so cometh as a thief in the night" (v. 2), Concerning the day of Christ, he said, "I would not have you to be ignorant, brethren" (4:13). Some people take 1 Thessalonians 5:1–10 to teach that the church will go through the tribulation; it teaches exactly the opposite. If we note the use of pronouns in this passage—*they, them, they, ye, ye, we, us, us, they, they, us, us, us, we, we*—we will see how carefully Paul distinguished between "us" and "them." Note his conclusion: "For God hath not appointed *us* to wrath, but to obtain salvation by our Lord Jesus Christ" (v. 9). The two events (the rapture and the day of wrath) are discussed in the same context (4:13–5:10) because of their close proximity in time. But the day of Christ comes first. When God takes out the salt, the resulting corruption precipitates the day of wrath.

Paul's explanation concerning the day of the Lord is most instructive. For the *sons of men* there can be no escape from its *impact* (5:1–3). That day is *already decreed*: "The day of the Lord so cometh as a thief in the night" (v. 2). That is, though the Lord's coming is a close-guarded secret as to the *time*, the *truth* of the day is thoroughly revealed. All speculation as to the time of the rapture is useless. All we can do is watch and be ready.

Then, too, the day is *accurately described*: "For when they shall say, Peace and safety; then sudden destruction cometh upon them, as travail upon a woman with child; and they shall not escape" (v. 3). The church will be gone! The man of sin will have appeared! The Devil's "millennium" will have dawned! Then suddenly, when man has "arrived," so to speak, when God has been voted out of the earth, when man has achieved a society based on science, sociology, and sin, presided over by Satan, the superman and the seer from the pit, suddenly the whole thing will explode! Sin, being a disruptive force in the universe, will cause the whole thing to collapse from within. And, from without, God will intervene. The Son of God will step back once more into the arena of human affairs. "And they shall not escape," says Paul. For the sons of men there is no escape from its impact.

For the *sons of God* there is no escape from its *import* (vv. 4–13). Paul tells us what we are to do in the light of it. First, we are to *watch*. "But ye, brethren, are not in darkness, that that day should overtake you as a thief. Ye are all the children of light . . . Therefore let us not sleep, as do others; but let us watch and be sober" (vv. 4–6). The world is in total darkness about what lies ahead; not so the Christian. The Word of God gives us ample warning. The "signs of the times" are written large for us to read. The Belshazzars of this world cannot read the signs that God is writing with unerring hand today upon the plaster walls of man's gilded palaces of pride. The Daniels in the household of faith can read them, however. We watch and marvel as each succeeding day brings increasing evidence that the day is approaching. Watch and pray!

Then, too, we are to *war*: "Let us, who are of the day, be sober, putting on the breastplate of faith and love; and for an helmet, the hope of salvation" (v. 8). In the day of the Lord, the earth will resound to the din of battle as the earth's millions are mobilized and marshaled at Megiddo. The battle of Armageddon, however, is the climax of a conflict that has been going on down here since Adam surrendered his sovereignty to Satan. We are all deeply involved in that battle; every time we kneel in prayer we invade the realm of the prince of the power of the air. So we are to gird on our armor and fight.

Moreover, we are to wait: "For God hath not appointed us to wrath, but to obtain salvation . . ." (v. 9). This verse is conclusive that the church will not go through the great tribulation, the time when God's wrath will be poured out upon this planet. That the "salvation" referred to here has to do with salvation or deliverance from the coming day of wrath is clear from the context, which has to do with "that great and terrible day of the Lord." We are not waiting for wrath but for the Lord Jesus, whose coming at the rapture will save us from that wrath.

In the meantime, we are to *work*: "We beseech you, brethren, to know them which labour among you, and are over you in the Lord, and admonish you; And to esteem them very highly in love for their work's sake" (vv. 12–13). Waiting does not mean being idle. Jesus said, "Occupy till I come" (Luke 19:13). There are still untold millions still untold, still two thousand tongues to go before all people have the Bible in their own language. The work of God worldwide is vast, and most of it is in desperate need of more men and more money and more mediators.

B. By Way of Exhortation (5:14–24)

This is twofold. First, we are to walk *virtuously*: "Now we exhort you, brethren, warn them that are unruly" (v. 14); there has to be an emphasis in the church on *government*: "Comfort the feebleminded, support the weak, be patient toward all men" (v. 14); there has to be an emphasis on *grace* in the church: "See that none render evil for evil unto any man; but ever follow that which is good, both among yourselves, and to all men" (v. 15); there has to be an emphasis on practical *goodness* in the church.

In addition to this, we are to walk *victoriously*. These closing exhortations of Paul are a series of short, sharp jabs to the conscience. They affect our approach to God (vv. 16–21), and our appeal to men (vv. 22–24). The man who knows how to rejoice evermore . . . pray without ceasing . . . in everything give thanks . . . quench not the Spirit . . . hold fast that which is good . . . abstain from all appearance of evil . . . that man, that woman will have power both with God and man. That person's life will make an impact. The coming of the Lord in that person's life will be indeed a sanctifying truth. "And the very God of peace will sanctify that person wholly—his whole spirit and soul and body will be preserved blameless unto the coming of our Lord Jesus Christ" (see v. 23).

VII. CONCLUSION (5:25–28)

The letter to this infant church ends with a final greeting. Then, having urged that its contents be made as public as possible, Paul commends his new converts to the Lord's grace.

It might be said in closing that eschatology is probably not what *we* would think should be drilled into babes in Christ. Paul evidently thought it a vital key to all growth in grace and godliness.

CHAPTER 17

2 THESSALONIANS

Second Thoughts on the Second Coming

Afterwriting his first letter to the Thessalonians, Paul received further disturbing news. The believers were being shaken in their faith on the matter of the Lord's return. Someone, it appears, had caused them to be troubled as to their relation to "the day of the Lord." Paul reminded the Thessalonians that he had already told them about these things (2:5), yet some were propagating the error that that day had already begun (2:2). Paul told them that two things must happen before the day of the Lord begins: there must be an apostasy, and the Man of Sin must appear on the earth.

Paul's two Thessalonian letters have much in common. The first has to do mainly with the church, and the second mainly with the world; the first tells of Christ's appearing in the air, and the second tells of His advent to the earth; the first has to do chiefly with "the day of Christ," and the second chiefly with "the day of the Lord." Both contain important passages on the Lord's coming (1 Thess. 4:13–18; 2 Thess. 2:1–12).

I. Introduction (1:1–2)
II. Paul's Word of Admiration (1:3–12)
   A. Undiluted Praise (1:3–4)
   B. Undisputed Promise (1:5–10)
   C. Undefeated Prayer (1:11–12)
III. Paul's Word of Admonition (2:1–3:15)
   A. The Greatness of the Coming Lie (2:1–12)
      1. The Immediate Deception Paul Fought (2:1–2)
      2. The Immense Deception Paul Foresaw (2:3–12)

a. The Man of Sin Revealed (2:3–4)
   (1) The Unveiling of Satan's Man (2:3)
      (a) His Coming
      (b) His Character
   (2) The Unveiling of Satan's Plan (2:4)
b. The Mystery of Iniquity Restrained (2:5–7)
   (1) Its Actuality (2:5–6)
   (2) Its Activity (2:7)
c. The Might of Satan Released (2:8–12)
   (1) A Dark Discovery (2:8)
      (a) A Revelation from Hell
      (b) A Proclamation from Heaven
   (2) A Deep Dishonesty (2:9–10)
      (a) Lying Miracles (2:9)
      (b) Lying Messages (2:10)
   (3) A Dreadful Destiny (2:11–12)
      (a) The True Source of Their Blindness (2:11)
      (b) The True Significance of Their Blindness (2:12)
B. The Greatness of the Christian Life (2:13–3:15)
  1. We Are Chosen (2:13–14)
    a. The Proof (2:13a)
    b. The Purpose (2:13b)
    c. The Process (2:14)
  2. We Are Challenged (2:15–3:5)
    a. To Trust (2:15–17)
    b. To Travail (3:1–2)
    c. To Triumph (3:3–5)
  3. We Are Charged (3:6–15)
    a. The Need for Discipline (3:6–11)
      (1) Explained (3:6)
      (2) Exemplified (3:7–11)
    b. The Nature of Discipline (3:12–15)
      (1) The Rule Established (3:12–13)
      (2) The Rebel Expelled (3:14)
      (3) The Reason Explained (3:15)
IV. Conclusion (3:16–18)

The unique revelation unfolded in this letter has to do with the coming of a world ruler. He will be the incarnation of all evil and of whom past wicked rulers have been but faint types.

I. Introduction (1:1–2)

Paul's introduction to this letter is identical to the one that opened his first letter to the Thessalonians, except for the additional statement that grace and peace are "from God our Father and the Lord Jesus Christ" (v. 2). Thus, God and His Son are put in the first place in this letter to overshadow all future references to Satan and his "son."

II. Paul's Word of Admiration (1:3–12)

He begins with a word of *undiluted praise* for their faith and their love (1:3–4). In his first letter he made mention, in addition, of their "patience of hope." The great hope of the church is the coming again of the Lord Jesus. Perhaps the fact that the Thessalonians were in difficulty again over this doctrine is why Paul does not again commend them for their hope. Nevertheless, Paul was quick to praise them for their bold stand in the face of persecution and tribulations.

He continues with a word of *undisputed promise* (1:5–10). They were going to inherit the kingdom of God, and as for those who were persecuting them, God would certainly visit them with tribulation. Paul pauses here to anticipate the coming day when the Lord will be revealed in glory, coming with His angels to pour out His vengeance in flaming fire upon the ungodly, and to display His glory in His own people. Paul writes these great truths down with bold assurance. Nothing can be more certain.

Then comes a word of *undefeated prayer* for the continued spiritual growth of the believers in the light of these great certainties (1:11–12). Supremely he wanted the Lord Jesus to be glorified in them *now* as He will be one day at His coming again.

III. Paul's Word of Admonition (2:1–3:15)

The great theme of the letter is in two contrasting parts. First comes a most remarkable and interesting discussion of the great delusion that will take over the world in the last days.

A. The Greatness of the Coming Lie (2:1–12)

It all began with a local deception that had taken root at Thessalonica. There were some who were teaching that "the day of the Lord" had already come.[1]

It seems that the erroneous teaching was well documented, but Paul repudiates the supporting "proofs" as fraudulent. The Thessalonians had been deceived by a spirit utterance, by a prophetic "word," and by a forged letter supposedly from Paul. Satan's attempt to deceive this local church turned out, though, to be too clever for his own good because Paul used the local deception at Thessalonica as a springboard to launch a full-scale exposure of Satan's most secret plans for the ages.

Paul tells how *the man of sin will be revealed* (2:3–4). He says, "Let no man deceive you by any means." There is a double negative in the text, which cannot properly be rendered in English. To state it ungrammatically we would have to render it, "Let no man deceive you by no means." Before the Devil's messiah can come there has to be "a falling away first" (v. 3), an *apostasia*, from which we get our English word "apostasy." There has to be a wholesale turning away from God—a process that appears to be well under way today with the advance of Communism, humanism, and cultism around the world.

When he is finally revealed, Satan's man will stand forth as the "man of sin" and as "the son of perdition" (v. 3, the only other person called the "son of perdition" in Scripture is that arch-apostate, Judas, in John 17:12). Doubtless the Antichrist's propensity for sin, his love of sin, his promotion of sin will be masked at first. He will seem to be a wonderfully attractive person, filled with charm and charisma, diabolically clever, tremendously persuasive and influential, able to sway the minds and hearts and wills of most of the unregenerate masses of mankind.

He will come swiftly to the seat of supreme power on earth. He will bend the world to his will, then seize the rebuilt temple of the Jews in Jerusalem and seat himself in the holy of holies, proclaiming himself to be God and demanding universal worship of himself.

As Paul goes on to explain, however, *the mystery of iniquity will be restrained* (2:5–7). There is One who restrains, holds back this full and final development of the actively working "mystery of iniquity" at the present time. This Restrainer is the Holy Spirit operating in the church. Time and again, down through the centuries, Satan has sought to finalize his plans for bringing his man on stage. He has always been frustrated by the Holy Spirit. The rapture of the church will signal the end of this age-long restraint. The Holy Spirit will then step aside and allow Satan to have his brief day.

For then *the might of Satan will be released* (2:8–12). "*Then,*" says the Holy Spirit, "shall that Wicked be revealed" (v. 8). All attempts to identify this coming ruler of wickedness with anyone living today are foolish. He may be in the world but he will not be revealed until the Holy Spirit ceases to restrain, which, in turn, will not be until after the rapture of the church.

The coming of this evil person will be accompanied by many lying miracles poured out to accredit Satan's man to a gullible world, and his coming will also be accompanied by every form of deceitful philosophy Satan can devise. All this will eventually lead to a universal rejection of the truths of God and the enthronement of the lie.

God warns that those who deliberately reject His truth now will automatically embrace Satan's lies then. There will be no second chance for those Christ-rejecters left behind after the rapture. Millions of souls will be saved (Rev. 7), but those who have heard, understood, and ignored the gospel of God's grace will not believe the gospel of the kingdom. That fact is solemnly avowed here.

B. The Greatness of the Christian Life (2:13–3:15)

Having dealt with the error, Paul characteristically turns to practical issues. He tells his friends at Thessalonica four things. First, *we are chosen* (2:13–14). Again we are confronted with the mystery of *God's* sovereign, election choice and man's volitional accountability for *his* choice. "God hath from the beginning chosen you," says Paul (v. 13). Nobody questions that. The sovereignty of God was exercised when He sovereignly elected to create man, endowed with intellect, emotions, and will, knowing full well that man would fall into sin. He also sovereignly chose to provide salvation for men and elected the way it should be provided—by the death of Christ at Calvary. He further sovereignly chose to offer His salvation to man "by grace through faith" (see Eph. 2:8). By grace—available to all equally and without favor or cost, through faith—available to all upon repentance and trust in Christ. Having sovereignly set the terms of His salvation, God chose all those He foreknew would respond to them. This choice was made, in His omniscience, "before the foundation of the world" (Eph. 1:4).

Then, *we are challenged* (2:15–3:5). "Therefore, brethren, stand fast, and hold the traditions which ye have been taught, whether by word, or our epistle" (2:15). The word "tradition" here is the same word translated "ordinances" in 1 Corinthians 11:2. It implies that the teacher is not expressing his own ideas but is handing over (*paradidosis*) a message received from someone else. The word is related to the teaching of the rabbis who made God's truth void by handing on wrong teaching; it is used in 1 Corinthians 11:2 of apostolic teaching; it is used in 2 Thessalonians 2:15 of Christian doctrine in general. The apostle's use of the word here is a denial that what he taught originated with himself; rather, it is a claim for its divine origin.

The word *hold*—"hold the traditions"—implies "a vigorous, tenacious grasp"; it is used of the lame man clutching the apostles (Acts 3:11). Believers are not to allow Satan to deceive them by their accepting as from God teachings that came from another source. Paul reinforces this exhortation by contrasting "our epistle" (2:15) with the "[epistle] as from us" (2:2). First they had his oral teaching; now it was confirmed in two epistles. They must pay no heed to contrary teaching.

Moreover, *we are charged* (3:6–15). It seems there were some at Thessalonica who refused to earn their living, expecting to share the wealth of more affluent believers. Paul issues a command, with all the apostolic authority vested in him as a called apostle: "Withdraw yourselves from every brother that walketh disorderly" (3:6). The word (as in 1 Tim. 5:1e) is a military metaphor applied to those who refused to keep in step or those who went absent without leave. Paul emphasizes the fact that secular employment is expected of believers. Christians are not to sponge off others and the church. Far from supporting such laziness, the church is to withdraw fellowship from those who refuse to work. Such disciplinary action, however, while necessary, is not to extinguish love. The offending believer is not to be counted an enemy but is to be admonished as a brother.

IV. Conclusion (3:16–18)

The letter ends with Paul's prayer that the Thessalonians might be at peace. Truth on the Lord's second coming was under such attack by Satan, and was the topic of so many various and conflicting and often erroneous views, that a special prayer for peace was breathed by Paul at the end of both these epistles dealing with eschatology. He had put them right; now let there be peace. Let there be an end to further discordant views! To achieve this he invoked the Lord by a unique title that occurs only here—"the Lord of peace" (v. 16).

Still rankled by the forged letter, Paul says, "The salutation of Paul with mine own hand, which is the token [sign] in every epistle . . ." To guard against forgery, Paul says that in all his epistles he adds his own distinctive seal in his own handwriting. We should remember that, in all probability, these two letters, after Galatians, were the first he wrote. He was going to make sure that all his future epistles would be in his own handwriting, or would contain some authenticating mark.

CHAPTER 18

1 TIMOTHY

An Aged Apostle and a Youthful Colleague

Any consideration of the two letters to Timothy needs to be accompanied by a good look at Timothy himself. Timothy, the son of a Gentile father and a Jewish mother, was probably born at Lystra. His father seems to have died when he was young, resulting in his being raised by his godly mother, Eunice, and his saintly grandmother, Lois. These two conscientious women instilled into the boy a good grounding in the things of God. When Paul first visited Lystra on his first missionary journey, Timothy was likely about fifteen or sixteen years of age. He seems to have been led to Christ by Paul at this time. Paul speaks of him affectionately as his son in the faith, as his dearly beloved son, and as his son Timothy.

When Paul came back to Lystra on his second missionary journey, Timothy was nearly twenty. Even at this early age he had already won his spurs in the Lord's work, for he "was well reported of by the brethren that were at Lystra and Iconium" (Acts 16:2). Paul decided that Timothy would be an excellent replacement for Mark, who had deserted the mission field on Paul's first expedition before getting so far as Lystra. It could have been no light thing for Eunice and Lois to part with their beloved Timothy. They knew, from what had happened when Paul was in their area the last time, that this intrepid gospel pioneer did not shrink from danger in doing the Lord's work.

Since Timothy was half Jew, half Gentile, Paul circumcised him to make him more acceptable to Jews. His being circumcised would not make him repugnant to Gentiles, whereas his being uncircumcised would greatly hinder him in any work among the Jews. So, in order to give Timothy the widest possible ministry, Paul, scorning to be petty, circumcised the young man. Since Timothy was already half a Jew he might as well go all the way and make himself acceptable to Jews. Perhaps, too, Paul wanted to put Timothy to the test to see if he would shrink from an unpleasant experience or if he would try to challenge Paul's authority.

Thereafter we see Timothy much in the company of Paul, and we find his name closely linked with Paul's in half a dozen epistles. In fact, of the four letters Paul wrote to individuals, two are addressed to Timothy. He was active in the Lord's work at Philippi, Thessalonica, Corinth, and Ephesus. He was with Paul after his release from his first Roman imprisonment and, when Paul was back in prison again for the last time, we find him urging Timothy to hurry to his side. Timothy, at the time, was at Ephesus as Paul's delegate, seeking to deal with heresies that had entered the church there.

Some review of Paul's movements as well as the march of events will also be helpful in considering the three so-called "pastoral epistles." The following is suggested tentatively from clues connected with the various places named in these letters—Ephesus, Macedonia, Philippi, Crete, Nicopolis, Asia, Rome, Antioch, Iconium, Lystra, Thessalonica, Galatia (possibly Gaul), Dalmatia, Troas, Corinth, and Miletus.

Paul was under house arrest in Rome when he wrote Colossians, Philemon, and Ephesians, and in the custody of the praetorian guard when he wrote Philippians. He was tried and acquitted, probably in A.D. 63. When the great fire of Rome broke out in A.D. 64, Paul was on a fourth missionary journey (A.D. 63–67), which took him to Philippi (Phil. 2:24), to Colossae (Philem. 22), and perhaps on to Spain (Rom. 15:28). He then came back to Ephesus, where he found that the heresies he had anticipated (Acts 20:28–30) had already taken root. He left Timothy behind to continue dealing with the situation while he himself went on to Macedonia (1 Tim. 1:3). While there, he doubtless visited Philippi and Corinth and wrote his first letter to Timothy. Paul then went on to Crete (Titus 1:5), found disorders there, too, and left Titus behind to minister to the believers on the island and to tackle the situation that had arisen. Paul seems to have hurried back to Ephesus to give Timothy assistance in that key church and, while there, wrote his letter to Titus. Next the tireless apostle went on to Miletus, where he left Trophimus sick (2 Tim. 4:20). He hurried on to Corinth (2 Tim. 4:20) on his way to Nicopolis (probably in Epirus), where he planned to spend the winter (Titus 3:12). The apostle seems to have been driven by the knowledge that his time was now very short.

In the meantime, Nero had launched the first great persecution of the church, and had murdered his tutor Seneca (A.D. 65). Also the Jewish war had broken out (A.D. 66). In A.D. 67 Paul was re-arrested, either at Nicopolis, Corinth, or Troas and, instead of spending the winter as planned, he spent it at Rome under harsh conditions. He was re-tried and gave his "first answer"; then, realizing his days were numbered, he wrote his second epistle to Timothy, the last of his letters. Paul was executed in A.D. 67–68; Nero was assassinated in A.D. 68; Jerusalem fell in A.D. 70.

Both of the letters to Timothy are full of exhortations. Timothy was not physically strong—he apparently had some kind of stomach disorder—and was of a much more timid and retiring disposition than Paul, something Paul always had to take into account when sending Timothy off to deal with difficult situations. Paul expected Timothy to be as zealous in soul winning and gospel preaching as he was, even though Timothy's gift was that of a pastor rather than that of an evangelist. Thus we find Paul urging his younger colleague to "war a good warfare" (1:18), not to let anyone despise his youth, not to neglect his gift, to be willing to suffer hardship, to flee youthful lusts, and so on. Remember that these challenges were given to Timothy, not when he was starting out in the Lord's work, but after he had been engaged in it for some sixteen years.

I. INTRODUCTION (1:1–2)

"Timothy, my own son in the faith" (v. 2). The yearning, the tenderness, the comradeship Paul felt for Timothy comes through at once. Paul was at least thirty years older than Timothy, and the entire period covered by the book of Acts is long since past. The two missionaries had shared many an experience together. Timothy was now in a place of great responsibility at Ephesus, for the key church there, one to which Paul had written the most magnificent of all his epistles, was in deep trouble. Timothy was the man on the spot—responsible to hold the line for the truth of God. Paul assures him that he is backing him up with all the weight of his apostolic authority and all the warmth of his heart. More, he directs his attention to "God the Father" and to "Jesus Christ our Lord" (v. 2) as standing beside him there, pouring into his heart grace, mercy, and peace.

II. HOW TO BUILD AN EFFECTIVE CHURCH (1:3–3:15)

A. The Church and Its Doctrine (1:3–20)

Everything has its foundation there. If truth is missing, if the teaching is wrong, all is wrong. I once knew a man, getting on in years, who was polished, successful, friendly, and hospitable, a man who was educated and respected and the leading pastor of a local church. He seemed to have all the gifts and all the graces; but he was a heretic. He held and taught views concerning the person of Christ that were, in the final analysis, an outright attack upon the deity of Christ. He was very persuasive, carrying the majority of the congregation with him for years until a young missionary the church supported dared to come home and challenge him. The older man's teaching was wrong, everything was wrong. The man's very charm, ability, and subtlety with the Scriptures only made him that much more dangerous. No wonder Paul always begins with doctrine. Nobody can build an effective church without sound doctrine. They can build successful religious systems, but not a church.

In the opening verses, Paul confronts Timothy and the beloved Ephesian church with *the loss of truth*: "Charge some that they teach no other doctrine, Neither give heed to fables and endless genealogies" (vv. 3–4). It would seem that the church was being plagued by some form of Judaism.

Paul mentions next *the law of God* (vv. 5–11). The essence of everything, the law included, is love, Paul says. However, "the law is good, if a man use it lawfully" (v. 8). As Christians, we accept the law as a *standard*, though we are not under the law as a *system*. If we are living the kind of life God expects, then we do not even need the law as a standard. Love makes sure we do anyway what the moral law demands. Paul described the teaching of the legalists, who wanted to impose on Christians the law as a system, as "vain jangling" (v. 6).

Next, Paul emphasizes *the love of Christ* (1:12–17). It is the love of Christ that saves people, not the law of God. Paul cites himself as an example and introduces the first of half a dozen "faithful sayings" (see v. 15) that occur in these pastoral epistles (1 Tim. 1:15; 3:1; 4:8–9; 2 Tim. 2:11–13; Titus 1:9; 3:4–8). These all appear to be fragments of early church hymns or catechisms.

Then he endorses *the life of faith* (1:18–20). He cites an illustration, the case of one Hymenaeus and the case of Alexander, two men Paul says he had "delivered unto Satan, that they may learn not to blaspheme" (v. 20). Hymenaeus is mentioned again in Paul's second letter to Timothy, and Alexander may be the same one referred to by Paul in his second letter as the "coppersmith" (2 Tim. 4:14) and the man who did him much harm. Likely, too, he is the same man mentioned in Acts 19:33.

B. The Church and Its Devotions (2:1–15)

Paul now has some things to say about prayer, preaching, and position in the church. He deals first with *the practice of worship in the church* (2:1–8). We should pray for all men. This will result in a desire to reach all with the gospel, for God "will have all men to be saved, and to come unto the knowledge of the truth" (v. 4).

Paul has something to say, too, about *the place of women in the church* (2:9–15). He says they are to "learn in silence" (v. 11), and they are not to teach, nor "to usurp authority over the man" (v. 12). Such teaching is rejected out of hand by modern feminists. We cannot have it both ways, however; either this is the Word of God, inspired and "God-breathed" by the Holy Spirit—in which case it must be accepted at its face value—or else it is not God's Word and must be dismissed as Pauline prejudice. To write it off as Pauline prejudice is to attack the inspiration, inerrancy, and infallibility of the Bible—a very serious position to take indeed. The Holy Spirit's upholding the ruling that the woman is not to usurp a man's role goes back to the creation and to the fall. There is evidently a deep underlying principle involved in this ruling regarding the ministry of women in the church, one that has to do with human nature, and particularly fallen human nature. We cannot afford to set aside this ruling just to accommodate popular opinion. This teaching, unpopular as it may be, is part of the Holy Spirit's teaching on how to build an effective church. Who should know that best, Paul or us? The Holy Spirit or the modernist?

C. The Church and Its Duties (3:1–15)

Now comes some practical advice on church leadership. Paul envisions two kinds of office: that of the *episkopos*, the elders, the spiritual shepherds of the local congregation; that of the deacons, those responsible for the more secular and mundane matters of the local church. The New Testament knows nothing of an ordained priesthood, of an episcopal hierarchy, or of a papacy. The qualifications given by the Holy Spirit are very high, but they do not include what seems most important in so many churches today—success in business.

III. How to Become an Effective Christian (3:16–6:19)

A. Walk with God (3:16–4:16)

We must walk a straight line. On the one side we have *the mystery of godliness* (3:16–4:7a) asserted by the saints of God (3:16) and assailed by Satan himself (4:1a). In this memorable passage, we have what is believed to be one of the great hymns of the infant church (3:16), a magnificent statement of Christ's coming, character, and career.

In stark contrast to the words of this hymn is the coming of the end-time apostasy, as Paul foretells, the dawn of an age when people will give heed to seducing spirits and to doctrines of demons, rather than to the Holy Spirit and biblical truth. The demonic characteristic of much of the apostasy is seen in its attack upon the institution of marriage and in its appeal for a vegetarian diet (both hallmarks, incidentally, of spiritism and of occult and oriental religion).

On the other side we have *the manifestation of godliness* (4:7b–16). Here, Paul gives Timothy some practical advice for living a godly life in a godless world.

B. Witness for God (5:1–6:19)

Again, Paul advances two concepts. First we must pay heed to *the people of God* (5:1–6:2). Here, Paul discusses our relationship as Christians to other believers, to widows, and to elders who are set by God to rule the local church. Here, too, Paul is down to earth with his counsel. While, for instance, urging Christians to take care of widows, he sensibly insists that they should be "widows indeed" (5:3). If they have family members who can support them, then they should not be a charge to the church. And, bluntly, Paul adds, "If any provide not for his own, and specially for those of his own house, he hath denied the faith, and is worse than an infidel" (5:8).

But Paul has another practical word. If our witness for God will be affected by our relationships at home, at church, at work, so will our attitude to money affect that witness. He speaks of *the peril of gold* (6:3–19). In that famous, but oft misquoted statement, he asserts that "the love of money is the root of all evil" (6:10). It is not money that is the root of all evil, but the *love* of money. Paul says that the desire to be rich is perilous, and that only people with perverse minds mistake gain for godliness. As for those who are rich, let them see to it that they are also "rich in good works" (6:18), giving generously to the Lord's work, laying up true treasure in heaven.

IV. CONCLUSION (6:20–21)

"O Timothy," Paul writes, "keep that which is committed to thy trust, avoiding profane and vain babblings, and oppositions of science falsely so called: Which some professing have erred concerning the faith. Grace be with thee. Amen."

The word for "trust" here is *parathēkē*, which literally means a deposit; it is the word for money deposited in a bank. Paul has just been speaking about a Christian and his money. But let us remember this—God has invested in us a trust. He has made a deposit in us. When we deposit money in a bank, we expect that our trust will be honored, that we shall get the money back when required. The Christian faith is like that—a sacred trust. We are responsible for what we do with it.

Paul has one last word for his younger colleague, who is struggling to hold the line for God against the cultists who have invaded the Ephesian church. He tells him to beware of false intellectualism and controversy. We are not here to argue. We are here to proclaim God's Word and to adorn the doctrine with our lives. Our adversaries may be very clever, but "God be with thee," says Paul. Truly "greater is he that is in you, than he that is in the world" (1 John 4:4). The Devil—even with all his clever sophistries—is no match for the Holy Spirit.

CHAPTER 19

2 Timothy

Paul's Famous Last Words

We give a person's last words a special place in our thinking. More so if that person has commanded an important place in our thinking. We can think of many examples of famous last words. When Sir Walter Raleigh was being executed, the headsman asked him whether he would not prefer to face the east. He replied, "So the heart be right it is no matter which way the head lieth." When Tallyrand, the infidel French statesman, was dying, he was asked by King Louis XVIII how he felt. He replied, "I am suffering, Sire, the pangs of the damned!" For two months, the dying infidel, Voltaire, cried out, "I must die—abandoned of God and of men!" D. L. Moody had a glorious death. His last words were, "Earth recedes—heaven opens up before me!" Edgar Allan Poe's haunted and drunken life came to an end full of delirium and despair: "Lord, help my poor soul," were the last words he uttered. When Anne Boleyn, the unfortunate wife of King Henry VIII, faced the executioner she said, "I pray to God to save the king." The great Bohemian reformer, John Hus, was burned at the stake as a heretic in Constance, Germany. He said, "You may cook the goose today [*Hus* in Bohemian means "goose"] but God shall raise up a gander and him you'll never roast" (the name *Luther* is derived in German from the word *gander*). Luther had not even been born at the time.

Paul was one of the greatest men ever to live, which invests this particular letter with such interest. For here we have the last words of the noblest Christian of them all, the greatest thinker and theologian of the church age, and the grandest missionary of all time.

When Paul wrote his first letter to Timothy he was traveling in Europe, having left his younger colleague behind at Ephesus. When he wrote his second letter—his last letter—Timothy was still at Ephesus; Paul was in prison in Rome; Nero was on the rampage; the church was undergoing a baptism of fire, and the great apostle was anticipating martyrdom. One of the stellar lessons to be learned from this last letter is how a Christian should face death. Paul faced it as he lived—with courage and with Christ. When my own grandfather was dying, he said to my father, "There's nothing to dying, Leonard; it's the living that matters. If you live right, you'll die right." And he died as he lived—a quiet, confident believer in the Lord Jesus.

    I. Introduction (1:1–2)
   II. Present Testings (1:3–2:26)
      A. Timothy's Personal Responsibilities: The Past (1:3–18)
         1. To Develop His Faith (1:3–6)
           In view of:
           a. His Family Connections (1:3–5)
           b. His Formal Call (1:6)
         2. To Dispel His Fears (1:7–18)
           a. The Exhortation (1:7–11)
              (1) Remember God's Spirit (1:7)
              (2) Remember God's Son (1:8–10)
              (3) Remember God's Servant (1:11)
           b. The Examples (1:12–18)
      B. Timothy's Pastoral Responsibilities: The Present (2:1–26)
        He was to be:
         1. A Steward (2:1–2)
         2. A Soldier (2:3–4)
         3. A Success (2:5–7)
           a. The Test of His Mastery as an Athlete (2:5)
           b. The Taste of His Ministry as a Husbandman (2:6–7)
         4. A Sufferer (2:8–13)
         5. A Student (2:14–19)
         6. A Servant (2:20–26)
           a. The Capacity of Service (2:20)
           b. The Condition of Service (2:21–23)
           c. The Character of Service (2:24–26)
  III. Predicted Testings (3:1–4:18)
      A. The Approaching Day of the Great Apostasy (3:1–4:5)
         1. The Pattern that Will Announce It (3:1–9)
         2. The Persecution that Will Accompany It (3:10–13)
         3. The Persons Who Will Anticipate It (3:14–4:5)
      B. The Approaching Death of the Great Apostle (4:6–18)
         1. Paul's Hope (4:6–8)

2. Paul's Hardships (4:9–15)
3. Paul's Heroism (4:16–18)
IV. Conclusion (4:19–22)

Paul has something to say to Timothy about the past (chap. 1), the present (chap. 2), and the prospect (chap. 3).

I. INTRODUCTION (1:1–2)

"Paul, an apostle of Jesus Christ by the will of God . . ." Nero might be Caesar, with supreme power on earth; Paul was an apostle of Jesus Christ with power in heaven. So much for Nero! "According to the promise of life which is in Christ Jesus" (v. 1). The promise of life! So much for Nero's headsman! "To Timothy, my dearly beloved son . . ." How Paul's great yearning for Timothy comes through! The name "Timothy" in full is *Timotheus*, made up of two Greek words—*timē*, which means "honor," and *theos*, which means God. So Timothy's very name was an exhortation—"Honor God!" One can almost hear Paul saying, "My dearly beloved son, live up to your name!" Timothy was indeed a son to Paul. If Paul had been blessed with a son, he would have wanted one just like Timothy, and doubtless Timothy (whose own Gentile father seems to have died when Timothy was still young) found in Paul the finest father a young man could ever have.

II. PRESENT TESTINGS (1:3–2:26)

A. Timothy's Personal Responsibilities: The Past (1:3–18)

First and foremost, Timothy's responsibility was to *develop his faith* (1:3–6). Paul's heart was full of gratitude at every thought of Timothy and he responds in kind to Timothy's sorrow at their separation. Timothy was the kind of man who makes a good lieutenant but who is a poor general. He needed the stimulation of a man like Paul. So Paul, while expressing his thanks for Timothy's own faith, sought to strengthen that faith by reminding Timothy of the faith of his mother and grandmother.

He was to *dispel his fears* (1:7–18). There was good reason for fear. Nero had blamed the great fire of Rome on the Christians and was exacting a terrible vengeance. Then, too, Timothy was of a retiring disposition and he was being opposed by formidable false teachers. "Be not thou ashamed of the testimony of our Lord," urges Paul. "[And don't be ashamed] of me his prisoner: but be thou partaker of the afflictions of the gospel according to the power of God" (v. 8). As for Paul himself, he states the source of his own boldness: "I know whom I have believed, and am persuaded that he is able to keep that which I have committed unto him against that day" (v. 12). Paul does not say, "I know *what* I have believed," although, of course, nobody knew better than he the glorious truths of the gospel. He says, "I know *whom* I have believed." It is a personal, dynamic acquaintance with the Lord Jesus that is the real anchor for our souls and our bright hope for the future. It is this that diminished Nero to nothing in Paul's calculations of the future. Paul had no fears, for he knew Jesus too well. For Paul, living or dying, all was Christ.

B. Timothy's Pastoral Responsibilities: The Present (2:1–26)

Paul introduces half a dozen illustrations of the Christian life and ministry. First, Timothy was to be a *steward* (2:1–2). In a statement of singular point and purpose, Paul gives the essence of Christian witness and discipleship: "The things that thou hast heard of me . . . the same commit thou to faithful men, who shall be able to teach others also" (v. 2). We should all be engaged in handing on the torch of truth, and in training those we reach to teach others.

Timothy was also to be a *soldier* (2:3–4). Paul had close acquaintance with many soldiers. He knew of the sacrifice, the courage, the obedience, and the loyalty of a good soldier. We are in a battle, and there is no discharge in this warfare.

Timothy was to be a *success*. He was to develop the persistence of the athlete (2:5) and the patience of the farmer (2:6–7). To "strive lawfully" (v. 5) comes from a Greek phrase (**athlein nomimōs**) used to describe the professional athlete, the man whose struggle was no part-time affair. A part-time Christian is a contradiction. As for the farmer, of all occupations, his calls for learning patience. There are no quick results.

Timothy was to be a *sufferer* (2:8–13), like Paul himself who could say that because he boldly preached the gospel he suffered trouble as an evildoer, even unto bonds. The word Paul used for "evildoer" (v. 9) is used elsewhere in the New Testament only to describe the malefactors (criminals) crucified with Christ.

Timothy was to be a *student* (2:14–19). "Study to show thyself approved unto God, a workman that needeth not to be ashamed, rightly dividing the word of truth" (v. 15). The expression "to rightly divide" comes from the word for driving a straight furrow across a field, the word for cutting and squaring a stone so that it fits correctly into place.

Timothy was to be a *servant* (2:20–26). In a great house are many vessels and each has its use. Some are vessels of high honor, others have much more mundane uses; all are important. Paul was "a chosen vessel" (Acts 9:15). Timothy could never be a Paul, but Timothy, in his own sphere, according to his own capacity, was to be just as much a vessel "meet for the master's use" (v. 21).

III. PREDICTED TESTINGS (3:1–4:18)

A. The Approaching Day of the Great Apostasy (3:1–4:5)

Any consideration of this passage that restricts it to the Gnostic heresy— which was raising its head in the early Christian church—is wholly inadequate.

Paul distinctly relates it to "the last days" (3:1), which he characterizes as *chalepos* (perilous), the word used to describe the Gadarene demoniacs (Matt. 8:28). Paul is pointing to that coming time in history when wickedness will come to full flower and fruit. We can see the beginnings of that age today.[1]

Paul envisioned a world in which self-love would reign supreme; where craving for money would be a compulsive drive; where men would be arrogant and boastful and blasphemous; where disobedience to parents would be the great characteristic of youth; where people would scorn life's ordinary decencies, being decadent and debased, parading their obscenities; a world where natural affection would be abandoned and where people would become implacable in their hatreds; where slander would be devilish in character and where people would not only be ungovernable in their desires but would become savage, like animals; a world where good people would be scorned; where treachery would be commonplace; where people would be reckless and swelled-headed and addicted to pleasure with little or no use for God. He saw a world where deceitful teachers would use their position to seduce women. He saw a time when, even in the church, people would repudiate doctrine, preferring teachers who will tell them what they want to hear, and who omit what they don't want to hear.

Over against all this, Paul points Timothy back to the Bible, the Scriptures he had known from childhood. "All scripture is given by inspiration of God, and is profitable for doctrine, for reproof, for correction, for instruction in righteousness" (3:16). And he urges his younger colleague, battling Judaistic-Gnostic heresy at Ephesus, to watch, to endure afflictions, to do the work of an evangelist, and to make full proof of his ministry. Good advice for us, too, facing as we are today the beginning of this ultimate apostasy.

B. The Approaching Death of the Great Apostle (4:6–18)

When Paul wrote this, his last letter, he had already made his "first answer" before Nero (v. 16). He was now "ready to be offered" (v. 6), to have his life poured out as a drink offering, a libation to God. He knew the time of "departure" (v. 6) was at hand, using a word for the unyoking of an animal at the end of the day, the word for untying a captive's bonds, the word for loosening the ropes of a tent.

He had everything to look forward to. He said, "I have fought a good fight, I have finished my course, I have kept the faith: Henceforth there is laid up for me a crown" (vv. 7–8). In the Grecian games, the greatest prize was the laurel wreath, which the victor wore with great pride as the highest honor. The honor Paul was looking forward to, however, was not an imperial honor. As someone has put it,

> Proud were the mighty conquerors
> crowned in Olympic games;

They deemed that deathless honors
were entwined around their names.
But sere was soon the parsley wreath,
the olive, and the bay,
While the Christian's crown of amaranth
will never fade away.

—Author unknown,
"Crown Eternal"

Paul was facing death with perfect equanimity. Yet his situation, humanly, was very terrible. And he was increasingly lonely. This colleague and that had departed to various outlying parts of the empire in the cause of Christ. Sadly, Demas had forsaken him and gone off to Thessalonica, in love with "this present world" (v. 10). Only his faithful Luke was with him. Alexander the coppersmith had done him much harm, possibly playing the part of an informer.

Paul asks Timothy to come to him and bring Mark with him. He pleads with him to bring his warm cloak, his books, and his parchments. He was now in the terrible Tullianum prison in Rome, a notorious hole in the ground known as "the sepulcher," because many in it were eaten alive by rats. He was old, cold, lonely, cut off from his beloved library. But even though he had been left to face his first hearing alone, he was not discouraged. "The Lord stood with me," he said (v. 17).

IV. CONCLUSION (4:19–22)

There come some final greetings to Christian friends and a last plea to Timothy to "do thy diligence to come before winter" (v. 21). Did he come? In the church of San Paulo at Rome, the traditional tomb of Paul is surmounted by a magnificent baldacchino. Near to it, in front of the high altar, is a shrine, much more modest and unpretentious. On it is inscribed one name: TIMOTHEI. We are tempted to leave it at that, to accept as fact that, whether or not Timothy made it in time, whether or not he stood by his dear friend to the last, he now lies beside him awaiting the morn of resurrection.

CHAPTER 20

TITUS

Letter to a Young Man

Titus was converted at a comparatively early period in Paul's ministry. We know this because he accompanied Paul and Barnabas as part of the Antioch delegation to Jerusalem to settle the matter of Gentile freedom from the ceremonial law (Gal. 2:1–4). One of Paul's converts, Titus seemed to have a home at Antioch in Syria. It was no easy thing for this young Gentile to accompany Paul and Barnabas to Jerusalem for that all-important conference. Paul intended to make him a test case. The Jerusalem church never seemed to have much use for Paul, and, in fact, it distrusted him. Titus must have received many sour looks from the legalist party in the church, especially when it became evident that Paul intended to make an issue of his reception by the Jerusalem church into its fellowship—without being circumcised. These things do not seem to have bothered Titus; he seems to have been made of tougher fiber than Timothy.

There is no mention of Titus in Acts. Since Titus is not mentioned directly in Acts, we have to glean our knowledge of him from Galatians, 2 Corinthians, 2 Timothy, and the letter Paul sent to him while he was at Crete. From 2 Corinthians 8:16–17 and 12:18, we learn that when Titus was sent to Corinth, another believer accompanied him, one "whose praise is in . . . all the churches," usually identified as Luke (2 Cor. 8:18). The interesting suggestion is that Luke and Titus were brothers. Indeed, in the "we" passages in Acts, where Luke accompanied Paul, some have seen an oblique reference to Titus.

On Paul's third missionary journey, Titus was sent from Ephesus to Corinth to see what impact the epistle of 1 Corinthians had made on the church at Corinth (2 Cor. 2:12–13; 8–9). He caught up with Paul in Macedonia with good news (2 Cor. 7:5–6) and was sent back bearing 2 Corinthians and charged by Paul with attending to the collection being taken for the poor saints in Jerusalem (2 Cor. 8:6–17).

In the interval between Paul's two Roman imprisonments, Titus accompanied the apostle to Crete (Titus 1:5). Titus remained behind when Paul left, charged with dealing with disorders in the church on the island, and while still there he received this letter from Paul to guide him and support him in his task. Paul was discriminating in the use he made of the young men around him. He chose Timothy to deal with the situation at Ephesus but Titus for the tougher crisis at Corinth and for the harder task on Crete. It is just as important in the Lord's work as in any other kind of work to have the right man for the job.

Crete, an island southeast of Greece, was a mountainous but populous place boasting an ancient civilization. The Cretans were great sailors and famous bowmen but had a bad moral reputation. We have no information about the founding of the church at Crete, although we do know that Cretans were present at Jerusalem on the day of Pentecost.

  I. Introduction (1:1–4)
     A. Paul's Status (1:1)
     B. Paul's Salvation (1:2–3)
        1. Promised (1:2)
        2. Preached (1:3)
     C. Paul's Son (1:4)
 II. The Naming of Elders in the Local Church (1:5–9)
     Elders are to be:
     A. Family Men (1:5–6)
     B. Faultless Men (1:7)
     C. Friendly Men (1:8)
     D. Faithful Men (1:9)
III. The Nature of Error in the Local Church (1:10–16)
     A. The Motives of False Teachers (1:10–11)
     B. The Menace of False Teachers (1:12–13)
     C. The Message of False Teachers (1:14)
     D. The Morals of False Teachers (1:15–16)
 IV. The Need for Exercise in the Local Church (2:1–3:11)
     A. Personal Exercise (2:1–15)
        1. About Behavior (2:1–10)
        2. About Beliefs (2:11–15)
           a. In View of Present Grace (2:11–12)
           b. In View of Promised Glory (2:13–15)
     B. Practical Exercise (3:1–11)

1. As Subjects of the Land (3:1–2)
2. As Saints of the Lord (3:3–11)
    a. Remembering What We Were (3:3–8)
    b. Remaining Where We Are (3:9–11)
V. Conclusion (3:12–15)

This is one of the last letters Paul wrote, probably about the same time he wrote 1 Timothy.

I. Introduction (1:1–4)

As always, Paul begins by affirming his *status*. He was "Paul, a servant of God" (v. 1). Nowhere else does he use this exact expression *doulos theou*, God's slave. Only a man who has learned to obey is fit to command. In giving orders to Titus, Paul is careful to first state his own right to so speak. His authority was derived from his apostleship.

Next we have his *salvation*, that "hope of eternal life, which God, that cannot lie, promised before the world began" (vv. 2–3). When God decided to act in creation He foreknew He was also to have to act in redemption. It was this "so great salvation" (Heb. 2:3), rooted in eternity, which was under attack at Crete. It was this salvation that Paul and the apostles and other true servants of God were now preaching. Paul makes an interesting reference here to "God our Savior" (v. 3) and to "the Lord Jesus Christ our Savior" (1:4). This not only affirms that behind the whole plan and process of salvation is the heart and mind and will of God, but it also affirms the essential deity of Christ.

Then we have mention of his *son*: to "Titus, mine own son after the common faith" (v. 4). Paul had great affection for these converts and colleagues of his. The "common faith" was the mainstream of Christian truth, the genuine apostolic teaching, which was fast being committed to writing so that it might be preserved in permanent form, and which was so heavily under attack from Gnostics, Judaizers, and other cultists and heretics.

II. The Naming of Elders in the Local Church (1:5–9)

The first chapter has to do with the appointment of elders over local churches on the island of Crete. As in his letter to Timothy, Paul spelled out carefully what Titus should look for in those set to rule over the house of God. One important qualification was that of teaching ability, since false teachers had to be exposed and expelled from the fellowship. It was always Paul's plan to appoint elders (bishops) as soon as practical after a church was founded to oversee its spiritual affairs. As in 1 Timothy, Paul here elaborates on the qualifications for such under-shepherds of the sheep. Paul does not suggest appointing people who were successful in business or people who had social status or political influence. Elders over God's flock must be, above all else, men of character and spiritual conviction.

Paul's first criterion was that an elder should be *a family man* (1:5–6)—a man who had proved his fitness to rule over God's family in the way he had brought up his own family. That rules out the idea of a celibate priesthood.

Then an elder should be *a faultless man* (1:7). Here, Paul emphasizes what he should not be. He must not be intolerant or a man who nurses anger, or a man given to beating or browbeating people, or a man unscrupulous in his business dealings. Moreover, he must be *a friendly man* (1:8), addicted to hospitality. He must be prudent (sober, right-minded) and just. He must be one who upholds the fundamental decencies of life, and he must be self-controlled, for any man who is to rule others must be able to rule himself.

Then, he must be *a faithful man* (1:9), one able to exhort the believers and silence the "gainsayers," those who would contradict. He must be able to "convict" them by proving beyond question the truth of his teaching.

III. THE NATURE OF ERROR IN THE LOCAL CHURCH (1:10–16)

The Cretans had a bad reputation. Titus had no easy task finding the kind of people qualified to run the various local churches on the island. Were it not for salvation's changing people he might never have found them. His task was made more difficult, however, by the presence of false teachers who were seeking to undermine the Cretan church.

Paul exposes *the motives* of these false teachers (vv. 10–11). Most of them were Jews. They were unruly—people who refused to accept the essential tenets of the gospel; they were glib talkers whose talk amounted to nothing—certainly it produced no goodness of life. They were deceivers, upsetting whole families, in it for the money. Paul says they were to be silenced. The way to do that was not by persecution but by patiently proving them to be in error.

Paul exposes, too, *the menace* of these people (vv. 12–13). The Cretan character made them particularly susceptible to these deceivers. Paul's description of the Cretans, as a people, was a quote from Epimenides, one of their own "prophets," who said "the Cretans are always liars, evil beasts, slow bellies" (v. 12). Epimenides lived about 600 B.C. and was regarded as one of the seven wise men of Greece. Paul affirms the soundness of his criticism. So notorious were the Cretans that "cretizing" was a common word for lying and cheating and "to play the Cretan with a Cretan" meant to out-cheat a cheat. Since deception was the Cretan stock in trade, they were not only very clever at it but also particularly vulnerable to it. Paul says that those trying to "cretize" the Christians were to be sharply rebuked.

Then Paul exposes *the message* of these false teachers. He describes their teaching as "Jewish fables" and "commandments of men" (v. 14). The Jews were given to all kinds of subtle stories and fanciful allegories and long genealogies. All such rab-binical nonsense was to be exposed and expunged from the church.

Finally, Paul exposes *the morals* of these false teachers (vv. 15–16). To them nothing was pure since both their minds and consciences were defiled. Their claim to know God was disproved by their evil conduct. Paul describes them as "repro-bate" (v. 16), *adokimos*, a word used to describe a counterfeit coin, or a cowardly soldier, or a flawed stone rejected by the builder.

IV. The Need for Exercise in the Local Church (2:1–3:11)

The last two chapters deal with Christian conduct. The instructions given to old and young, men and women, and to servants (slaves) make interesting reading in view of the Cretan character. The gospel changes people.

The great inspiration to godly living is the second coming of Christ (2:13) and the tremendous cost of Calvary (2:14). Moreover, the Christians were to be law-abiding citizens. Paul deliberately reminds the Cretan believers how they once behaved in their unregenerate state, but only to underline the contrast expected of them now. And they must avoid the contentious and unprofitable wrangling of the Judaizing cult. Indeed, they must go further: a proven heretic, after two admoni-tions, must be rejected.

V. Conclusion (3:12–15)

Paul's conclusion contains some *personal notes* (3:12–13). He obviously intended to replace Titus on the island, either with Artemas of whom we know nothing, or Tychicus, one of Paul's trusted messengers (Eph. 6:21; Col. 4:7). Paul wanted Titus to join him at Nicopolis in Epirus, a logical center for the evangelization of Dalmatia. Paul had decided to spend the winter there, though Nero's net was closing fast about him. In the meantime, Titus was to help "Zenas the lawyer and Apollos on their journey" (v. 13), and he was to see to it that they lacked for nothing. Zenas is unknown to us. He was a lawyer—the word used can denote just that or it can simply mean a scribe, in which case Zenas might have been a converted rabbi. Apollos, of course, we know as a gifted Bible teacher of great elo-quence. No two better men could have visited Crete to help the resident workers with their task of silencing the lying Judaizers.

Then concluding *practical notes* carry a special emphasis on "good works" (v. 14), not as the way to salvation, but as the proof of genuine salvation.

PHILEMON

Plea for a Runaway Slave

Far, far away and long, long ago there existed in a little corner of the Roman world a little country town known as Colossae. It was notable for almost nothing at all. Once, in its remote history, the mighty Persian emperor Xerxes had halted there on his way to the Grecian wars. Once, too, another Persian, Cyrus the younger, had stopped there on his way to attack his brother. But apart from these two isolated footnotes on the pages of history, Colossae was simply a slumbering, sleepy little town at the mouth of a ten-mile glen.

A hard day's walk away, in the same Lycus Valley, lay Laodicea. A hundred miles to the west was the great, thriving city of Ephesus. The whole area was earthquake-prone, and just a scant two years after Paul wrote this little note to Philemon, the little town was, indeed, devastated by shocks. Nowadays, the site of the city is represented by a heap of ruins—broken structures, mutilated columns and, at a little distance, another field showing the rubble of a cemetery.

But at the time of which we are speaking, Colossae was a country town. And, as such, it was just like any other country town. It had its brighter side of close neighborhood and domestic friendships. It had its sadder side, the kind of stagnation that usually marks a little country community.

There had been one burst of excitement, the tides of which had sent its wavelets lapping even into Colossae. In Ephesus there had been a spiritual revival, a great moving of the Holy Spirit, one of those awe-inspiring spiritual awakenings that take place from time to time when the Spirit of God descends in power upon a preacher's ministry.

To Ephesus had come a small, wiry little Jew, a tentmaker by trade, and an evangelist by calling. He had stayed in Ephesus for three whole years, during which time all of proconsular Asia "heard the word" (Eph. 1:13). His preaching had turned Ephesus upside down and inside out. Thousands had been converted to Christ. The most remarkable scenes had been witnessed, giving abundant evidence of the gospel's power to change men's lives.

The revival was well-nigh epidemic. From town to town, from village to village, the longing to hear the heavenly message spread. Smyrna, Pergamos, Thyatira, Sardis, Philadelphia, Laodicea, Hierapolis, Colossae . . . in town after town news of the spiritual awakening spread. Men were hungry for such living bread, parched for a drop of water from such a satisfying spring.

So we see them come, a group of friends, coming down the Maeander Valley from the quiet old town among the limestone hills. Philemon is there, perhaps, and Apphia his wife, and Archippus their son. And perhaps Onesimus is there to minister to their wants along the way. They find the new teachers, and some, at least, including Philemon and his wife and son, open their hearts to the life-transforming story of Jesus.

We may well suppose that Epaphras was there. He, too, opened his heart to the gospel. He, too, took Jesus as Savior and Lord. And that little Jewish tent-maker, Paul by name, soon recognized that Epaphras had a vital spiritual gift. In due time, he put his hand upon him and sent him back to Colossae to spread further the tidings of the cross.

Our story concerns three men—Philemon, the wealthy slave owner of Colossae; Onesimus, a runaway slave, who could expect a fate worse than death if ever caught; Paul, the great apostle living in Rome under house arrest as the prisoner of Nero, and awaiting trial.

To understand the story we need to go back into that ancient Roman world and consider, for a moment, the lot of the slave. Rome was a great slave-maker. From the time she crushed Hannibal, Rome set out to enslave mankind. Roman conquests turned great numbers of people into slaves—in Gaul and Macedonia and Greece and Asia Minor and Britain and wherever the imperial eagles spread their relentless wings. The coast of the Adriatic opposite Italy, alone, yielded a hundred thousand slaves.

An ordinary day laborer would bring one hundred dollars. A craftsman or a good clerk was worth much more. An attractive young woman with some ability to entertain would fetch ten times as much. The Roman world was flooded with slaves. Some of the better-educated slaves, those skilled in art or medicine or law, were often pampered by their masters, although even if so, the master's whim could send the slave to be mutilated and scourged and crucified. But for the majority, the life of a slave was worse than death. The treatment they received was so unbearable that, from time to time and from place to place, they rose against their masters. In Sicily, rebellious slaves, some sixty thousand strong, rose against their lot, slew their masters, captured towns, and set up a kingdom. It took a Roman consul at the head of an army and a war lasting several years to subdue them.

Slave owners in the empire sometimes held great numbers of men in captivity. It was not uncommon for a patrician Roman family to own as many as seven thousand slaves—scribes and carpenters, litter-bearers and sculptors, cooks and musicians—even half-witted dolts kept for the entertainment of guests.

A slave was merely a slave. The gulf between slave and master was as vast as the gulf between a man and a beast. It was a social disgrace if a slave owner did not scourge and crucify a rebellious slave. Such leniency threatened the whole system, endangering the lives of all slave owners. The slave owner who hesitated to flog or sell or crucify a stubborn slave was looked upon as deranged, insane!

Vedius Pollio, an associate of the Emperor Augustus, kept a shoal of conger eels in a tank in his garden to which he fed offending slaves. One day when the emperor was dining with him, a slave dropped and broke a crystal cup and was promptly sentenced to the tank. The emperor was not disturbed—after all the offender was only a slave! Half a century later, when Paul was writing, four hundred slaves, men and women alike, including many of high culture as well as wretched menials, were executed in a brutal way under express and deliberate sanction of the Senate. One of them had murdered their master.

Death by crucifixion was a common punishment for petty theft by slaves. The whole world of Roman power sanctioned slavery. Plato, in his ideal *Commonwealth*, gave ample room for slavery; the master who murdered a slave was punished with ceremonial purification only. Aristotle, in his *Polity*, defines a slave as being one who is by nature the property of another—merely an extension of his master's limbs and without any personal rights.

Philemon was a slave owner. He was a slave owner, however, who had been converted to Christ by the personal ministry of the great apostle Paul. Onesimus was his slave. We do not know how or when or why Philemon acquired Onesimus. Perhaps it was in Ephesus, perhaps it was at Rome. Slaves were sold by public auction in the Forum—the slave market. Each wore a tablet hung about his neck by a cord. On this was written the chief merits of the wearer and also a list of his or her defects, so that the buyer might know what to expect. There were Phrygians with fair, curly hair and delicate hands. There were Numidians with skins of ebony and keen, black eyes, agile in the chase, able to capture a lion or trap a beast for sale to the circus. There were Greeks who could make music with a lyre. There were swarthy Spaniards who could fashion breastplates of steel and fine chain mail to resist an assassin's knife. There were musicians and cooks and mechanics and physicians and scribes and laborers—all up for sale.

Into the Forum, perhaps, Philemon came one day, looking for another slave for some task he had in his palatial home. We can see him, joining the pushing crowds. As trade becomes more brisk, the work of the lictors becomes more arduous as they ply their flails to keep order among the slaves. Philemon inspects the merchandise for sale. He listens to the voice of the auctioneer on the rostrum as he sings the praises of his wares, shouting incessantly in fluent Latin but with a foreign lisp, and stopping every now and then to mop his brow and to refresh his parched throat from a leather bottle of wine.

"What am I bid for this German giant? Look at his massive frame! Look at his hairy arms. Look at his mighty fist. He can fell an ox. A useful man with harrow or plow and a skilled smith for good measure. Gentlemen, come and examine his teeth, feel his muscles, look at the calves of his legs." So Philemon strolled about the market, looking for a slave. And one, perchance, he found. The tablet about this neck proclaimed him as Onesimus! "Profitable!" And the auctioneer proclaimed him to be a profitable investment indeed.

So, for this reason or that, Philemon bought him and took him home and set him to work. And doubtless forgot all about him until one day he was told that Onesimus was gone! He had run away! He had put himself under the law of torture, the law of the cross. He was a man, now, marked out for death.

And it is here that our story begins. For Onesimus, the runaway slave, is the great theme and subject of this brief little note from the persuasive pen of Paul. There, in far-off Rome, Onesimus had run into Paul, and Paul had led him to Christ. Now Onesimus must return to Philemon—and the only thing that stands between him and the cross is a little note that contains less than 140 words.

The brief note we call *Philemon* is acknowledged as one of the masterpieces of writing in the world. Nothing can more vividly reveal the genius of Paul as a writer than the facility with which he passes from the writing of *Colossians* to the writing of *Philemon*. The letter to the Colossians is deep and profound; the note to Philemon is simple and sweet. It is as though Michelangelo had gone straight from smiting out of his massive marble the magnificent statue of Moses to chiseling out, with light tracery, a tiny figure of love or friendship on a cameo. Short as the letter is, no less than eleven people are mentioned—five at the beginning, five at the end, with Onesimus in between. The letter is not only a plea, it is a parable. And as such we shall view it in this survey.

Seven striking items leap from the page to arrest us as we read. We are confronted with an *injury*, an *intercessor*, an *injunction*, an *influence*, an *indebtedness*, an *insurance*, and an *intention*. We shall now examine these, one by one, and see that behind the plea for Onesimus is the story of the cross.

I. THE INJURY

Onesimus had a master who was conspicuous for his goodness. The very name "Philemon" is significant. It means "the affectionate." But, for one reason or another, Onesimus stole some money and fled from his master. Out from the house he crept one dark night, out past the gate and on down the glen. On one hand towered the heights of Mount Cadmus, called by the Turks today "Father of the Mountains." On the other hand ran the Lycus, the Wolf-stream, hurrying on to join the Meander and thus on to the sea. On every hand were traces of volcanic fires. But Onesimus would have no thought for the beauty of nature. He had but one thought—to put as much distance as he could between himself and the master he had wronged. For in running away, Onesimus cast a grave slur on Philemon. He testified thus to the world that Philemon was a tyrant, a cruel and oppressive master, a hateful person—when he was nothing of the kind. Moreover, he set an example of lawlessness to the rest of Philemon's slaves. He taught them how to rebel.

Says Martin Luther in his preface to the book of Philemon, "We are all the Lord's Onesimi." For Onesimus, whose name means "profitable," had become unprofitable after all. And here the parable begins.

Like Onesimus, we have no independent life of our own. Our very breath is loaned us by God. We live as those who have nothing and are nothing in a world His hands have made. Yet by nature and by practice we are rebels against His laws and against His love. We have robbed Him of what rightfully belongs to Him—our allegiance, our adoration, and our praise. And, by our lawlessness and self-will, we slander Him, proclaim to all the world that God is a tyrant. We deny His true nature, we injure Him, we cast a slur upon both His character and His name. And, like Onesimus, it is man's nature, born and bred into his bone and marrow, to put as much distance as possible between himself and God.

Onesimus fled to Rome. We are not told how he arrived there or how long it took him to get there. We do not know whether he took to the hills and found his way to that ancient Babylon of wickedness by means of the haunts of the highwaymen, or whether he stowed away aboard a vessel heading to Rome from Ephesus. All we know is that he came to Rome. And there, in that vast city of slums, Onesimus concluded he would be safe. Philemon would never find him in Rome. But Onesimus reckoned without God. God does not give up on His

Onesimi. He sends the Holy Spirit into the world to hunt them down, to mark them out, to arrest them in the name of Calvary love. It is that love that finds us at last. God has His servants everywhere.

II. THE INTERCESSOR

The main characters are etched in with consummate skill. There is Philemon—wealthy, loving, wronged, hurt. There is Onesimus—a runaway, a thief, an outcast, a criminal. And in between the two appears Paul, a sufferer, a sympathizer, an intercessor. Between the deeply wronged Philemon and the now hopelessly condemned Onesimus appears a mediator, a daysman, a go-between.

Thus, indeed, the gospel story runs as well. For between the guilty sinner, who has awakened the fires of righteous wrath and divine vengeance, and the Almighty Creator, who has been slandered before the entire universe, there appears a Mediator. Says Paul, "There is . . . one mediator between God and men, the man Christ Jesus" (1 Tim. 2:5). Not the Virgin Mary, not a priest ordained by human hands, not a preacher nor a pastor nor a Pope—but Christ! And what a perfect Mediator He is. Being fully and absolutely and eternally God, He can put one hand on Deity; and being perfectly and truly and really man, He can place the other hand on humanity.

Apart from such a mediator there was no way that the guilty Onesimus could be restored to his master. In the first place, he had no desire to go back—he had no love for Philemon. In the second place, the law stood between them, the fierce Roman law that demanded death for the rebel slave. The law would have seized Onesimus long before he ever arrived at Philemon's door.

Someone had to intervene on behalf of the fugitive, and Paul was that man. We do not know how or when or exactly where Onesimus met Paul. But he did. Paul was under house arrest in Rome. Perhaps, looking out of the window of his house one day, he saw this figure hurrying by and hailed him. Perhaps he heard about Onesimus from one of the other believers in Rome and sent after him and fetched him to his house. We do not know. All we know is that Paul and Onesimus met, and Paul promptly led Onesimus to Christ and then became the mediator between him and Philemon.

Apart from Christ, there is no way that a guilty sinner can be reconciled with God. By nature we have no love for God at all. Our behavior has raised between us and God a barrier we cannot scale even if we would. Besides, the law of God stands astride the path to arrest us, for the sentence of death has already been passed: "The soul that sinneth, it shall die" (Ezek. 18:20); "The wages of sin is death" (Rom. 6:23); "It is appointed unto men once to die, but after this the judgment" (Heb. 9:27). But Christ has come to be a Mediator—to reconcile us to God. And He is the only One who can. So somewhere, sometime, we must have a living, vital contact with the Lord Jesus.

III. THE INJUNCTION

The first thing Paul did, when he won Onesimus to Christ, was to send him back to Philemon. And that is the first thing Christ does—send us back to God. We must all get back to God. All religions proclaim this. The great question is *How?*

The answer of this little book is simple. With a covering letter. No excuses! No denials! No vows! No promises! No offers to pay our debt! No attempt to work out our own salvation to make it on our own! Onesimus silently pointed to the letter in his hand. He staked everything on Paul's influence with Philemon. We must stake everything on Christ's influence with God.

But there is another lesson here. The gospel is very practical. It is not merely some kind of intellectual exercise or emotional experience. It confronts us, at each issue, at the point of the *will*. It insists on our doing what is right. Paul would have liked to keep Onesimus with him. That would not have been right, for Onesimus, by the law of the land, belonged to Philemon. Onesimus would rather have done anything than return to Colossae. But what was right? He had wronged Philemon— so back he must go and do what was right. It was not enough for him to have met Christ; he must now go and get right with the one he has wronged. Any kind of gospel preaching that does not insist that, once we are saved, we must at once go and put things right with our fellow men is a shallow, unscriptural gospel. When a man gets right with God through Christ, he then through Christ turns around and gets right with men.

IV. THE INFLUENCE

Paul was demanding a very hard thing. While the act of salvation is very simple— just a committal of one's whole being and need to the Lord Jesus Christ—the subsequent demands of Christ are often not simple at all. But Onesimus did not have to go it alone. Paul wrote to Philemon for him and he called him "my child" (v. 10 PHILLIPS). "Onesimus," he says, "that I have sent back in his own person, that is my very heart" (see v. 12). "If thou count me therefore a partner, receive him as myself" (v. 17). Onesimus came back to Philemon not just as Onesimus but as part of Paul.

This, indeed, is the sheer genius of the gospel. We come back to God in Christ—as part of Him. It is the most telling argument in the universe. When a person becomes a Christian he is instantly baptized by the Holy Spirit into the body of Christ. Henceforth he is part of Christ. It is one of the most basic concepts of the New Testament. God accepts *us* because He accepts *Christ*.

But more! Because Paul adopted this position in relation to Onesimus, now Onesimus had something he never had before—the strength and desire to return to Philemon. He was coming back to the one he had wronged, coming not in his own strength but in the strength of another. In actual fact, he was coming back in the strength of Christ Himself. For when we yield to the claims of Christ, He gives us power to do what we don't naturally want to do, and what, indeed, often we are quite unable to do. There is a new influence at work in our lives, as there was in the life of Onesimus, one that was never there before.

V. THE INDEBTEDNESS

But Onesimus was a bankrupt slave and his debt remained unpaid. Philemon might justly say, "If my slave can rob me with impunity and I merely cancel his debt, how can this be just to my other slaves?" Paul answers, "If he hath wronged thee, or oweth thee ought, put that on mine account; . . . I will repay it" (vv. 18–19). Paul had not robbed Philemon, but the liability for his debt passed now from Onesimus to Paul. After that, Onesimus was in debt no more.

This is exactly what the Lord Jesus has done for the sinner's soul. The entire indebtedness of our sin was transferred to His account. Crucifixion, the extreme penalty for a runaway slave, has been paid in full. The redeemed person is in debt to God no more. Christ took the full liability; we take the complete discharge. God added up the enormous debt of human sin. We were, to use the Lord's own expressive language, "ten thousand talent" debtors (Matt. 18:24). The number ten thousand was the highest number; the talent was the heaviest weight. Our debt was the highest possible to owe, and we had nothing with which to pay. But Jesus paid it all, paid it to the very last penny. The believer stands before God in debt no more. His debt has not been merely forgiven; it has been paid in full.

VI. THE INSURANCE

Philemon might have argued, "But how can I take back one so false and untrust-worthy—such a rebel? He might rob me a second time, he might ruin me the next time, he might sow seeds of discord among my other slaves, he might lead riot and insurrection in my home, he might murder me in my bed. What insurance do I have that he will not do me even greater harm?" Paul says, "He is my child, whom I have begotten in my bonds" (see v. 10). He is saying, "I am not sending back the old Onesimus; I am sending back another man altogether. I am sending one who has been born over, born again, one who has been recreated by power divine, one who is now just like me. I am sending back one who has a new nature."

Is that not exactly what the gospel is all about? The child of God is begotten in the bonds of Calvary. The Lord Jesus sends us back to God made anew, born again, made in His own image and after His own likeness, with a new nature.

Thus Philemon received back far more than he lost. This is exactly the biblical philosophy of the fall, in the first Adam, and the restoration through the second Adam (Rom. 5). Because of Calvary, God gets back far more than was ever lost—He receives back an individual with a new nature, made just like Jesus, recreated by power divine.

VII. The Intention

What was Onesimus to Philemon now? He was no longer a slave; he was more than a slave—he was "a brother beloved" (v. 16). He was Philemon's in body before; now he is Philemon's in body and soul. And why? Simply because, through Christ, Onesimus had entered into a relationship that binds man to man and man to God. He had entered into love.

So Onesimus went back to Colossae determined to live Christ before Philemon, before all the brethren, before the other slaves in the household, and before all the world. He had been converted. Two changes had taken place in his soul—two changes that ensured that never again would Philemon have cause to rue the day he invested in an Onesimus.

He now had a *happiness* that made hard duties easy, and he now had a *holiness* that made all duty divine. He was determined to be in Christ—as the master, controlling force in his life—a willing, devoted bond slave. No matter how repellent the task, no matter how long the day, no matter how galling the load—he was no longer the bond slave of Philemon, he was the bond slave of Jesus Christ. Every task, great or small, whether to rule an empire or to sweep a chimney, was to be done as unto Christ! Henceforth Christ was to be magnified in his body.

That is the divine intent with every born-again, blood-washed, ransomed soul. In Christ we are transformed. The Christian employee should be the very best employee that ever was hired; the Christian boss should be the most thoughtful, considerate, desirable boss that ever was.

Legend has it that Onesimus eventually became a bishop—bishop of Ephesus. Perhaps he did. But one thing is sure. He went back to Colossae first determined to be the best slave in the vast empire of Rome, and he went back because he had met a man named Paul and—more important still—because he had met a Man named Jesus.

That is what the gospel is all about. We can become one of God's Onesimi.

CHAPTER 22

HEBREWS

Outside the Camp

There is widespread difference of opinion as to who wrote the book of Hebrews. Luke, Barnabas, Clement of Rome, Apollos, and the apostle Paul have all been suggested. The arguments for a Pauline authorship are weighty enough despite the objections made. It is claimed by some that Paul could not have been the author of Hebrews because the language, the style, the arguments are not Pauline. Moreover the epistle is anonymous, whereas Paul's other epistles all bear his signature. Against this it can be argued that, whatever differences in style and language Hebrews may contain as compared with the known Pauline epistles, the thoughts and the reasoning are very much like Paul's. Moreover all of Paul's other epistles were addressed to Gentiles, whereas Hebrews was written for Jews. But it should not be forgotten that Paul could describe himself as a "Hebrew of the Hebrews" (Phil. 3:5). The suspicion with which the Jews regarded Paul and their deep hatred of him would, in itself, be ample reason for his withholding his name from any general epistle addressed to them. The closing verses of the epistle, however, could well have come from Paul (13:18–19). The reference made to "my bonds" (10:34) and to Timothy (13:23), the characteristically Pauline "Grace be with you all" (13:25)—these suggest that the epistle may not be so anonymous as is sometimes claimed. Indeed, some think that the last chapter of Hebrews is really a covering letter from Paul, which accompanied the epistle itself. By itself, few would fail to recognize chapter 13 as Pauline.

The two monumental epistles of Hebrews and Romans have certain similarities. Romans heads the list of the Pauline epistles, and Hebrews heads the list of the general epistles; Romans expounds and explains the believer's relationship to the moral law, and Hebrews expounds and explains the believer's relationship to the ceremonial law. Romans moves from law to grace, and Hebrews moves from shadow to substance.

I. The Superior Person of Christ (1:1–2:18)
   A. Superior in His Majesty as Son of God (1:1–2:4)
      1. How This Is Expressed (1:1–3)
      2. How This Is Exemplified (1:4–14)
         a. His Excellent Name (1:4–5)
         b. His Earthly Fame (1:6–7)
         c. His Eternal Claim (1:8–14)
      3. How This Is Experienced (2:1–4)
         a. By Appropriating the Gospel (2:1–3a)
         b. By Appreciating the Gospel (2:3b–4)
   B. Superior in His Ministry as Son of Man (2:5–18)
      1. His Sovereignty as Man (2:5–9a)
      2. His Sufferings as Man (2:9b–10)
      3. His Sympathy as Man (2:11–18)
II. The Superior Provisions of Calvary (3:1–10:39)
   A. We Have a Better Savior (3:1–8:5)
      1. His Preeminence (3:1–4:13)
         a. Two People Considered (3:1–6)
         b. Twin Perils Considered (3:7–4:3)
            (1) God's People in the Wilderness in Old Testament Times (3:7–19)
            (2) God's People in the World in New Testament Times (4:1–3)
         c. True Peace Considered (4:4–13)
            (1) Creation Rest (4:4–5)
            (2) Canaan Rest (4:6–8)
            (3) Calvary Rest (4:9–13)
      2. His Priesthood (4:14–8:5)
         a. He Is a Real Priest (4:14–5:3)
            (1) His Name (4:14)
            (2) His Nearness (4:15–16)
            (3) His Nature (5:1–3)
         b. He Is a Rightful Priest (5:4–6:20)
            (1) The Choice of Christ as Priest (5:4–10)
            (2) The Challenge of Christ as Priest (5:11–6:20)
               (a) To Those Who Are Weak (5:11–6:3)
               (b) To Those Who Are Wicked (6:4–8)
               (c) To Those Who Are Wise (6:9–20)
         c. He Is a Royal Priest (7:1–8:5)

          (1) His Lordship as Priest (7:1–10)

          (2) His Legality as Priest (7:11–22)

          (3) His Life as Priest (7:23–8:5)

  B. We Have a Better Security (8:6–13)

     1. Based on an Improved Covenant (8:6)

     2. Based on an Imperative Covenant (8:7–8)

     3. Based on an Important Covenant (8:9–12)

     4. Based on an Implemented Covenant (8:13)

  C. We Have a Better Sanctuary (9:1–12)

     1. The Human Tabernacle (9:1–10)

     2. The Heavenly Tabernacle (9:11–12)

  D. We Have a Better Sacrifice (9:13–10:39)

     1. What Was Wrought by Christ's Sacrifice (9:13–28)

        a. The Old Transgressions Are Removed Forever (9:13–14)

        b. The New Testament Is Ratified Forever (9:15–28)

          (1) Our Benefits (9:15)

          (2) Our Benefactor (9:16–28)

             (a) His Death Conveys Our Inheritance (9:16–22)

             (b) His Life Confirms Our Inheritance (9:23–28)

     2. What Was Sought by Christ's Sacrifice (10:1–18)

        a. As to the Past (10:1–4)

        b. As to the Present (10:5–12)

          (1) The Descent of God's Son (10:5–9)

          (2) The Decease of God's Son (10:10–12)

        c. As to the Prospect (10:13–18)

     3. What Was Taught by Christ's Sacrifice (10:19–39)

        a. A Tremendous Word of Welcome (10:19–25)

        b. A Terrible Word of Warning (10:26–31)

        c. A Timely Word of Wisdom (10:32–39)

III. The Superior Principles of Christianity (11:1–13:17)

  A. The Walk of Faith (11:1–40)

     1. Faith Defined (11:1–2)

     2. Faith Demonstrated (11:3–38)

        a. By Glorious Illustration (11:3–31)

          (1) The Present Age (11:3)

          (2) The Primeval Age (11:4–7)

          (3) The Patriarchal Age (11:8–22)

          (4) The Patriotic Age (11:23–31)

        b. By General Allusion (11:32–38)

     3. Faith Decreed (11:39–40)

B. The Wisdom of Hope (12:1–29)
  1. Running in the Heavenly Race (12:1–13)
    a. The Call to Self-Discipline (12:1–3)
    b. The Call to Spiritual Discipline (12:4–13)
      (1) The Explanation (12:4)
      (2) The Exhortation (12:5–6)
      (3) The Expectation (12:7–8)
      (4) The Example (12:9–10)
      (5) The Experience (12:11–13)
  2. Resting in the Heavenly Grace (12:14–29)
    a. The Stringent Command (12:14–17)
      (1) The Need for Holy Living Declared (12:14–15)
      (2) The Need for Holy Living Demonstrated (12:16–17)
    b. The Striking Contrast (12:18–24)
      (1) Distance Imperative (12:18–21)
      (2) Distance Impossible (12:22–24)
    c. The Stirring Conclusion (12:25–29)
C. The Way of Love (13:1–17)
  1. Christian Compassion (13:1–3)
  2. Christian Chastity (13:4)
  3. Christian Contentment (13:5)
  4. Christian Courage (13:6)
  5. Christian Consideration (13:7)
  6. Christian Consistency (13:8)
  7. Christian Conviction (13:9)
  8. Christian Communion (13:10–14)
  9. Christian Consecration (13:15–16)
  10. Christian Concern (13:17)
IV. Conclusion (13:18–25)
A. A Word of Exhortation (13:18–19)
B. A Word of Benediction (13:20–21)
C. A Word of Supplication (13:22)
D. A Word of Information (13:23)
E. A Word of Salutation (13:24–25)

To understand the primary emphasis of Hebrews, we must remember it was written to recently converted Jews in the very early days of Christianity. The old religious customs of Judaism still exerted a powerful force upon these new Jewish converts. The Jewish temple, for example, was still standing, crowning the summit of Mount Moriah with magnificent splendor. Its gorgeous rituals and its elaborate system of sacrifices beckoned the Jewish convert to Christ to come back to the fold. Jewish traditions, born and bred into the Jewish believer's heart, still had a powerful hold upon him and called him to come back to Judaism. The grandest names in history were associated with that religion. Traditions, hoary with antiquity, pulled upon all the pious emotions, the national sentiments, and even the religious superstitions of the Jewish believer. The temptation to go back must have been great indeed.

Jewish ties of family, friendship, and fellowship were very strong. These ties had enabled the Jew to overcome persecution and resist assimilation for centuries. Now, by his conversion to Christ, those ties were all threatened with severance.

During Christ's life on earth, the Pharisees had opposed the gospel; now, during the period covered by the book of Acts, the Sadducees resisted the gospel. Jewish opposition commenced with the persecution of Peter and climaxed in the persecution of Paul; it began in Jerusalem and spread far and wide throughout the dispersion. Moreover, the church was becoming increasingly Gentile in composition, and this was an added problem to the Jewish convert.

Then, too, Jewish teachings were hard to renounce. Hot and fierce were the debates against Christianity in those early days. How dare these Jewish Christians set aside the law of Moses, the Aaronic priesthood, the solemn rites and rituals of the sacrificial system? So all in all the new convert from Judaism to Christianity had many problems to face, all of which the epistle to the Hebrews was designed to answer.

One of the key words in Hebrews is *better* (1:4; 6:9; 7:7, 19, 22; 8:6; 9:23; 10:34; 11:16, 35, 40; 12:24). The writer wanted his fellow Jewish believers to see that in Christ they gained much more than they had renounced in Judaism. Christ is better than the prophets and the angels, superior to Moses and to Joshua, and has a priestly ministry far superior to that of Aaron. The Christian has better promises, a better sanctuary, a better covenant, a better country, and a better resurrection. It is far better to worship in the true heavenly tabernacle than in a man-made temple on earth. The sacrifice of Calvary renders obsolete all the ceremonial washings and offerings required under the Mosaic Law.

The writer of Hebrews repeatedly emphasizes the word *heavens* and often employs the adjective *heavenly* (1:10; 3:1; 4:14; 6:4; 7:26; 8:1, 5; 9:23–24; 10:34; 11:16; 12:22–23, 25–26). His purpose is to show that, in contrast with Judaism, which is earthly and concerned with physical ceremonies, Christianity is heavenly and spiritual.

Another vital truth is connected with the word *once* and the thought "once for all" (6:4; 7:27; 9:12, 26, 28; 10:2, 10; 12:26–27) intended to convey the truth of the absolute finality of the Christian revelation. It can readily be seen how these truths would encourage Jewish Christians, who, for Christ's sake, had gone "without the camp, bearing his reproach" (13:13).

I. THE SUPERIOR PERSON OF CHRIST (1:1–2:18)

Christianity does not supplement Judaism; it replaces it altogether. With the coming of Christ, the descent of the Holy Spirit, and the advent of the church, Judaism is rendered null and void. When Jesus died on the cross of Calvary, God reached down and rent the temple veil, making Judaism obsolete—just as a few days earlier, Caiaphas, the High Priest, in a fit of fury at the claims of Christ, had rent his priestly robe, signifying, though he did not know it in his blindness, that the Old Testament priesthood had come to an abrupt and utter end.

The writer of this epistle lets it be known that Christ is superior to all Old Testament worthies.

A. Superior in His Majesty as Son of God (1:1–2:4)

The writer brings on stage two representative classes—the prophets of Israel and the angels of God. Christ is first shown as superior to *all human messengers*. The writer begins: "God, who . . . spake in time past unto the fathers by the prophets, Hath in these last days spoken unto us by his Son" (v. 1–2). Christ is God's last word to man; He eclipses all the prophets of the past.

Bring on Moses and Malachi; bring on Jeremiah, Jonah, and Job; bring on David and Daniel—Jesus outshines them all as the sun outshines the moon. They brought only reflected light; He is the Light.

Christ is next shown to be superior to *all heavenly messengers*. The angels dispensed the law, but they are just ministering spirits, no more, just glorified servants. Their job is to run errands on behalf of the children of God. But Jesus is the Son, eternal, uncreated, over all, blessed forevermore. Between Him and them, even the greatest of them, is a great gulf fixed—the gulf that separated the Creator from a mere creature.

B. Superior in His Ministry as Son of Man (2:5–18)

This time the writer brings four people on stage and stands them alongside Christ. Again it is obvious there is no comparison.

Take, for instance, *the practical leaders of the past*, Moses and Joshua. Moses brought Israel out of Egypt, and Joshua brought Israel into Canaan. But Moses, after all, was only a servant, and Joshua was only a soldier. As a servant, Moses was unable to enjoy rest, and as a soldier, Joshua was unable to impart rest. Both come far short of Christ, who not only brings us out of bondage but who brings us into rest.

Or take *the priestly leaders of the past*, Aaron and Melchizedek. Aaron was *a ritual priest*; he was nothing compared with Melchizedek who was *a royal priest*. Aaron was a sacrificing priest; Melchizedek was a sovereign priest. Christ was both! As *the* Priest, He has superseded the sacrifices of the Aaronic priesthood and the sovereignty of the Melchizedek priesthood. Both Aaron and Melchizedek were, at best, but feeble types of Christ. They were the shadows; He is the substance. He is superior in His ministry, whether the practical ministries of Moses and Joshua or the priestly ministries of Aaron and Melchizedek.

That is the first major point the author makes. There were many stars of great magnitude in the Hebrew sky, but Jesus outshines them all. He is greater than any of them, both in majesty and ministry. So why go back to the inferior?

II. THE SUPERIOR PROVISIONS OF CALVARY (3:1–10:39)

In this epistle there are twenty-nine quotations from the Old Testament and fifty-three direct allusions to the Old Testament. The writer quotes thirty-nine times from the Pentateuch, eleven times from the Psalms, four times from the Prophets, once from the Proverbs, and once from the Histories. Thus, in these thirteen short chapters of Hebrews, there are no less than eighty-two references to the Old Testament. It is very evident that the purpose of the epistle is to show that the Old Testament revelation is consummated in the person and work of Christ.

A. We Have a Better Savior (3:1–8:5)

The writer sets before his Hebrew readers the *preeminence* and the *priesthood* of the Lord Jesus Christ. To introduce that priesthood, he first disarms the anticipated refusal of the Jews to accept that priesthood (on the ground that since Jesus came from the royal tribe of Judah and the royal family of David instead of the Levitical tribe and the priestly family of Aaron, He could not be a priest) by introducing the name Melchizedek. He was a royal priest, whose order took precedence over that of Aaron. Moreover, he inserts a sobering warning against turning back from this better Savior to dead Judaism.

B. We Have a Better Security (8:6–13)

There was a covenant in the Old Testament, a covenant ratified at Sinai. But even in Old Testament times, when the Mosaic covenant was still in force, God promised to write a *new* covenant. That covenant has been signed, sealed, and delivered in the blood of Christ. "Christ," says our author, "is the mediator of a better covenant, which was established upon better promises" (v. 6). This new covenant contains two major clauses—*eschatological* clauses (prophetic elements that anticipate the glorious millennial reign of Christ) and *soteriological* clauses (redemptive elements into which all true believers enter today). The eschatological clauses belong exclusively to the nation of Israel; the salvation clauses belong inclusively to the church. In the upper room, as the Lord Jesus took the cup, He said, "This cup is the new testament in my blood" (1 Cor. 11:25). We can rest today in absolute security, a security paid for and purchased at Calvary by the precious blood of Christ.

C. We Have a Better Sanctuary (9:1–12)

There was a sanctuary in the Old Testament—in fact there were two of them. First there was the tabernacle, then there was the temple. Both were temporary structures. Both served their purpose and both were rendered obsolete by the march of events.

The writer of Hebrews says, "But Christ being come an high priest of good things to come, by a greater and more perfect tabernacle, not made with hands, that is to say, not of this building" (v. 11). Both the tabernacle in the wilderness and the temple in Jerusalem were mere models of the true and heavenly tabernacle, which God built and not man. Through Christ we have access to the true tabernacle, to the tabernacle in heaven.

D. We Have a Better Sacrifice (9:13–10:39)

Hundreds of thousands of animals were sacrificed in Old Testament times. Jewish altars ran red with rivers of blood. But it was not possible that the blood of bulls and goats could take away sin. The law, indeed, was only a shadow of good things to come. The shadow of a key cannot open a prison door; the shadow of a meal cannot satisfy a hungry man; the shadow of Calvary could not take away sin.

In the Old Testament, all God did was *cover* sin, sweep it under the rug, so to speak. In the New Testament, He has *canceled* sin, willed it out of existence. Instead of the many, many sacrifices of the Old Testament there is now only one sacrifice. We read, "But this man, after he had offered one sacrifice for sins for ever, sat down on the right hand of God" (10:12).

We have a better sacrifice which gives us total and absolute cancellation of all our sin and which gives us immediate and unceasing access into the immediate presence of God. That was something no Hebrew ever had—not even the properly constituted, duly anointed high priest himself.

The author of this epistle, then, makes his second great point. Calvary covers it all! So why go back to dead ritual, which never did cleanse from sin anyway.

III. THE SUPERIOR PRINCIPLES OF CHRISTIANITY (11:1–13:17)

The Old Testament was thorough, detailed, and inspired of God, and its law was written on tables of stone. That law probed every nook and cranny of life. "Do this! Don't do that! Beware of the other!" And oh! what a burden it was. And worse! Nobody could keep it in the letter, let alone the spirit.

Christ has delivered us from all that. In His life He kept to the letter every jot and tittle of the law; in His death He fulfilled to the full every dictate and demand of the system of sacrifice. And now, instead of works—works we cannot produce—we have faith and hope and love. In three chapters, the writer of Hebrews takes up each of these cardinal principles of Christianity and shows their many-sided splendors.

He rises at length with rapture to say, "Now the God of peace, that brought again from the dead our Lord Jesus, that great shepherd of the sheep, through the blood of the everlasting covenant, Make you perfect in every good work to do his will, working in you that which is wellpleasing in his sight, through Jesus Christ; to whom be glory for ever and ever. Amen" (13:20–21).

The book of Hebrews is punctuated by five warning passages and no survey can be complete that does not take them into consideration. Because these warnings are varied in character and scope, they need to be studied in two ways: first in light of their *context* to see why they were introduced and where they lead, and in light of their *content* to see what they say and to whom they are addressed.

1. Warning against *disregarding the salvation of God* (2:1–4). This warning is brief. The writer has just finished setting before us the superior majesty and ministry of Christ. He warns us that we need to pay special heed to what God has to say about His Son. To "neglect so great salvation" (v. 3) as that provided in Christ is a deadly sin. The punishment is *spiritual*. Those who neglect God's salvation never enter into spiritual life. For them there is no escape.

2. Warning against *disbelieving the sufficiency of God* (3:7–4:13). The context deals with Israel's sad failure, in the Old Testament, to enter into rest. God brought a whole generation of Hebrews out of Egypt, but they would not let Him bring them into Canaan. He talks about creation rest and Canaan rest and then of Calvary rest. He warns that it is possible to have a saved soul but a lost life. The punishment is *temporal*. The unbelievers in the Old Testament lived a second-class life in the wilderness instead of entering into Canaan rest. It is possible for the Christian, too, to miss the joy, the blessing, the fullness, the fruitfulness, and the rest that God offers in Christ. In other words—to be saved, but "so as by fire."

3. Warning against *discrediting the Son of God* (5:11–6:20). The context speaks of Christ as our Great High Priest—a real, rightful, and royal priest, His priesthood based on the superior order of Melchizedek. The warning is threefold. One part is addressed to those who are weak, one part to those who are wicked, and one part to those who are wise. At the heart of the warning is a solemn statement about the impossibility of ever bringing back to the point of salvation those who, having been fully enlightened, turn away and thus crucify the Son of God afresh. The punishment is *eternal*. The key word is *impossible*. It is a terrible word. Other uses of it in the epistle underline its finality. "It [is] impossible for God to lie" (6:18). "It is not possible that the blood of bulls and goats should take away sins" (Heb. 10:4). "Without faith it is impossible to please [God]" (11:6).

4. Warning against *despising the Spirit of God* (10:26–39). The context is solemn. The greatest spiritual privilege was accorded just once a year in Israel to only one man. Once a year, after elaborate preparation, the high priest could venture inside the veil. *Now* all believers can come, as often as they like, for as long as they like, whenever they like. The writer warns his readers that it is sadly possible for a person to examine this new covenant and then to deliberately turn back to a dead religion. In so doing, they do despite to the Spirit of grace. The punishment is *judicial*. Such apostasy means that the transgressor will fall into the hands of the living God—something so fearful that such a possibility should be shunned at all costs.

5. Warning against *disobeying the summons of God* (12:15–29). The writer has been talking about the heroes of faith. He has been telling of men and women who, in the face of all kinds of pressure, dared to believe God. He urges the true believer to emulate their example and press on, and not be like Esau who traded spiritual things for carnal things. Then, when he wanted the spiritual too, he found he had lost out forever. The punishment is *millennial*. The writer draws a vivid contrast between Sinai and Zion in order to press home his point. It is possible to be in the family of God and yet to be a sad loser in the kingdom of God.

IV. CONCLUSION (13:18–25)

Truly, Hebrews is one of the most magnificent books in the Bible. Its teaching is particularly relevant to those coming to Christ out of a dead, Christ-denying religious system.

CHAPTER 23

JAMES

A Belief That Behaves

There has been considerable controversy about the author of this book. The writer calls himself "James, a servant of God and of the Lord Jesus Christ" (1:1). The traditional view is that he was "the Lord's brother" (Gal. 1:19), prominent in the Jerusalem church, who took a leading part in the Council of Jerusalem (Acts 15; see also Matt. 13:55; Gal. 2:9). During the Lord's earthly life, James was not a believer, but the Lord appeared to him after His resurrection and dispelled all his former doubts (1 Cor. 15:7).

The epistle is addressed to "the twelve tribes which are scattered abroad" (1:1), but it is evident from its contents that it is primarily addressed to Jewish Christians. It is generally agreed that the epistle was written before the fall of Jerusalem and probably even before the Council of Jerusalem. It belongs to the period before the inclusion of Gentiles into the church, when the whole church was Jewish and when their meeting places still bore the designation "synagogues."

Some maintain that it is the earliest of all the New Testament documents. It could well have been written to those who had been present in Jerusalem on the day of Pentecost and who had carried away with them the barest essentials of Christianity—in fact, little more than the Messiahship of Jesus.

James wrote in the style of an Old Testament prophet. His language is vivid and picturesque. He covers a wide range of subjects and draws repeatedly on the Old Testament, even the Apocrypha. It has been pointed out that, more than any other book of the New Testament, the book of James reflects the language of the Sermon on the Mount. The book is quite evidently not intended to be a theological treatise but rather a moral appeal.

I. Introduction (1:1)
II. The Christian and His Battles (1:2–16)
    A. The Testings of Christians (1:2–12)
        1. The Purpose of Testings (1:2–11)
            a. Our Enlargement (1:2–4)
            b. Our Enlightenment (1:5–8)
            c. Our Ennoblement (1:9–11)
        2. The Profit of Testings (1:12)
    B. The Temptations of Christians (1:13–16)
        1. The Source of Temptation (1:13–14)
        2. The Course of Temptation (1:15–16)
III. The Christian and His Bible (1:17–27)
    A. The Bible Likened to a Gift (1:17–18)
        1. It Brings Divine Light (1:17)
        2. It Brings Divine Life (1:18)
    B. The Bible Likened to a Graft (1:19–22)
        1. It Will Change the Fruit of Our Lips (1:19–20)
        2. It Will Change the Fruit of Our Lives (1:21–22)
    C. The Bible Likened to a Glass (1:23–27)
        1. In Which We Look to Be Challenged (1:23–24)
        2. In Which We Look to Be Changed (1:25–27)
IV. The Christian and His Brethren (2:1–13)
    Partiality is a sin against:
    A. The Lord (2:1–7)
    B. The Law (2:8–13)
V. The Christian and His Beliefs (2:14–26)
    The truth that "faith without works is dead" is:
    A. Forcefully Declared (2:14–17)
    B. Fully Debated (2:18–20)
    C. Firmly Demonstrated (2:21–25)
    D. Finally Decided (2:26)
VI. The Christian and His Behavior (3:1–4:12)
    A. Sin in the Life Must Be Revealed (3:1–4:4)
        1. In the Mouth (3:1–12)
        2. In the Mind (3:13–18)
        3. In the Members (4:1)
        4. In the Motives (4:2–4)
    B. Sin in the Life Must Be Resisted (4:5–10)
        1. Admit (4:5)
        2. Submit (4:6–7)

3. Commit (4:8–10)
    C. Sin in the Life Must Be Repudiated (4:11–12)
VII. The Christian and His Boasting (4:13–5:6)
    It is wrong for the Christian to boast about:
    A. Plans (4:13–17)
    B. Prosperity (5:1–6)
VIII. The Christian and His Burdens (5:7–20)
    A. The Burden of Poverty (5:7–11)
    B. The Burden of Proof (5:12)
    C. The Burden of Prayer (5:13–18)
    D. The Burden for People (5:19–20)

The epistle of James is very practical. James insists throughout that we have a belief that behaves.

I. INTRODUCTION (1:1)

The epistle belongs to the Pentecostal period when the whole church was Jewish. James identifies himself as "a servant of God and of the Lord Jesus Christ." He knew by now the vast gulf that separated him, as a son of Joseph and Mary, from the Lord Jesus, the Holy Spirit-conceived Son of the Virgin Mary. There could be no trading upon the half-brother relationship he sustained to that glorious Jesus of Nazareth, with whom he had shared for so long (and in chronic unbelief) that Nazareth home.

He writes to "the twelve tribes scattered abroad" as one of the recognized leaders of the Jerusalem church. No man in apostolic circles had the ear of the Jewish Christians as did James, and in this letter his address is brief and business-like. He is evidently not writing to a local church but to Jews scattered far and wide in the Gentile world. At the time James wrote, Jews were very numerous in all the great commercial centers of the world, but probably James had in mind, especially, the vast numbers still residing in the East, in Babylonia and Mesopotamia. If so, his epistle is the counterpart of Peter's letters addressed to the western dispersion. While it is possible James had all Jews in mind, it is most likely he was addressing Christian Jews outside of Palestine, many of whom had been converted on the day of Pentecost itself.

II. THE CHRISTIAN AND HIS BATTLES (1:2–16)

In these early verses, James discusses two quite different forms of experience—different, yet in some ways much the same—the *testings* of the Christian and the *temptations* of the Christian. Briefly, we may say that there is a basic and fundamental difference: God tests to bring out the good in us; Satan tempts to bring out the bad.

A. The Testings of Christians (1:2–12)

James gives us *the purpose of testings* (1:2–11). We are to count it all joy when God tries us, because it is a high privilege to be tried by God. Abraham was tested but not so Lot. The testings are designed to show us how far we have progressed in the school of God, and we shall be tested continually until we graduate to glory. James shows that God has a threefold objective in mind when He tests us. He wants to enlarge us, enlighten us, and ennoble us.

James gives us also *the profit of testings*. "Blessed is the man that endureth temptation: for when he is tried, he shall receive the crown of life, which the Lord hath promised to them that love him" (v. 12).

B. The Temptations of Christians (1:13–16)

We are to mark well *the source of temptations*. "Let no man say when he is tempted, I am tempted of God: for God cannot be tempted with evil, neither tempteth he any man: But every man is tempted, when he is drawn away of his own lust, and enticed" (v. 13–14). Man has a depraved and fallen nature and temptations boil up from within. Every man is built around a volcano that seethes and surges within his breast, and which at any moment can erupt in sin.

We are also to mark well *the course of temptations*. "Then when lust hath conceived, it bringeth forth sin: and sin, when it is finished, bringeth forth death. Do not err, my beloved brethren" (vv. 15–16). God does not condemn sin in the sinner and then condone it in the saint. There is an inevitable law of sin and death, which is as certain in its workings as the laws of gravity, magnetism, or electricity. When the atomic scientists first began to think about splitting the atom, they were afraid of what they called a chain reaction. We need to be desperately afraid of the chain reaction that is set in motion when lust is given its reign in our lives.

III. THE CHRISTIAN AND HIS BIBLE (1:17–27)

James gives us three illustrations of the Bible and its importance in our lives.

A. The Bible Likened to a Gift (1:17–18)

"Every good gift and every perfect gift is from above, . . . from the Father of lights, with whom is no variableness, neither shadow by turning. Of his own will begat he us with the word of truth, that we should be a kind of firstfruits of his creatures." This gift brings us *divine light*. God is described as the giver of this supernatural gift and as "the Father of lights." His first act in creation was to dispel darkness by means of light, and His word was the active agent. He said, "Light be"—and light was! His first act in redemption is to dispel the darkness by means of light—likewise, by His Word.

The Bible also brings us *divine life*. James says, "Of his own will begat he us with the word of truth" (v. 18). "Being born again," Peter is saying, "not of corruptible seed, but of incorruptible, by the word of God" (1 Peter 1:23). The Word of God is a seed that contains the germ of life in its kernel. When mixed with faith, it germinates in the soul and springs up into everlasting life. Thus, the Word carries with it the gift of divine life. When a person believes the written Word and opens his heart to the incarnate Word ("the Word was made flesh" [John 1:14]) then God's omnipotent power regenerates that person with life anew.

B. The Bible Likened to a Graft (1:19–22)

James now changes the metaphor and shows us that we are to "receive with meekness the engrafted word" (v. 21). When a gardener wants to improve the quality of fruit on a tree, he will sometimes do so by means of a graft. Grafting is a task that calls for great skill and patience on the part of the gardener and cooperation on the part of the plant.

When we allow the Word of God to become an integral part of our lives, it becomes the means in God's hand of *changing the fruit of our lips*. "Let every man be swift to hear, slow to speak, slow to wrath" (v. 19).

It is also the means of *changing the fruit of our lives*. "Wherefore lay apart all filthiness and superfluity of naughtiness . . . be ye doers of the word, and not hearers only, deceiving your own selves" (vv. 21–22).

C. The Bible Likened to a Glass (1:23–27)

Once again James changes the figure and likens the Word of God to a looking glass. As we look into this glass we are *challenged*: "If any be a hearer of the word, and not a doer, he is like unto a man beholding his natural face in a glass . . . and goeth his way, and straightway forgetteth what manner of man he was" (vv. 23–24). The function of God's Word is to show us ourselves as God sees us. Often, it is not a very pleasant picture!

Moreover we are *changed* (1:25–27). When we see what we are like, as our reflection gives us the uncompromising picture in the Word, we are moved to do something about it. Probably James had in mind the laver that stood in the outer court of the tabernacle. It was made of the mirrors of the women so that it reflected to the worshipper a true picture of himself and his defilement. But the laver also contained water so that the defilement thus revealed could be removed. The psalmist wrote, "Wherewithal shall a young man cleanse his way? by taking heed thereto according to thy word" (Psalm 119:9).

IV. THE CHRISTIAN AND HIS BRETHREN (2:1–13)

Next, James discusses the problem of partiality among Christians. He shows that having cliques and showing special favors to those we admire is sin.

A. Partiality Is a Sin Against the Lord (2:1–7)

He says that to give special preference to the rich man and to be rude to the poor man is actually an offense against Him who "for [our] sakes he became poor" (2 Cor. 8:9). James argues that all too often the rich man not only oppresses the believer but actually blasphemes "that worthy name by the which ye are called" (James 2:7). Therefore, to show partiality to any rich man is a sin against the Lord.

B. Partiality Is a Sin Against the Law (2:8–13)

He says, "If ye fulfill the royal law according to the scripture, Thou shalt love thy neighbor as thyself, ye do well" (v. 8). James goes on to show that if a man breaks one law he cannot plead as an excuse that he keeps another law. The law makes no such discrimination.

V. THE CHRISTIAN AND HIS BELIEFS (2:14–26)

"What doth it profit, my brethren, though a man say he hath faith, and have not works? can faith save him?" (2:14). Some think this statement puts James in conflict with Paul. Martin Luther certainly seemed to think so. Since "the just shall live by *faith*" (Heb. 10:38) was the watchword of the Reformation, he called this letter of James "an epistle of straw" because of its emphasis on works.[1] But there is not really any conflict here. The issue is not "faith" versus "works."

A. "Faith Without Works Is Dead" Is Forcefully Declared (2:14–17)

According to James, it is nonsense to say we have saving faith if we can see a brother in need and content ourselves with a pious, "Depart in peace, be ye warmed and filled" (v. 16). We are self-deceived if we think we can be genuinely saved and have no feeling for other members of the body of Christ, who are in need, if we can know about their needs and make no practical effort to help them.

B. "Faith Without Works Is Dead" Is Fully Debated (2:18–20)

"Yea, a man may say, Thou hast faith, and I have works: show me thy faith without thy works, and I will show thee my faith by my works" (v. 18). James produces a powerful argument next: "Thou believest there is one God; thou doest well: the devils also believe, and tremble." Evidently, belief must go beyond mere knowledge of certain facts.

C. "Faith Without Works Is Dead" Is Firmly Demonstrated (2:21–25)

James now gives two telling illustrations to prove his point that faith is valueless unless given a practical expression. "Intellectual assent" to a truth is not saving faith.

He cites the example of Abraham, who was willing to offer up his beloved Isaac on the altar of sacrifice as a practical demonstration of his faith. Abraham did not believe for a moment that, even if it came to the actual slaying of Isaac, matters would end there. God had said, "In Isaac shall thy seed be called" (Gen. 21:12). So death would have to be followed by resurrection.

The other illustration goes to the opposite side of the human spectrum. It was a far cry from Abraham, the founding father of the Hebrew people, to Rahab, a pagan, Canaanite harlot of Jericho. Yet her faith was as real and as practical as Abraham's. She demonstrated her faith in saving the two spies and asking that she and her family might be saved in turn.

D. "Faith Without Works Is Dead" Is Finally Decided (2:26)

"For as the body without the spirit is dead, so faith without works is dead also." There is no disagreement between Paul and James. In the New Testament we are justified by *blood*—that's the godward side of the issue; we are justified by *faith*— that's the selfward side of the issue; we are justified by *works*—that's the manward side of the issue. It is by our works that people can tell whether or not we are saved.

VI. The Christian and His Behavior (3:1–4:12)

The argument of James that we must have a belief that behaves leads quite naturally to a discussion of Christian conduct. This is by far the longest section in the epistle.

A. Sin in the Life Must Be Revealed (3:1–4:4)

First, there is *sin in the mouth* (3:1–12). Here, James gives us one of the greatest passages in literature on sins of the tongue. He likens the tongue to horses, to ships, to fire, to beasts, birds, and serpents, to a fountain, and to fruit. He has a very potent argument: "If any man offend not in word, the same is a perfect man, and able also to bridle the whole body" (3:2).

Then there is *sin in the mind* (3:13–18). "Who is a wise man and endued with knowledge among you?" (v. 13). He speaks of man's natural wisdom, which he castigates as "earthly, sensual, devilish" (v. 15) and contrasts it with the wisdom that comes from God, which is "pure, then peaceable, gentle, and easy to be entreated, full of mercy and good fruits, without partiality, and without hypocrisy" (v. 15). These verses give us a real clue for understanding human behavior and for understanding the way people think.

Next, there is *sin in the members*: "From whence come wars and fightings among you? come they not hence, even of your lusts that war in your members?" (4:1).

Finally, there is *sin in the motives*: "Ye lust, and have not: ye kill, and desire to have, and cannot obtain: ye fight and war, yet ye have not, because ye ask not. Ye ask, and receive not, because ye ask amiss, that ye may consume it upon your lusts" (4:2–3).

B. Sin in the Life Must Be Resisted (4:5–10)

At this point, James sounds very much like Paul! He has a threefold secret to victory over sin! Admit! Submit! Commit!

First we must *admit*: "Do ye think that the scripture saith in vain, The spirit that dwelleth in us lusteth to envy?" (v. 5). "Face up to it!" James says, "You're not perfect! You have an evil nature!" (The word *spirit* in this passage is used in a psychological way of the human soul.) Man's natural disposition is bent toward sin.

Then, we must *submit* (4:6–7). James says, "Submit yourselves therefore to God. Resist the devil, and he will flee from you" (v. 7). We often misquote this verse, taking it out of context and exhorting one another with the words, "Resist the devil and he will flee from you." But that is not true. The Devil will not flee from us for he is not the least bit afraid of us. That is not what the Holy Spirit says. He says: "*Submit yourselves unto God*; resist the devil and he will flee from you." That makes all the difference. When we first submit ourselves to God, the Devil is then left facing Him, and he is deathly afraid of God. Then, too, we must *commit*. James says, "Draw nigh to God, and he will draw nigh to you. . . . Humble yourselves in the sight of the Lord, and he shall lift you up" (vv. 8–10). No greater recipe could be given for a holy life. If we "practice the presence of God," sin will lose its power, for it cannot flaunt itself in the presence of God.

C. Sin in the Life Must Be Repudiated (4:11–12)

"Speak not evil one of another, brethren" (v. 11). This is a command. There must come a time when we resolutely turn our backs on sin and deliberately embrace God's will for our lives. Mere wishful thinking and reciting spiritual truths will not make us holy. We must demonstrate a deliberate, step by step, walk with God in newness of life.

VII. THE CHRISTIAN AND HIS BOASTING (4:13–5:6)

James next turns his attention to another aspect of the Christian life—that of having too much confidence in ourselves.

A. It Is Wrong for the Christian to Boast About Plans (4:13–17)

"Go to now, ye that say, Today or tomorrow we will go into such a city, and continue there a year, and buy and sell, and get gain: Whereas ye know not what shall be on the morrow" (vv. 13–14). This is a challenge to Christian businessmen who leave God out of account in their plans for the future. There is nothing essentially wrong in wishing to make money or in setting up business establishments in one place after another. The harm comes in ignoring God when making these plans. God refuses to be left out of our affairs. A heart attack, a sudden stroke, is all it takes to bring our plans to nothing.

B. It Is Wrong for the Christian to Boast About Prosperity (5:1–6)

"Go to now, ye rich men, weep and howl for your miseries that shall come upon you" (v. 1). This passage of Scripture needs careful consideration by every student of prophecy. It contains a remarkable prediction of the days in which we live. Communism drew its original inspiration from *Das Kapital* and from Engel's writings, which were based on the dreadful conditions in England's factory towns a century ago. Nothing is more deadly, more soul-destroying than tainted wealth and ill-gotten gain. Christ claims the right to be the Senior Partner in all our business affairs.

VIII. THE CHRISTIAN AND HIS BURDENS (5:7–20)

In this last section, James deals with four burdens, of different kinds but of practical significance.

A. The Burden of Poverty (5:7–11)

"Be patient therefore, brethren, unto the coming of the Lord" (v. 7). The purpose of James was to hearten the scattered Jewish Christians in their trials and to protest against the oppressions under which so many were suffering. "Be patient unto the arrival of the Lord," James says. As one writer puts it, "In the Christian race one cannot afford to be short of wind." The race is a long one. God's view of time and ours are quite different. "Behold, the judge standeth before the door," said James (v. 9), obviously looking at things from heaven's point of view. If it sometimes seems to us that justice is long overdue, that is because this is a day of grace and the hand of mercy is holding back the hand of vengeance.

B. The Burden of Proof (5:12)

James turns his attention now to a different problem—that of using extravagant language to back up one's assertions. "But above all things, my brethren, swear not, neither by heaven, neither by the earth, neither by any other oath: but let your yea be yea; and your nay, nay; lest ye fall into condemnation."

James warns frequently against sins of the tongue—against talkativeness, unrestrained speaking, love of correcting others, railing, cursing, boasting, murmuring (1:19, 26; 3:1–12; 4:11; 5:9). Now he warns against profanity, of wanting to back up one's simple denial or affirmation with oaths. Our word should be our bond. We should give our word and such should be our character and our reputation that all will know that our word is enough.

C. The Burden of Prayer (5:13–18)

"And the prayer of faith shall save the sick" (v. 15). This passage needs to be studied in its context. James is not giving us blanket insurance coverage against sickness here. The statement, "If he have committed sins, they shall be forgiven him" (v. 15), and the calling in of the elders suggests that the sickness in view here is of a judicial nature, doubtless brought on by church discipline. The circumstances are those of 1 Corinthians 11:30. The offender is one who has wronged his brethren, shown an unbrotherly spirit, or committed some flagrant sin that has brought chastisement upon him. When a true spirit of repentance is shown, the elders can come, pray for the brother's recovery, and confidently expect their prayer of faith to have effect. James puts the elders in this case on the same plane as Elijah.

That is not to say that God does not sometimes heal in answer to believing prayer. There is plenty of proof that He does. But we should be careful not to use this passage as some sort of guarantee that He will always do so. We have plenty of proof that He doesn't.

D. The Burden for People (5:19–20)

"Brethren, if any of you do err from the truth, and one convert him: Let him know, that he which converteth the sinner from the error of his way shall save a soul from death, and shall hide a multitude of sins."

James has in mind here those who have gone astray. The word for "err" comes from a Greek word for one lost on the mountains, one who has missed the path. There is no nobler work than rescue work. It is no easy task to get a man back on the right track.

James leaves us with a final picture—that of "hiding a multitude of sins," or "covering with a veil" the sins of the poor wanderer who is now brought back. So James begins by reminding us of the testing and temptations of life and ends by urging us to be out after the souls of men, covering as much as possible the transgressions of those who do come back.

This tender note on James ends his epistle and gives us a fleeting glimpse at another side of his character. The general impression we get of James is that of a severe and austere man, rigidly orthodox, meticulously correct and scrupulous about religious detail. He is moral, upright, and cold. His closing word, however, especially shows us the other side of his nature. He suddenly seems human, after all, with an unexpected fund of warmth, and possessed of an unsuspected compassion for those who are weak and those who fall.

CHAPTER 24

1 PETER

Salvation and Suffering

In this letter, Peter says he is in Babylon. That is not surprising. Babylon was still a great city. There were a million Jews in Babylon in early New Testament times—they had been there since the Babylonian captivity. When the remnant came back in the days of Zerubbabel, Ezra, and Nehemiah, to lay claim to the Promised Land in view of the coming of Christ, the majority of Jews stayed behind. Like many American Jews today—quite willing to support the State of Israel with their money and their influence, but not willing to go there to live—many Babylonian Jews elected to stay where they were. Business was good, the political atmosphere was congenial. Why go roughing it in the Promised Land? Why deliberately court hardship and danger?

Peter was the apostle to the Jews. So, when he says that he was in Babylon, we can take it he was in Babylon.

Some say that when Peter writes "Babylon" he means "Rome." It is true that when John writes about "Babylon" in Revelation 17, he means Rome but that is because he is writing about "mystery Babylon"—the Roman church in its full and final development, heir and successor of Babylonian religion, power, worldliness, and pride. In any case, John leaves enough clues in the chapter, enabling us to identify the city of which he is writing as Rome. It is a different matter in Revelation 18, where the symbolic gives way to the literal and where Babylon is Babylon—a literal city, the rebuilt Babylon of the Beast's tomorrow.

Many who claim that when Peter wrote "Babylon" he actually meant "Rome" have a vested interest in putting Peter at Rome. They want to make him the first Pope.

The "Historical Index" at the back of one Roman Catholic Bible, under the date A.D. 39, says, "He [St. Peter] is thought to have gone about this time to Antioch in Syria, and to have founded the episcopal see" (of Antioch). The generally received account among Roman Catholics, and one that can claim a long traditional acceptance, is that St. Peter came to Rome in the second year of Claudius (that is A.D. 42), and that he held the see twenty-five years. The "Historical Index," under the date A.D. 68, says; "About this time St. Peter and St. Paul came to Rome . . . not long after they were both put in prison, and suffered martyrdom."

Since so many millions of people take these bald and unsupported statements at their face value, we need to put them to the test. First, Peter was supposed to have founded the episcopal see of Antioch and to have been its bishop from A.D. 39 until A.D. 44. Here are the biblical facts:

1. three years after Paul's conversion, Peter was living in Jerusalem (A.D. 38–40; Gal. 1:15–18),
2. then he was at Lydda (Acts 9:26–32);
3. next at Joppa (Acts 10);
4. then at Caesarea (Acts 10);
5. next we find him back at Jerusalem (Acts 11:2);
6. where he was imprisoned by Herod Agrippa I (A.D. 44; Acts 12).

So he seems to have had little time for his supposed Bishopric.

As to the claim that he was Bishop of Rome beginning with A.D. 42—the following biblical facts make this virtually impossible:

1. In A.D. 44 he was in prison in Jerusalem (Acts 12).
2. He was a prominent member of the Council of Jerusalem in A.D. 49 (Acts 15).
3. Soon afterward he was at Antioch, where Paul rebuked him for dissembling, and for dividing the church (Gal. 2).
4. Paul wrote his epistle to the Romans in A.D. 56. The epistle makes no mention of Peter and contains no apology for interfering in the sphere of another apostle's labors. On the contrary, Paul says that he would not "build upon another man's foundation" (Rom. 15:20). There is no hint in this letter of anything like an apostolic visit to Rome by Peter or any other apostle hitherto. Paul is evidently looking forward to his own proposed visit as being an occasion when the Roman church would receive spiritual gifts, which were at present lacking.
5. In this same epistle, Paul greets two dozen people by name. The name of Peter is conspicuously absent.

6. When Paul at last arrives in Rome, he is met by a company of believers. Again no mention is made of Peter (Acts 28:15).

7. Paul met with a company of Jews while imprisoned in Rome, whereupon they stated they had heard nothing about Christianity (Acts 28:22). This hardly seems evidence of Peter's by now supposed seventeen-year residence in the city as its chief bishop, considering he was especially commissioned to be the apostle to the Jews.

8. While a prisoner at Rome (A.D. 59–61), Paul wrote four epistles (Ephesians, Philippians, Colossians, and Philemon) and names numerous people who were his helpers in the work in the city. No mention is made of Peter, which, to say the least, is very strange if Peter was Bishop of Rome.

9. Paul was back in Rome expecting martyrdom in A.D. 68 or thereabouts and wrote his last letter (2 Timothy). Not only does he not mention Peter, he states, "Only Luke is with me" (4:11). He says that at his first trial "no man stood with me, but all men forsook me: I pray God that it may not be laid to their charge" (4:16). Are we to suppose that Peter, if he were Bishop of Rome, would have deserted Paul?[1]

In the light of *biblical* evidence, it is very difficult to support the idea that Peter was Bishop of Rome from A.D. 42 to A.D. 68. It is not at all certain he was ever there at all. In this epistle he says he is at Babylon. Evidently he was ministering to the church in that city, though he was writing to churches in far-off Pontus, Galatia, Cappadocia, Asia, and Bithynia—in other words, to churches pioneered by Paul.

Something must have prompted the writing of this letter. Why should Peter feel the compulsion of the Holy Spirit to write to the "elect sojourners of the dispersion" (as he calls them [see vv. 1, 2])? These were doubtless Christian Jews, scattered abroad throughout the Roman Empire. And why should he write to Jews and Gentiles in areas of the Roman Empire he himself had seemingly never visited?

In the first place, his name would be well known to all Christians. It was a name that carried tremendous weight in the early church. After all, Peter was one of the very chiefest of the apostles. He had been an intimate, personal follower of the Lord Jesus when He had lived on earth. A letter from Peter would be read and prized by Christians everywhere. But why did he write—and when?

The letter seems to have been written between A.D. 63 and 67. So it was written during that first great persecution of the church instigated by Nero. That persecution started in November of A.D. 64 and lasted until Nero's death in A.D. 68. This was a widespread persecution, not confined to Rome but extending more or less over the whole empire. It was one of the most savage and terrible persecutions in all the church's long and checkered history.

There are many clues that this persecution was raging when this letter was penned. Peter speaks of the "trial of your faith, being much more precious than of gold that perisheth, though it be tried with fire" (1:7). He says, "Beloved, think it not strange concerning the fiery trial [the word has to do with "burning" and with a furnace] which is to try you [literally, "the burning which is taking place among you]" (4:12). All the way through the epistle are references to terrible, false accusations being made against the Christians. Peter issues exhortations such as, "Fear not their terror." This, then, is the background of the epistle. Nero's persecutions! What a flood of light that casts on this letter. It should be read in the light of that.

    I. Introduction (1:1–2)
   II. The Question of Salvation (1:3–9)
     A. We Have an Expectant Hope (1:3–4)
       1. A Triumphant Exit from the Grave (1:3)
       2. A Triumphant Entrance into Glory (1:4)
     B. We Have an Experiential Faith (1:5–7)
       1. It Sees Beyond the Temporal (1:5)
       2. It Sees Beyond the Temptations (1:6)
       3. It Sees Beyond the Trial (1:7)
     C. We Have an Expressive Love (1:9)
  III. The Question of Scripture (1:10–12)
     A. Its Message (1:10a)
     B. Its Mystery (1:10b–11a)
     C. Its Meaning (1:11b)
     D. Its Majesty (1:12)
  IV. The Question of Sanctification (1:13–25)
     A. The Character of God (1:13–17)
       1. His Fatherly Character (1:13–14)
       2. His Fearful Character (1:15–17)
     B. The Cross of Christ (1:18–21)
       1. The Price of Redemption (1:18–19)
       2. The Plan of Redemption (1:20)
       3. The Point of Redemption (1:21)
     C. The Control of the Spirit (1:22–25)
       1. A New Pattern of Life (1:22)
       2. A New Principle of Life (1:23–25)
   V. The Question of Separation (2:1–12)
     A. Its Requirement (2:1)
     B. Its Reasons (2:2–11)
       1. Separated by Birth from the Old Life (2:2–3)

The outline contains more detail, perhaps, than might be warranted in the survey of such a short letter, but it is given deliberately to stimulate more detailed study of this important letter. After all, this letter gives the lie to so many false claims about the church, and it is written by an apostle who is exalted by many to a place he himself would have rejected with vigor (Acts 10:24–27).

We can picture Peter, perhaps sitting in the luxurious home of some wealthy, influential Babylonian Jewish Christian, or in the home of some humble, believing peasant. The news has come of the terrible things Nero is doing to the Christians at Rome and of the rapid spread of the persecution into areas pioneered by Paul. He decides to write to these people—and to all of God's persecuted, suffering people everywhere in all ages. What should he say to them? What would we say to them?

I. INTRODUCTION (1:1–2)

"Peter!" The letter begins with his *signature*. It was a signature to command attention, the signature of a man who had been one of the foremost and most famous disciples of the Lord Jesus. A humble fisherman, he had become a diligent shepherd of God's sheep. Everyone would want to read a letter from Peter.

The letter continues with his *status*—"an apostle of Jesus Christ." He is not writing as the Bishop of Rome, the incumbent of the church, the Vicar of Christ, the Pope of Rome. He knows of no such title, no such position. He has a higher authority, a grander position—one he shared with James and John, Thomas and Matthew, Andrew and Phillip, and half a dozen others, including that greatest of all the apostles, Paul. It was a disappearing office. The work of an apostle was to lay down the foundations of the church (Eph. 2:20). With the death of a dozen men, this unique position of apostle would vanish forever from the earth. But, while it lasted, it gave Peter a status not given to many but shared equally with others. This status enabled these men to set the church upon its course for its voyage over the seas of time from Pentecost until the rapture.

The letter continues with mention of the *saints*—Peter's chief concern. They are described as "the strangers scattered [abroad] . . . elect" or better, "the elect sojourners of the dispersion." Peter was writing to areas that had been evangelized by Paul, but his chief concern was the Christian Jews of the dispersion. Peter knew he was particularly the apostle of the circumcision, of the Jews, as Paul was the apostle to the Gentiles. We gather from his description of his readers as "strangers" that he had never met them. Technically the word *parepidēmos* means "a sojourner among a people not one's own." In Hebrews 11:13, it is translated "pilgrims." (It is also so translated in 1 Peter 2:11 and these are the only times the word is used.) Peter makes no mention of any of them by name. The teaching of "our beloved brother Paul" (2 Peter 3:15) and his fellow workers is referred to by Peter as "the true grace of God wherein ye stand" (5:12).

II. THE QUESTION OF SALVATION (1:3–9)

That is the place to begin. Peter is saying, "I'll remind them of what a wonderful salvation we have—a salvation that triumphs over even the terror of the grave." And so he does. He picks up three of Paul's favorite words—faith, hope, and love— and weaves them into a glorious garland of encouragement. He reminds his readers they have "an inheritance incorruptible, and undefiled, and that fadeth not away, reserved in heaven" (v. 4). He lifts their eyes above these scenes of time and reminds them of the second coming of Christ. He urges them to so live in the light of Christ's return that praise, honor, and glory will be theirs at His appearing. "We have a living hope," he says (see v. 3).

What a prospect! And what a person! He directs their attention to the Lord—he calls Him by His human name, "Jesus." "Whom having not seen, ye love; in whom, though now ye see him not, yet believing, ye rejoice with joy unspeakable and full of glory" (v. 8). Peter had seen Him. They hadn't seen Him, but the reality of Jesus is the same—seen or unseen. The very thought of Him fills the believing heart with joy. It became, indeed, a source of wonder and amazement to the pagans that the Christians could face the most fearful terrors with joy unspeakable and full of glory. This is the secret of it—*Jesus!*

What a prospect! What a person! Yes, and what a possession! "Receiving the end of your faith, even the salvation of your souls" (v. 9). That is what salvation is all about. Men might be able to destroy the body—but they can never destroy the soul.

> The soul that on Jesus hath leaned for repose,
> He will not, He will not desert to its foes.
>
> —John Rippon,
> "How Firm a Foundation"

After Peter's opening statement, he next writes about the Word of God.

III. THE QUESTION OF SCRIPTURE (1:10–12)

Our faith and our hope are not founded on vague uncertainties. People sometimes say, when faced with someone's misfortunes, "It'll be all right! Don't worry! Everything is going to be fine!" Such assurances are usually vain platitudes based on nothing but wishful thinking. Our assurance is based on something solid and substantial, something that has stood the test of time. It is based on the Scriptures.

Peter refers his readers to the Bible. There are two great themes in the Bible, he says, "the sufferings of Christ, and the glory that should follow" (v. 11). The sufferings are never mentioned without the glory. Christ suffered—yes! But glory followed. You are suffering? Yes! But glory will follow.

He reminds God's people that those who wrote the Old Testament Scriptures often did not understand what they had written. They wrote things down—then stared in amazement at the words before them on the page, wondering what they meant. They could not unravel words from God that spoke of a *sovereign* Christ and a *suffering* Christ. The prophets knew they had written Scripture, but they did not understand its significance.

The Holy Spirit, says Peter, has made it clear as crystal to us. The sufferings were to come first; the glory was to follow. First the cross—then the crown. Christ came first to redeem—He is coming back to reign. The literal fulfillment of the one is the guarantee of the literal fulfillment of the other.

Then he adds something of great interest: "Which things the angels desire to look into" (v. 12). The word translated "look" literally means "to stoop down to look." These are matters of such vast import that the shining ones who surround God's throne, who are occupied with Him, who awake the echoes of the everlasting hills with the thunder of their praise, who live on high in the eternal courts of bliss—these stoop down to look into the great truths that fill the pages of this Book! They are intensely interested in them. The great truths of the incarnation of the Son of God, of His resurrection, His ascension on high, His coming again—these majestic themes that fill the pages of this Book, and the angels are fascinated by them! How strange that we are so careless of them. If the angels had a Bible they would memorize it, study it, revere it, proclaim it. They don't have one, so they stoop down to look into ours. Every time we open a Bible, we have a crowd of angels peering over our shoulders!

"There!" says Peter, "that should encourage these dear saints of God! Nero can never rob them of that! Their faith is securely founded on the true sayings of God!"

IV. THE QUESTION OF SANCTIFICATION (1:13–25)

Peter goes back to the Old Testament. In the Mosaic Law, all kinds of ritual taboos hedged in the Hebrew kitchen. The people could eat this, but they couldn't eat that; food for the table had to be prepared in a certain way, meat had to be free from blood, meat and milk must not be mixed in the same dish. Peter had lived almost all of his life governed by these ritual rules. And he had almost missed the point and purpose of it all. For right in the heart of the chapter dealing with these things was a blinding flash of light. God said, "Ye shall be holy; for I am holy" (Lev. 11:44). These ritual food laws were intended to sanctify. The Jews were to be set apart from all other people, separate unto God.

The Jews, of course—and Peter was an example of this—placed all the emphasis on the *ritual* and forgot the *reason*. Now Peter, having learned that the ritual was obsolete, picks up the reason. He quotes a text without a context. In this case it was all that mattered: "Be ye holy, for I am holy" (see v. 15). God expects His people to be sanctified, set apart from all other people for Himself. They are to be like Him. He is holy; we are to be holy. The former lusts are to be replaced by the family likeness.

"There!" says Peter, "I know that your accusers are saying all kinds of foul things about you. Put the lie to their accusations by your life. Be holy! And remember—God's commands are His enablings. His words are not only legislative but executive."

We know from our history books what terrible things were being said against the Christians. Tacitus, writing at the end of the first century, said the Neronic persecutions were directed against "a set of people who were held in abhorrence for their crimes, called by the common people Christians." He describes their faith as a "detestable superstition," accuses them of "hatred to mankind."[2]

V. THE QUESTION OF SEPARATION (2:1–12)

God's people are to be "strangers and pilgrims" on the earth, for this world is not our home. A stranger is a man who is away from home; a pilgrim is a man who is going home. People feel ill at ease in the presence of both. Strangers bother people because they are *different*; pilgrims bother people because they are *dedicated*.

This is what bothered people about the early Christians. The Christians were different and they were dedicated. Their hopes and affections were set on things above, not on things on the earth. Their citizenship was in heaven; thus, they were heaven-born and heaven-bound. That citizenship is one of the great features of the abiding presence of the Holy Spirit in the heart of a believer. He is likened to a dove, as coming from another world and having strong homing instinct. The Holy Spirit in our hearts will head us for home!

Peter says that by birth, by belief, and by behavior you are to be different. Separation from the world is one of the marks of a believer in a God-hating, Christ-rejecting, Bible-denying, Spirit-resisting age.

VI. THE QUESTION OF SUBMISSION (2:13–3:13)

Peter's demands in regard to submission are sweeping. As citizens, we are to submit to the government; as employees, we are to submit to our employers; as believers, we are to submit to Christ; as wives, we are to submit to our husbands; as husbands, we are to submit to the best interests of our wives; as brethren, we are to submit one to another.

But, as might be expected, given the climate of the new and fearful persecution that had been launched by Nero, Peter has something to say about submission to government. This section of the epistle begins with that topic. Thus, we are to submit to every ordinance (the word used literally means "creation") of man. We are to submit to the government.

The government of Rome, when Peter penned these words, was the most corrupt, oppressive, and vicious on the face of the earth. The head of state was a monster, commonly regarded by Christians as the Antichrist—in fact, the belief soon took root that Nero would, indeed, come back as the Antichrist. Yet believers are told to submit to such a government as that! They are not told to fight, to demonstrate, to organize protest rallies and marches. They are to submit.

Such advice sounds strange to many today, especially in the United States, which traces its roots to revolution against constituted authority. But such was the mind of the Holy Spirit to believers—submit! That was what Jesus did; that is what we must do. As the poet Whitlock Gandy puts it,

> By meekness and defeat
> He won the throne and crown;
> Trod all His foes beneath His feet
> By being trodden down.

Meekness was the path that Jesus accepted. He could say to Peter, "There are twelve legions of angels, Peter, with drawn swords, straining over the battlements of heaven. One word from Me and I could wipe out all mankind. I could usher in Armageddon here and now." He could say to Pilate, "Thou hast no power over me at all." He submitted! He "became obedient unto death, even the death of the cross. Wherefore God also hath highly exalted him" (Phil. 2:8–9). That was His way. Peter says, "That is still His way."

VII. THE QUESTION OF SUFFERING (3:14–4:19)

This is the longest section in his letter. Peter examines the whole question of suffering, but the dark shadow that overlies these verses is the shadow of Nero.

Tacitus tells us how Christians were made to suffer: "The sufferings at their execution were aggravated by insult and mockery; for some were disguised in the skins of wild beasts and worried by dogs; some were crucified; and others wrapped in shirts dipped in pitch and set on fire when the day closed, that they might serve as lights to illuminate the night."[3] In the references to "fire" and to "burning," we can see the Christians standing as flaming torches to lighten the wild parties held in Nero's gardens.

Peter might have been reasonably safe in far-off Babylon when he wrote these verses on suffering. But his own turn was coming; he already knew that. He knew that he was to die, and to die by crucifixion, for Jesus had already told him so. These words of suffering were born out of a heart fully resolved now to be obedient unto death.

In the process of this great message on suffering, Peter makes a statement that has puzzled many. He says that Jesus went and preached to the spirits in prison—the spirits that were disobedient in the days of Noah. All kinds of interpretations are offered in order to escape the obvious—that Jesus went and preached to the spirits in prison!

Here are Peter's words: "For Christ also hath once suffered for sins, the just for the unjust, that he might bring us to God, being put to death in the flesh, but quickened by the Spirit: By which also he went and preached unto the spirits in prison; Which sometime were disobedient, when once the longsuffering of God waited in the days of Noah, while the ark was a-preparing, wherein few, that is, eight souls were saved" (3:18–20). Peter then goes on to speak of "the resurrection of Jesus Christ: who is gone into heaven, and is on the right hand of God; angels and authorities and powers being made subject unto him" (3:21–22).

The word for "preached" here is *kērussō*, which comes from a word meaning "a herald, a crier." This is not the same word Peter uses later (4:6). The word for "preach" in this case is *euangelizō*, "to evangelize"—the regular word for preaching the gospel, a word that means to make a glad announcement or to bring a joyful message. Jesus, however, went down into the underworld as a herald to make an announcement. The context makes it clear that included in this proclamation were the fallen angels responsible for the unnatural and deadly sins that made the flood such an absolute necessity if the human race were to be preserved from utter corruption. Very likely, too, Jesus proclaimed the triumph of Calvary to the imprisoned spirits of men in hades—to some a message of life, to others a message of deeper and darker doom. Then, having made His proclamation throughout the dark and dismal halls of hades, He rose in triumph over the tomb, and thereafter ascended, spirit, soul, and glorified body, to the right hand of God, where now He reigns in undisputed triumph over all angels, all authorities, and all powers, good and bad.

This great triumphant message occurs in the midst of Peter's lengthy word on suffering. The saints to whom he addressed this letter were being persecuted by a human monster. No matter! All Nero could do was put them to death in the flesh, but they would emerge from that ordeal triumphant. Human tribunals might condemn them to death in all kinds of horrible, nightmarish forms. They might well die as martyrs but an incorruptible, glorious triumph awaited them on the other side.

VIII. THE QUESTION OF SHEPHERDING (5:1–7)

For to be an acknowledged leader of the Lord's people in times of persecution is an added peril. Leaders are always hunted down. By destroying the leadership of the church, the enemy hopes to destroy the church itself. Peter tells these Christian leaders that he is an elder, an overseer, a shepherd himself. He does not endorse the claims of the Catholic Church, which bestows on him some kind of primacy or papacy, but says, "The elders which are among you I exhort, who am also an elder, and a witness of the sufferings of Christ, and also a partaker of the glory that shall be revealed" (v. 1). He was just one of them. He and Paul did indeed tower above many others—Peter was a witness of the sufferings (at Calvary) and a partaker of the glory (on the Mount of Transfiguration); Paul was a witness of the glory (on the Damascus road) and a partaker of the sufferings (in all the persecutions he endured for the sake of the gospel). But neither claimed any primacy over other elders.

IX. The Question of Satan (5:8–11)

"Be sober, be vigilant; because your adversary the devil, as a roaring lion, walketh about, seeking whom he may devour" (v. 8). Satan was behind the Neronic persecution as he is behind all persecution. He hates Christ, hates the church, and hates all Christians. But he cannot win. We are to resist him by being steadfast in the faith. We are to watch and war and win!

Peter's first epistle, against the lurid flames kindled by Nero's mad hate, shines as an apostolic gem. The dreadful human torches, dipped in coats of tar and set ablaze to lighten the spectacles of lust and sin in Nero's pleasure gardens are now flaming firebrands of God, ablaze with the light and luster of another world. The terrified men and women, boys and girls, who were wrapped in pigskins and goatskins, and who braved the wild dogs of the arena—they are now seated with Christ in glory. The countless thousands who faced death by crucifixion are now the crowned royalty of heaven.

Their tormentors have been burning in the flames of a lost eternity now for nearly two thousand years, while the faithful have been living in a tumult of "joy unspeakable and full of glory." This letter—written with the passion of one who had the sentence of death upon him already, which was written in the prophetic word of Christ—has become a treasured book in the library of God. It has helped smooth many a pillow, helped soften many an iron chain, helped many a brave believer to face the horrors of the Inquisition, the boot, the rack, the thumbscrew, and the stake.

For Satan still roars. He comes like that old serpent to instill poison wherever he may. He comes like an angel of light to deceive. His favorite guise is that of a roaring lion. He always falls back on that. Nor is the martyr roll of God's illustrious dead yet closed. The roaring lion is still abroad. "Never mind," says Peter. "The God of all grace, who hath called us unto his eternal glory by Christ Jesus, after that ye have suffered a while, make you perfect, stablish, strengthen, settle you. To him be glory and dominion for ever and ever. Amen" (vv. 10–11). We're on the victory side.

X. Conclusion (5:12–14)

Peter's conclusion contains a number of fascinating references. Evidently Silvanus (Paul's dear friend and fellow traveler Silas) was with Peter and, perhaps, gave Peter much background information about some of the areas to which Peter addressed his letter. He was probably the bearer of the letter and possibly Peter's amanuensis also.

Peter sends greetings from "the church that is at Babylon" (v. 13). Actually the words "the church" are much disputed. All kinds of suggestions have been made to define it as "the co-elect," an adjective needing a feminine noun. One popular view is that it is a reference to Peter's wife, who Paul says traveled with Peter. Another view is that it refers to the *diaspora*, the dispersion. No one has yet the last word on this topic. Perhaps we should simply let the words "the church" stand.

Peter also sends greetings from "Marcus my son" (v. 13). This is no doubt the well-known John Mark (replaced by Silas as Paul's co-worker on his second missionary journey) and the author of the gospel of Mark—addressed particularly to Romans.

"Greet ye one another with a kiss of [love]" (v. 14). What a blessing to be a Christian in a world so filled with hate! "Peace be with you all that are in Christ Jesus" (v. 14). What a blessing to be a Christian in a world so filled with war and strife! Peace! Paul generally ended his letters with the word "grace." Peter ended his with a word he had so often heard fall from the Lord's own lips—*peace!*

CHAPTER 25

2 Peter

Beware of Apostasy

I n some ways, this second letter of Peter is one of the most fascinating books in the Bible. First is the way it is written. Some people have, in fact, denied that Peter ever wrote it, mainly because of the divergence in tone between 1 and 2 Peter. This difference, however, has been exaggerated. Consider, the writer of the epistle claims to have been on the Mount of Transfiguration. He knows, from the lips of the Lord Himself, that he is to die—the only one of the apostles who did not have the blessed hope of seeing the Lord come in his own lifetime. He claims that this is the second epistle he has written to his readers. He speaks of Paul as a brother beloved.

So why should we doubt that Peter wrote this remarkable little note? Why cannot a person write in more than one style—especially if the subjects are different?

This epistle is intended by Peter for the same people who read his first one— Gentile converts of the apostle Paul in Europe, and Jewish believers of the dispersion. A note of urgency infuses Peter's first letter—Nero's persecutions were raging across the empire. There is an added note of urgency to this letter. The roaring lion has now become the old serpent. Persecution, raging fire from without, is now matched by apostasy working from within.

Adding to the note of urgency is Peter's conviction that his own martyrdom is not far distant. It is presumed that the second epistle was written soon after the first, probably before the fall of Jerusalem in A.D. 70. Peter's martyrdom took place about A.D. 68. Thus, 2 Peter and 2 Timothy have much in common, with both writers aware that martyrdom was near (2 Tim. 4:6; 2 Peter 1:14). Both warn of apostasy and both reflect the joyful spirit of the writers.

Although Paul and Jude had written warning letters against the heretical teachings now making drastic inroads into the church, Peter felt he must fling the weight of his own personal authority and influence into the scales. Peter enjoyed a tremendous reputation in the early church and a vast fund of goodwill. So, with the shadows lengthening as the first century of the Christian era moves into its second half, Peter writes. And some of the insights he has are astonishing, indeed. He even foresaw the dawning of the nuclear age as a herald of the great and terrible "day of the Lord."

I. Faith's Convictions (1:1–21)
   A. As to the Walk with God (1:1–15)
      1. The Secret of Commencing Well (1:1–4)
         a. How to Be Saved (1:1–3a)
         b. How to Be Sure (1:3b–4a)
         c. How to Be Sanctified (1:4b)
      2. The Secret of Continuing Well (1:5–9)
         a. The Path of Diligence (1:5–8)
            (1) Faithful Addition (1:5–7)
            (2) Fruitful Abundance (1:8)
         b. The Path of Delusion (1:9)
      3. The Secret of Concluding Well (1:10–15)
         a. Peter's Exhortation (1:10–12)
            (1) The Nature of It (1:10–11)
            (2) The Need for It (1:12)
         b. Peter's Example (1:13–15)
            (1) His Unfaltering Determination (1:13)
            (2) His Unforgettable Destiny (1:14)
            (3) His Unfailing Diligence (1:15)
   B. As to the Word of God (1:16–21)
      1. Its Integrity (1:16a)
      2. Its Instruction (1:16b–18)
      3. Its Importance (1:19a)
      4. Its Illumination (1:19b)
      5. Its Interpretation (1:20)
      6. Its Inspiration (1:21)
II. Faith's Contention (2:1–22)
   A. The Doctrine of the Heretics (2:1–3a)
      1. Their Lying Message (2:1)
         a. It Was Deceitful (2:1a)
         b. It Was Damnable (2:1b)

2. Their Loose Morals (2:2)
3. Their Low Motive (2:3a)
B. The Doom of the Heretics (2:3b–9)
   1. Its Nearness (2:3b)
   2. Its Nature (2:4–9)
      a. An Appeal in View of Past History (2:4–8)
         (1) The Flood in Noah's Day (2:4–5)
            (a) The Sinning Angels (2:4)
            (b) The Sinning Antediluvians (2:5)
         (2) The Fire in Lot's Day (2:6–8)
      b. An Application in View of Present Heresy (2:9)
C. The Deeds of the Heretics (2:10–22)
   1. An Exposure of Their Conduct (2:10–14)
      a. Its Brazenness (2:10–12)
      b. Its Boldness (2:13–14)
   2. An Exposure of Their Claims (2:15–19)
      a. A Biblical Sketch (2:15–16)
      b. A Biographical Sketch (2:17–19)
         (1) Their Empty Profession (2:17)
         (2) Their Empty Preaching (2:18)
         (3) Their Empty Promises (2:19)
   3. An Exposure of Their Converts (2:20–22)
      a. The Truth Revealed to Them (2:20)
      b. The Truth Rejected by Them (2:21)
      c. The Truth Related About Them (2:22)
III. Faith's Consummation (3:1–18)
  A. Peter Exposes the Scoffers (3:1–13)
   1. Their Insistent Denial of the Promise of the Lord's Return (3:1–4)
      a. Why This Denial Would Be (3:1–2)
      b. When This Denial Would Be (3:3)
      c. What This Denial Would Be (3:4)
   2. Their Ignorant Denial of the Promise of the Lord's Return (3:5–13)
     Their ignorance of:
      a. The Lord's Past Dealings with the Heaven and Earth—His Wrath Experienced (3:5–6)
      b. The Lord's Present Dealings with the Heaven and Earth—His Wrath Expected (3:7–12)
         (1) The Truth of This (3:7)
         (2) The Time of This (3:8–9)
         (3) The Terror of This (3:10–12)

        c. The Lord's Predicted Dealings with the Heaven and Earth—His
           Wrath Exhausted (3:13)
   B. Peter Exhorts the Saints (3:14–18)
     1. To Behave (3:14)
     2. To Believe (3:15–16)
     3. To Beware (3:17–18)

As we read this letter we must remember that Nero was still on the rampage, that apostasy was taking swift root, and that Peter was soon to die, and knew it.

I. Faith's Convictions (1:1–21)

In his opening chapter, Peter sensibly brings his readers back to two great factors.

A. As to the Walk with God (1:1–15)

We have what he calls "exceeding great and precious promises." Further, he says that we have been made "partakers of the divine nature," and that we have "escaped the corruption that is in the world through lust" (v. 4).

What an *eternity* is ours! Those "exceeding great and precious promises" are the pledge of it.

What an *experience* is ours! It was always intended that man should be inhabited by God—that the human spirit should be indwelt by the Holy Spirit, that man in his life down here should be the visible expression of God in His life over there. That has now become a reality. We have become partakers of the divine nature.

What an *escape* is ours! This world is a corrupt and filthy place. It is not getting any better; in fact it is getting worse. The indwelling power of the Holy Spirit enables us to escape all that.

The Christian life is eminently worthwhile, quite apart from all the untold blessings that await us in eternity. What a blessing not to have to carry around a load of guilt because of illicit affairs, not to have to battle every day with a craving for tobacco or alcohol or drugs, not to have to worry about things, but to have a loving heavenly Father interested in us and caring for us.

Ah! says Peter, but remember—the Christian life is not a static experience. We have to be growing! Peter's formula for a holy life is interesting. According to him it is largely a matter of addition. Add! he says. "To your faith virtue . . . knowledge . . . self control . . . patience . . . godliness . . . brotherly kindness . . . love" (see vv. 5–7). Most people look upon the Christian life as mostly a matter of subtraction—giving up this, giving up that, going without the other. Nonsense! says Peter. It is largely a matter of addition. "But, Peter, did you not have to give up anything?" we might ask. Peter would reply, "Of course! I can remember once having to give up a hundred and fifty-three fish!"

When one thing is lost, however, something else is gained. We have an oak tree in our garden. In the fall the leaves on that tree wither and die, but they are tenacious. Not even the winter winds seem to blow most of them down. That is no cause for worry. Nobody has to get a ladder and climb the tree and try to pluck off those unsightly dead leaves one at a time. All that is necessary is just to wait for the spring to come. When the new life surges up through the branches and makes its way to the twigs, those leaves drop off by themselves! It is not a matter of subtraction. We don't have to pluck off the dead leaves of our old bad habits, our old ways. We wait until the new life in Christ reaches these things. They then drop off and are replaced by the beauty and verdure of spiritual life.

B. As to the Word of God (1:16–21)

The things we have in Christ are almost too good to be true. Ah, says Peter, but "we have not followed cunningly devised fables" (v. 16). While experience is great, we must never trust experiences. That is the problem with many today. They want a "charismatic" experience, usually something extra-biblical. They want to speak in tongues and recover those temporary, transient sign-gifts of the early church, long since withdrawn.

Well, says Peter, I know all about experiences. I experienced the majestic spectacle of the unveiling of the Lord Jesus, in all His pristine glory, on the Mount of Transfiguration. I've seen Moses and Elijah! If it comes to voices and visions, I know all about it. But there is something more important than that. On the Mount, God said to us, "This is my beloved Son: hear him" (Mark 9:7). The teachings of the Lord Jesus are more important and more to be relied upon than all the voices and visions in the world.

In fact, he says, let us be quite sure about this—"We have also a *more sure word of prophecy*; whereunto ye do well that ye take heed . . . prophecy of the scripture . . ." (vv. 19–20). Peter deliberately turns us away from voices and visions, from extra-biblical experiences and phenomena, to the Book. *That* is the basis of our beliefs, the Bible, the Word of God.

With apostasy, heresy, and error invading the church, Peter was saying, "Let's get back to the Book, the inspired, infallible Word of God, the book written by men who were borne along by the Holy Spirit. And," he said, "let's interpret that book properly. Don't take texts out of context": "no prophecy of the scripture is of any private interpretation" (v. 20). The word *private* here means "by itself" or "individually." In other words, Scripture is to be interpreted in harmony with the whole of God's divine revelation, and according to sound hermeneutical principles. We do not interpret one Scripture in a way that contradicts another Scripture.

Peter begins, then, with the convictions of the faith—with things intended to safeguard the flock of God against the false shepherds who were now seeking to lead God's people astray.

II. FAITH'S CONTENTION (2:1–22)

He uses strong language, indeed, to describe those who were introducing heretical teachings. The Bible, in fact, always reserves its strongest language for such. They were teaching what Peter calls "damnable heresies" (v. 1)—that is, "heresies of perdition." Their teaching bore the hallmark of the Antichrist, the son of perdition. He describes their ways as "pernicious ways" (v. 2) or "lascivious ways." All kinds of moral perversions were being introduced. He speaks, for instance, of the "lust of uncleanness" (v. 10). The word is *miasmos*, which literally means to stain, to dye, to taint. He calls these false teachers "cursed children" (v. 14)—that is, "children of the curse."

Drawing on two previous ages, going back to the days of Noah and to the days of Lot, Peter illustrates what was happening. In *the days of Noah*, he reminds them, God spared not the angels that sinned. When Lucifer fell from glory and was transformed into the fearful being we now know as Satan, he dragged a third of the angelic host with him into sin. The majority of these fallen angels still roam the air. They are those "principalities, powers, rulers of this world, darkness, spiritual wickedness in high places" spoken of by Paul (see Eph. 6:12). These are the supernatural powers that oppose us when we pray. These are angelic beings of great power and malice, who hold this world in subjection under Satan.

But there are other fallen angels, the ones referred to here by Peter. These angels of Satan sinned in an even more flagrant way. We learn from Genesis 6 that they found a way to entangle themselves in forbidden union with the daughters of men, giving rise to a hybrid progeny on this planet. They spawned a fearful seed; men of great size, cleverness, and evil arose, a race of giants of whom men like Goliath of Gath were later-day specimens. For this sin of corrupting the human seed, these angels are now imprisoned in Tartarus. God "delivered them into chains of darkness, to be reserved unto judgment" (v. 4). It was this rebellion that spurred on the judgment of the *flood*—an outpouring of wrath so severe that only eight human beings survived.

Peter reminds his readers, too, of *the days of Lot*, when man's wickedness called down *fire*. Again, wickedness rose like a flood, and again people abused the normal functions of the body. In the days of Noah, women were prominent in the abuse; in the days of Lot, men were prominent. In the days of Noah there was a demonic penetration of the human race; in the days of Lot there was a depraved perversion of the human race. Both times God acted in judgment. In the days of Noah He destroyed the polluted earth by the flood; in the days of Lot He destroyed the perverted cities with fire. It is quite evident from what Peter says and from what Jude says, in a parallel discussion of these things, that times of apostasy are always accompanied by abnormal wickedness in society—wickedness marked by outbursts of socially approved demonism and depravity. This is significant to us today because both these marks of apostasy are present in our society. There is a growing fascination with all kinds of occult phenomena, with people becoming interested in witchcraft, Satanism, and astrology. Ouija boards can be bought as a child's toy. Talk shows regularly feature soothsayers and fortune-tellers who operate under the more respectable name of psychics.

In step with that is the growing acceptance and social approval of the very sins of Sodom. Sins that once hid their face in shame, slunk down back alleys, and met the scorn and outrage of normal people are now socially acceptable. People who practice these abominations are allowed to teach our children; books featuring their perversions are openly on sale. They band together in mass demonstrations; they taunt clean-minded people. They put pressure on politicians to vote for laws legalizing their perverted lifestyle. And an ever-increasing majority of people take it all in their stride as something about which they can be tolerant.

This, then, is the theme of Peter's second great section in his letter. He warns urgently against the inroads of apostasy in the church.

What was even worse, the Christian community was accepting in friendship and fellowship the people who advocated these vile lifestyles. "They are foul spots and blots, playing their tricks at your very dinner tables" is the way Peter puts it, as rendered by J. B. Phillips (v. 13). Some texts render it slightly differently, using the word *agape* instead of *apate*. According to this rendering, these people were taking their place at the love-feasts of the church, which were a common prelude to the Lord's Supper. In other words, they were practicing communicants. They were being accepted as members of the Christian brotherhood—even while publicly practicing their abominations.

"Their eyes cannot look at a woman without lust," says Peter, "they captivate the unstable ones, and their technique of getting what they want is, through long practice, highly developed." He continues, "They are born under a curse, for they have abandoned the right road and wandered off to follow the old trail of Balaam . . . the man who had no objection to wickedness as long as he was paid for it" (vv. 14–15 PHILLIPS).

Peter now turns to this third great theme.

III. FAITH'S CONSUMMATION (3:1–18)

Peter says, Look out for the scoffers of the last days. "Knowing this first, that there shall come in the last days scoffers, walking after their own lusts" (v. 3).

Peter says of these end-time mockers that they will ridicule the second coming of Christ and they will do so out of utter ignorance. They will be ignorant of

God's ways. "Where is the promise of his coming?" they will say, "people have been talking about that since the very beginning. Nothing changes. It's the same now as it was from the very beginning" (see v. 4). They are ignorant, however, of God's Word. Things have not been the same from the beginning. For one thing, the flood brought about a major change in things. Peter keeps coming back to the flood; evidently it effected massive change.

We have those scoffers with us today who sneer, "Where is the promise of His coming?" In June 1982, the prestigious *Atlantic Monthly* devoted not only its featured article but also its front cover to ridiculing the second coming of Christ. The lead article was titled "Waiting for the End." The cover showed a fussy little man dressed in a poorly tailored blue suit, a Bible tucked under his arm, his finger pointing to his watch. Coming toward him was an army of giant locusts. The author of the article ridiculed names revered among us—D. L. Moody, John Nelson Darby, and Dr. Scofield. He displayed some basic knowledge of the teaching in fundamentalist circles about the second coming of Christ, but the whole tone of his article was one of ridicule. He made such statements as "only moderate imagination is required to identify Russia as Rosh." And, "news that various forms of 666 are prominently in use spreads through fundamentalist networks as rapidly as the false reports that worms are used in MacDonald's hamburgers." He held up evangelical scholarship to ridicule, evidently preferring the liberal schools of Harvard, Yale, Princeton, Chicago, and the German liberal schools.

The article ends, "Barring nuclear holocaust or some shift in Israel's status that would necessitate a drastic reconstruction of end-time scenarios, the current wave of apocalyptic interest will surely maintain its force at least through the 1980s and probably to the year 2000, the numerical properties of which will likely encourage still more millennial speculation. But if Jesus keeps on not coming, interest will eventually crest and recede to await the next promising configuration of signs."[1]

Well, there you have Mr. William Martin's folly, published and printed and circulated by an esteemed magazine. Incidentally, some of the names he ridiculed are names of great luster. When it comes to sheer scholarship, J. N. Darby, for instance, could lose men like Mr. Martin. J. N. Darby translated the Bible out of Hebrew and Greek into English, French, German, and Italian, no mean accomplishment in itself. And the Scofield Bible will be read by millions long after the *Atlantic Monthly* has ceased from publication. As for D. L. Moody—he is a noble example of the fact that God does not need human wisdom in order to accomplish His sublime purposes on earth.

Mockers! "Where is the promise of His coming?" After telling us to look out for *the scoffers* of the last days, Peter tells us to look out for *the sign* of the last days (3:10–13). And here we have an astonishing thing—an ignorant and unlearned man, an unschooled Galilean fisherman, telling us in accurate language of the coming of the nuclear age. Hardly what might be so-called "foolish preaching."

The words Peter uses are accurate words in the Greek of his day. He says, "The day of the Lord will come as a thief in the night; in the which the heavens shall pass away with a great noise, and the elements shall melt with fervent heat, the earth also and the works that are therein shall be burned . . . all these things shall be dissolved" (vv. 10–11). The word translated "elements" comes from a Greek word that carries with it the meaning of the letters of the alphabet. In physics today, it would convey the thought of the components into which matter is ultimately divided—atoms. The word translated "dissolved" literally means "to break up" or "to destroy" or "to melt." In several places in the New Testament it is translated "unloose." John the Baptist said he was not fit to "unloose" or untie the latchet of the shoes of Jesus.

The phrase "a great noise" signifies "with a rushing sound as of roaring flames." The expression "with fervent heat" comes from a Greek word denoting a fever—Peter's is the only known use of the word in connection with inanimate objects.

So, while Peter used nontechnical language, he was scientifically accurate in foretelling, as the great sign of the day of the Lord, the dawning of the nuclear age. The elementary, basic building blocks of the universe, the atoms, would be destroyed—melted—broken up—untied. This would be accompanied by a tremendous noise and with fervent, fever heat. When the first atomic bomb was dropped on August 5, 1945, over a doomed Japanese city, the whole world of believing men and women turned instinctively to Peter's prophecy of the day of the Lord.

Finally, Peter says, look out for *the slackness* of the last days. Having urged upon his readers the significance of these end-time events, telling them to invest in "all holy conversation and godliness" (v. 11), he urges them to be "diligent" (v. 14) and to "beware" (v. 17). He directs their attention to Paul's writings: "As also in all his epistles, speaking in them of these things; in which are some things hard to be understood, which they that are unlearned and unstable wrest, as they do also the other scriptures, unto their own destruction" (v. 16).

"Beware lest ye also . . . fall from your own steadfastness. But grow in grace, and in the knowledge of our Lord and Savior Jesus Christ. To him be glory both now and for ever. Amen" (vv. 17–18).

Thus ends Peter's second epistle—his last word before Nero's men found him and took him away to be crucified. Thus Peter was ushered into glory.

CHAPTER 26

1 JOHN

Back to Basics

J ohn spent his later years, before his arrest and deportation to Patmos, at Ephesus. The church there had been under attack from pagan, Gnostic, and Judaizing influences. Indeed, a wholesale defection from apostolic teaching is implied from Paul's last words to Timothy: "all they which are in Asia be turned away from me" (2 Tim. 1:15). Just before the outbreak of the Jewish war in A.D. 66, numbers of the more progressive Jewish Christians left Palestine and settled in Asia Minor. Philip the evangelist and his daughters are believed to have settled in Hierapolis, and the apostle John came to Ephesus. What an addition he must have been to the Ephesian church and to the other churches in the area! How his ministry, his presence, his testimony, and his teaching must have been sought after by all those who still loved the Lord in spirit and in truth!

The Neronic persecutions ended in A.D. 68, by which time Peter and Paul were dead. Jerusalem fell in A.D. 70. There follows a quarter century of silence, broken in the last decade of the century by the writings of John. During this time, heresy took fresh root. The philosophy of Philo, which had so greatly influenced Jewish thought, spilled over into Christian thought with just as disastrous results. Gnosticism became more defined and more of a threat to the church. Large numbers of professing Christians, wanting to be in step with the times, abandoned simple apostolic teaching in favor of the new, supposedly intellectual ideas. John wrote to give the lie to these subtle and dangerous heretical ideas. Confrontation with pagan philosophy and Jewish legalism, so common in the Pauline epistles, becomes in John's writing confrontation with a more ominous and sinister entity— the world.

We know a great deal about John. His family residence, in his youth, was Bethsaida on the lake of Galilee. His brother was James, the first of the apostles to be martyred. His father was a prosperous fisherman. Jesus was related to John, who was his cousin—Mary and John's mother were sisters. He was one of the first disciples to be called, and he was the last to die. In temperament he was passionate (Jesus once called him and his brother "sons of thunder"); yet he was retiring, contemplative, and mystical.

John's writing style is a mixture of simplicity and complexity; it is both poetic and pragmatic. He picks up a word or a thought, then puts it down, only to pick it up again. His great words are *light, life,* and *love.* He does not argue. He simply makes forceful statements and leaves it at that. He knows no shades of gray. Things are either right or wrong, true or false, good or bad, black or white. His epistle is awkward to analyze because of his habit of jumping from this thought to that one and back again. Even a comprehensive analysis, such as the one that follows, is vaguely unsatisfactory, for we get the feeling that John would have recognized no such analysis at all!

Various themes run through this letter. John gives four reasons for writing: that we may enjoy fellowship with God and His Son (1:3); that our (his readers') joy might be full (1:4); that we may not sin (2:1); that we may know for sure that we have eternal life (5:13).

He gives six tests whereby we can know that we are born of God: the test of spiritual deportment (2:29); the test of spiritual desires (3:9); the test of spiritual disposition (4:7); the test of spiritual discernment (5:1); the test of spiritual deliverance (5:4); and the test of spiritual dominion (5:18).

In the opening chapters we note the repeated statement "if we say" or "he that saith." Also we note the repeated statement "I write" or "I have written."

We are impressed, too, with the number of things we know. Over two dozen times John puts before us the things we *know* in grand contrast with the speculations of the cults.

John's remedy for the widespread apostasy of his day was to take his readers back to the beginning. He refers to the past again and again with emphasis on Christ's life and death.

I. Living in God's Light (1:1–2:29)
   A. Communion with God Observed (1:1–2:2)
      1. Its Beginning (1:1–4)
      2. Its Basis (1:5–2:2)
         a. A Fact (1:5)
         b. A Formula (1:6–10)
         c. A Fundamental (2:1–2)

B. Commandments of God Obeyed (2:3–11)
   1. The Lord and His Person (2:3–6)
   2. The Lord and His Precept (2:7–8)
   3. The Lord and His People (2:9–11)
C. Commendation from God Obtained (2:12–29)
   1. The Family (2:12–14)
   2. The Foe (2:15–23)
      a. A Forbidden Sphere (2:15–17)
      b. A False Spirit (2:18–23)
   3. The Facts (2:24–29)
      a. Living in Him (2:24–25)
      b. Learning of Him (2:26–27)
      c. Looking for Him (2:28–29)
II. Living by God's Love (3:1–4:21)
   A. Love That Is Pure (3:1–10)
      1. Our High Calling as Sons (3:1–3)
      2. Our Holy Conduct as Saints (3:4–10)
         a. As to Our State (3:4–5)
         b. As to Our Standing (3:6–10)
   B. Love That Is Practical (3:11–24)
      1. The Truth of That Love (3:11–13)
      2. The Test of That Love (3:14–18)
      3. The Tenderness of That Love (3:19–22)
      4. The Triumph of That Love (3:23–24)
   C. Love That Is Perfect (4:1–21)
      1. A Serious Warning (4:1–6)
         a. A Wicked Spirit (4:1–4)
         b. A Worldly Spirit (4:5–6)
      2. A Spiritual Walk (4:7–21)
         a. Divine Love (4:7–10)
            (1) Its Overflow (4:7–8)
            (2) Its Object (4:9–10)
         b. Duplicated Love (4:11–21)
            (1) Its Cause (4:11–13)
            (2) Its Confession (4:14–16)
            (3) Its Consequence (4:17–19)
            (4) Its Counterfeit (4:20–21)
III. Living with God's Life (5:1–21)
   A. The Life Received (5:1–5)
      1. The Child of God (5:1–2)

    a. Knowing We Love God Personally (5:1)
    b. Knowing We Love God's People (5:2)
  2. The Challenge of God (5:3–5)
    a. Obeying the Word (5:3)
    b. Overcoming the World (5:4–5)
B. The Life Recorded (5:6–13)
  1. The Witness of the Spirit to the Son (5:6–8)
  2. The Witness of the Spirit to the Saint (5:9–10a)
  3. The Witness of the Spirit to the Scripture (5:10b–13)
    a. What John Wrote (5:10b–12)
    b. Why John Wrote (5:13)
C. The Life Revealed (5:14–21)
  1. In a Bold Way (5:14–15)
  2. In a Brotherly Way (5:16–17)
  3. In a Behavioral Way (5:18–19)
  4. In a Believing Way (5:20–21)
    a. Affirming the Truth (5:20)
    b. Avoiding the Trap (5:21)

I. Living in God's Light (1:1–2:29)

A. Communion with God Observed (1:1–2:2)

The *beginning* of living in the full blaze of God's unsullied light is historical (1:1–4)—it begins with Christ, the One who had dwelled in that light from all eternity and who was incarnated at Bethlehem. In his opening statement John plunges right into the Gnostic controversy. He, who was there, the last of the living disciples of Jesus, the one unimpeachable witness, declares "we saw Him, we studied Him, we handled Him. He was a real human being" (see vv. 1–2). In John's *gospel* he emphasizes the essential deity of Jesus; in his first *epistle* he emphasizes His essential humanity. To the fine-spun philosophies of the cultists, John brings the church back to basics. "Nonsense!" he says in effect, in refuting the cultists. "Of course He was real! I was there! I know!"

The *basis* of living in that light is forgiveness (1:5–2:2). God is of "purer eyes than to behold . . . iniquity" (Hab. 1:13), so sin in our lives has to be dealt with to His satisfaction. We cannot live in light and darkness at the same time. There is no twilight zone. Some of the false teachers were claiming that they had attained a state of sinless perfection; John bluntly calls them liars. The answer to sin is "the blood of Jesus Christ [God's] Son" (1:7). If we confess our sin He is "faithful and just" (v. 9) to forgive and cleanse. More! While we can never say that we have reached the place where we are *not able* to sin, we can certainly say that we are *able not* to sin.

But, if we do sin, then we not only have the vicarious death of Christ to maintain our forgiveness by God, but we also have the victorious life of Christ to maintain our fellowship with God—for "we have an advocate with the Father, Jesus Christ the righteous" (2:1). How much better that is than philosophical speculation and self delusion! In this section John begins the telling use of his formula "If we say." What we say is of no value if it runs contrary to what God has to say.

B. Commandments of God Obeyed (2:3–11)

First there is *the Lord's person* to be considered (2:3–6). The statement "I know Him" (2:4) must be backed by the proof of which He would approve. If I know Him I will want to be like Him.

John says, practically enough, "He that saith he abideth in him ought himself also so to walk, even as he walked" (2:6).

Next is *the Lord's precept* to be considered (2:7–8). The one commandment Jesus handed on to us, and which He exemplified in His life, was love—"no new commandment" indeed (v. 7). If we love as He loved, it will prove that "the darkness is past, and the true light now shineth" (v. 8).

Moreover, there are *the Lord's people* to be considered (2:9–11). "He that saith he is in the light, and hateth his brother, is in darkness even until now" (v. 9).

C. Commendation from God Obtained (2:19–29)

Evidence that we are living in God's light will be forthcoming in our relationship to *the family*—whether we are "little children" "fathers," or "young men" (2:12–14). All stages of spiritual growth, maturity, and ability are considered. Each has its own share of blessing and grace and its own responsibility. In connection with "fathers" it is the knowledge of *Christ* that predominates; with the "young men" it is love of the *Father*; with the "little children" it is the *Holy Spirit*. Thus God's commendation of our lives as believers results from the work of each member of the Godhead in our lives.

But John has something to say about *the foe* (2:15–23). The believer must beware of the world, the inveterate foe of God. The world is the Devil's lair for sinners and his lure for saints. It is defined by John as "the lust of the flesh, and the lust of the eyes, and the pride of life" (v. 16). This foe is already defeated and its power to deceive and enslave is only temporary. It will one day pass away, but those who "doeth the will of God" (v. 17a), who have obtained God's commendation, "will abide forever" (see v. 17b).

John warns, too, against what he calls "the antichrist," in this case the false teachers who were denying the true nature of the Lord Jesus Christ. Most likely John had in mind the heretic Cerinthus, who was prominent in the church about this time and whose teachings might well have prompted this letter.

Cerinthus taught the standard Gnostic nonsense about matter being evil and about various aeons and emanations that supposedly interposed between God and matter. Cerinthus further taught that Jesus was the ordinary son of Joseph and Mary. He claimed that the aeon Christ came upon this man Jesus at the time of His baptism, that it enabled Him to perform His miracles, that it left Him just before His crucifixion so that it was just a mere man, Jesus, who suffered on the cross, since an aeon was a spirit being incapable of suffering.

John says that genuine believers should not be deceived by such unfounded speculations. We have "an unction [an anointing] from the Holy One" enabling us to know the truth of the matter, to "know all things" (v. 20). The cultists had speculation; we have knowledge. As for the false teachers, John simply calls them liars. He said, "Who is a liar but he that denieth that Jesus is the Christ? He is antichrist, that denieth the Father and the Son" (v. 22).

John then comes back to *the facts* (2:24–29). The life that wins God's commendation is the one that maintains a threefold relationship to Christ—*living* in Him, *learning* of Him, and *looking* for Him. It is a question of abiding in Christ "that, when he shall appear, we may have confidence, and not be ashamed before him at his coming" (v. 28).

II. Living by God's Love (3:1–4:21)

John now comes to the second great word in his basic vocabulary. He has used it before in illustrating the significance of light; now he picks it up for emphasis—the word is *love*. He begins the section with a magnificent statement concerning our place in the royal family of heaven.

A. Love That Is Pure (3:1–10)

"Behold, what manner of love the Father *hath bestowed* upon us, that we should be called the sons of God" (v. 1, that has to do with the past); "beloved, now are we the sons of God" (v. 2a, that has to do with the present); "it doth not yet appear what we shall be: but we know that, when he shall appear, we *shall be* like him; for we shall see him as he is" (v. 2b, that has to do with the future). John adds, "And every man that hath this hope in him purifieth himself, even as he is pure" (v. 3). Such is our *high calling* as sons.

This purifying, however, has to be worked out in our *holy conduct* as saints (3:4–10). Here again we have one of John's uncompromising statements concerning sin: "He that committeth sin is of the devil" (v. 8a) balanced by "the Son of God was manifested, that he might destroy the works of the devil" (v. 8b). Then, "whosoever is born of God doth not commit sin" with the explanation, "for his seed remaineth in him" (v. 9). The old nature is incapable of holy conduct; the new nature in incapable of unholy conduct.

B. Love That Is Practical (3:11–24)

John draws our attention to the death of Christ for us. "Hereby perceive we the love of God, because he laid down his life for us: and we ought to lay down our lives for the brethren" (v. 16). If a man has plenty of this world's goods, says John, and sees his brother in need, and does nothing about it—how can God's love dwell in that man? "My little children, let us not love in word, neither in tongue; but in deed and in truth" (v. 18). Talk, after all, is cheap.

C. Love That Is Perfect (4:1–21)

God's love in this world is under constant attack by the Evil One. So John begins this section with *a serious warning* (4:1–6). This section places considerable emphasis on the world, the inveterate foe of God and His children. The section begins with a double warning—against *wicked spirits* and against having a *worldly spirit*.

The believer is warned emphatically not to believe every spirit (4:1–4). He is to try the spirits. Every spirit that confesses that Jesus Christ is come in the flesh is of God; every spirit that makes not this confession is not of God. It is the spirit of antichrist. Cerinthus manifested the spirit of antichrist by denying that Jesus Christ was a true human being.

The warning has a special application today in face of the claims of many to speak in tongues and to prophesy in the Spirit. These people are very foolish to take their utterances as coming from the Holy Spirit without testing the spirit speaking to see if it is indeed of God.

When the modern tongues movement broke out first, about a century ago, it was known as Irvingism after its chief proponent. D. M. Panton[1] in his *Present Day Pamphlets* studied the movement, its errors and its excesses, its claims and its dangers, and tells what happened when people like himself did go to the meetings of the Irvingites and challenged the spirits when people were speaking in tongues. That they spoke in tongues was not denied, but the source of their inspiration, then as now, was more than highly suspect.

It was discovered, for instance, that often the test question, "Do you confess that Jesus Christ is come in the flesh?" was ignored. Sometimes the controlling spirit made some statement that was true but that was not an answer to the question. Sometimes, when the soul of the person making the utterance was filled with ecstasy, an emotion was substituted for an answer. If the outside challenger persisted in seeking an answer to the question from the controlling spirit, it would withdraw into the background, push forward the Christian, and allow him to answer the question himself. All these methods of avoiding the test betray the presence of a deceiving spirit.

John follows this up with a warning against having *a worldly spirit* (4:5–6).

Those who embrace cultic teachings, John says, are "of the world" (v. 5). They may be able to produce some spectacular phenomena and collect a following, but "greater is he that is in you, than he that is in the world" (v. 4). John contrasts "the spirit of truth, and the spirit of error" (v. 6). The test of truth is apostolic doctrine—those who hold to it are "of God"; those who set it aside are "not of God."

This serious warning is followed by more instruction regarding *our spiritual walk* (4:7–21) and a fresh emphasis on the importance of love. John sets before us again *divine love* (4:7–10). "In this was manifested the love of God toward us, because that God sent his only begotten Son into the world, that we might live through him" (v. 9). He adds, "Herein is love, not that we loved God, but that he loved us, and sent his Son to be the propitiation for our sins" (v. 10).

That divine love is to become *duplicated love* (4:11–21) as it is reproduced in us. "Beloved," John begins, "if God so loved us, we ought also to love one another" (v. 11). The passage is full of practical assertions such as "God is love" (v. 16); "as he is, so are we in this world" (v. 17, an absolutely marvelous summary of Christian life and behavior in nine small monosyllables); "perfect love casteth out fear" (v. 18); "we love him, because he first loved us" (v. 19); "if a man say, I love God, and hateth his brother, he is a liar: for he that loveth not his brother whom he hath seen, how can he love God whom he hath not seen?" (v. 20).

III. Living with God's Life (5:1–21)

A. The Life Received (5:1–5)
This new life begins with a new birth—"Whosoever believeth that Jesus is the Christ is born of God" (v. 1). One of the evidences of this new life is a disposition to keep God's commandments because our heavenly Father's commandments are not grievous. Moreover, this new life expresses itself in victory over the world.

B. The Life Recorded (5:6–13)
There is a threefold witness of the Holy Spirit experienced by all who have this life of God within them. *He witnesses to the Son* (5:6–8). "This is he that came by water and blood, even Jesus Christ; not by water only, but by water and blood. And it is the Spirit that beareth witness, because the Spirit is truth. For there are three that bear record . . . the spirit, and the water, and the blood: and these three agree in one" (vv. 6–8).

This is an important statement in view of the heresy of Cerinthus. The statement of John reminds us that blood and water flowed from the Savior's riven side (John 19:34) when His dead body was rent by the soldier's spear—proof positive of the Lord's genuine humanity and His real death. But there is more. The order here is different—water and blood. Cerinthus taught that the aeon Christ, a spirit being, came down upon the man Jesus at His baptism (the water) but left Him before He died. The Christ Spirit, that is, came through *water* baptism but not through *blood*. "Nonsense!" says John, the eyewitness. "He came not only by water but with water *and* blood, *and* the Spirit bears witness to this." In other words, the One who died on the cross was as much the Christ, the incarnate Son of God, as the One who was baptized in Jordan. All this is reinforced by the threefold witness of the water, the blood, and the Spirit, "and a threefold cord is not quickly broken" (Eccl. 4:12). Three witnesses were required under Mosaic Law for full confirmation of affirmation. Moreover, John's affirmation is reinforced by the deliberate use of the polysyndeton, which reveals itself in our text by the repetition of the word *and* (a common literary device in the Bible for drawing attention to, and placing special emphasis on, each and every statement in the sequence). So much for Cerinthus, his teaching, and those who would resurrect his heresy again. The word of one credible and trustworthy eyewitness is worth more than any amount of philosophical word juggling by some later-day idea peddler.

The Spirit also *witnesses to the saints* (5:9–10a). "If we receive the witness of men, the witness of God is greater: for this is the witness of God which he hath testified of his Son. He that believeth on the Son of God hath the witness in himself" (vv. 9–10). The Holy Spirit has His own way of confirming divine truth in the hearts of God's believing saints. There is an inner confirmation to that which rings true, given by the Holy Spirit directly to our spiritual understanding. We have that inner witness, too, when something wrong is being proposed as truth. We may not be able to put our finger on the error but we have that instinctive sense of disquiet.

The Spirit *witnesses to the Scriptures* (5:10b–13). "He that believeth not God hath made him a liar; because he believeth not the *record* that God gave of his Son. . . . These things have I *written* unto you that believe on the name of the Son of God." We have not only subjective inner confirmation of God's truth, but also the objective revelation of truth in "the record" in God's revealed and recorded Word. Not to believe God's own record to His Son is to make Him a liar—it would be hard to think of a greater sin.

C. The Life Revealed (5:14–21)

John's closing remarks are down-to-earth. The new life we have in Christ, if genuine at all, will express itself in *a bold way.* "This is the confidence that we have in him, that, if we ask any thing according to his will, he heareth us: And . . . we have the petitions that we desired of him" (5:14–15). The life of the Lord Jesus is so reproduced in us that we can walk in such close fellowship with God that our prayers and His purposes go hand in hand.

It will express itself in *a brotherly way* (vv. 16–17). John urges us to pray for our fellow believers we see falling into sin—with one exception: those who are guilty of a "sin unto death." Several examples of such sins are found in the New Testament (Acts 5:1–11; 1 Cor. 5:5; 11:30). In the light of the repeated warnings in this particular epistle against *apostasy*, it is likely that this was the "sin unto death" John had in mind. We are not to pray for false teachers who have the spirit of the antichrist (2:18–23) and who have so repudiated the known truth of God that it is "impossible to renew them to repentance" (see Heb. 6:4–8).

It will express itself in *a behavioral way* (5:18–19). Again we have one of John's warnings against wickedness and worldliness, and an admonition to overcome sin and Satan in our lives.

Finally, it will express itself in *a believing way* (5:20–21). We note again here John's repeated use of the word *know* and his threefold emphasis on the word *true*. "We *know* that the Son of God is come." The heretics knew nothing. "We *know* Him that is *true*." John cannot seem to say it too often—"Jesus is the Son of God. The Man of Calvary is God's Son, Jesus Christ."

His very last word is one of warning. Having again and again underlined what is true, he leaves us face-to-face with the trap—"Little children, keep yourselves from idols." And an idol may be not only a molten one or a monetary one, it can be a mental one. The teaching of the heretics was a form of idolatry in which human thinking was elevated above God's Word. Whatever form it may take, we must keep ourselves from enthroning anything in the heart and life that takes the place of God and "His Son, Jesus Christ."

CHAPTER 27

2 AND 3 JOHN

A Pair of Postscripts

These two letters are quite evidently a couple of appendices to John's first letter. No new teaching is introduced, but in 2 John the danger of anti-Christian teaching taking hold among God's people is stressed. The writer remains anonymous as in John's other letters and his gospel, writing under the title of "the Elder." The recipients of John's letters, of course, would have no trouble recognizing the writer. The title does not necessarily signify old age, although John was indeed a very old man when he wrote. The title rather indicates spiritual position and that his knowledge of the gospel went back so very much further than his present contemporaries. For this reason he called them "little children."

2 JOHN

It is possible that this letter was written from Ephesus, but we have no certain knowledge as to its exact date and place of origin. Opinions differ as to whether this letter was addressed to a church or to an individual.

I. A Word of Commendation (vv. 1–4)
  A. The Lady as a Person (v. 1a)
  B. The Lady as a Partner (vv. 1b–3)
    1. In the Truth of the Gospel (vv. 1b–2)
    2. In the Triumph of the Gospel (v. 3)
  C. The Lady as a Parent (v. 4)
II. A Word of Command (vv. 5–6)
  A. Love Demanded (v. 5)
  B. Love Defined (v. 6)

III. A Word of Caution (vv. 7–11)
    A. Danger from the Deceiver (vv. 7–8)
        1. How to Recognize Him (v. 7)
        2. How to Regard Him (v. 8)
            a. As a Threat (v. 8a)
            b. As a Thief (v. 8b)
    B. Danger to the Doctrine (v. 9)
        1. Those Who Abandon the Truth (v. 9a)
        2. Those Who Abide in the Truth (v. 9b)
    C. Danger at the Door (vv. 10–11)
        1. Refuse the Apostate Your Hospitality When He Comes (v. 10a)
        2. Refuse the Apostate Your Handshake When He Goes (vv. 10b–11)
IV. A Word of Conclusion (vv. 12–13)
    A. What John Expected in the Future (v. 12)
    B. What John Extended to His Friends (v. 13)

We do not know why the writer of this letter keeps his own identity anonymous (though we can have little doubt that John wrote it) or why he keeps the name of the addressee anonymous, as well as the identity of her sister and her children. The suggestion has been made that the disclosure might have provoked some kind of persecution.

I. A WORD OF COMMENDATION (vv. 1–4)

Efforts have been made to identify the lady to whom John addressed this brief memo. The immediate occasion was his recent pleasant encounter with some of her children. John addresses her as "the elect lady." Some have tried to extract her name from the Greek *eklektē kyria*, which can be rendered "elect Kyria" or even "the lady Electa." The speculation is inconclusive.[1]

If indeed the letter is addressed to a lady, this is the only book in the Bible so addressed. We are impressed, too, with the apostle's restraint. He uses the term "beloved" when writing to a church or to a man but he uses no such familiarity in addressing a woman, not even when writing to a sister in Christ.

Just the same, John does not deny the bond that exists between him and this lady "whom I love in the truth," he says (v. 1). It is the truth of God that binds together all those who love the Lord. More! He was delighted, having met some of her children, to know that they, too, were as zealous for the truth as she was. He commends her for being such a faithful parent.

II. A WORD OF COMMAND (vv. 5–6)

John repeats, in abbreviated form, similar thoughts to those expressed in his first epistle. John was delighted to find some members of the Christian community still seeking to live by that one great word of command given by the Lord Jesus—that we love one another. For

> Love never faileth
> Love is pure gold.
> Love is what Jesus
> Came to unfold.

In his first epistle, John reiterated the same command (2:7–8); he used the word four times in one passage. Love without obedience is sentiment; obedience without love is servitude.

III. A WORD OF CAUTION (vv. 7–11)

John has a threefold word of caution. There was danger abroad—danger first *from the deceiver* (vv. 7–8). This repeats the warning against "many antichrists" John had already given in his first general epistle (1 John 2:18–24; 4:1–6). Dangerous heretics were abroad, and these deceivers were striking at the very roots of Christianity. Although this unknown Christian lady was a stalwart for the truth, and had brought up her children in a way that won the warm commendation of the aged apostle John, he still felt the need to warn her, and all like her, especially women, to be on guard against these subtle deceivers.

There was also *danger to the doctrine* (v. 9). John warns his friend against those who transgress (the word used literally means "to go onward"), a sarcastic reference to those who claimed to have advanced knowledge. The false teacher invariably pretends to have some new teaching—something that goes beyond what the Bible teaches. These false claims are one of the marks of an apostate. There is nothing beyond; the claims of the cultists are false.

There was *danger at the door* (vv. 10–11). John bluntly warns this lady not to receive such a teacher into her house. Perhaps this is one reason why this particular letter is in the New Testament. A lady naturally tries to avoid being rude, and it would seem the height of bad manners not even to invite into the home someone who came to the house claiming to be a believer, even a preacher. John says she is to let prudence take precedence over politeness. It is good advice. It is a favorite practice of cultists, to this day, to try, literally, to get a foot in the door. John adds that, if she were to accidentally make a mistake and have one of these deceivers in her house, as soon as she detects the mistake she is to send him on his way and not to wish him a good day. To knowingly receive a false teacher, to extend him hospitality, to send him on his way with a Christian farewell is to give him a measure of credibility with others and to become a partner in his evil deeds.

IV. A Word of Conclusion (vv. 12–13)

John had much more to say, but much of it he had already said in his gospel and first epistle. He forebears to write more, having said enough to give this urgent warning to his friend. That warning was intended to show that combating and discouraging false teaching regarding the person of Christ is as much an individual responsibility as it is the corporate responsibility of the church.

John's last word assures this lady that he hopes to see her soon, and conveys greetings from some of her sister's children who, evidently, were in the same place John was when he wrote.

Thus ends a brief but pointed little memo on personal responsibility in the matter of faith and family alike.

3 John

Similarities and contrasts can be pointed out between John's last two letters. The second letter was sent to a woman, the third to a man; the second urges against receiving false messengers, the third warns against rejecting true messengers; anonymity marks the second letter, naming of individuals highlights the third; the second letter warns against being too soft, the third against being too hard; one warns against the deceiver, the other against the dictator.

These last two letters of John are very touching. We get a picture of the aged apostle, concerned about the inroads of apostasy in the church, writing his impassioned first epistle. He adds a postscript, then another. Brevity is the hallmark of all three letters. In the first there are about 2,350 words, in the second only 245, in the third fewer still, a bare 219—only a few more than 2,800 words in all. We get a picture in this of John's feeling for the desperate urgency of the situation. He puts down his pen, picks it up again, puts it down again, picks it up again, and puts it down a third time. He is the last of the apostles, he is old, the times are uncertain; Nero has gone but Domitian will soon pick up Nero's policy of persecution; error is abroad, tares are growing profusely, springing up everywhere among the wheat; Christians are squabbling.

So John writes and writes and writes. His last two letters are mere memos, but the Holy Spirit urged him to write them, breathed into them, saw to it that they were preserved, brought them into the divine library, added them to the Book as almost His very last word. We should certainly not make the mistake of underestimating their importance simply because they are brief. In the things of God, as we learn from the so-called "minor" prophets, it is a mistake to measure the man by the size of his manuscript; the Holy Spirit does not always inspire long books in order to convey vital beliefs. Weighty things can often be stated in a few dynamic words—"I love you," for instance, or "Don't touch," or "Exit," or "Help!" We certainly don't expect a drowning man to express his urgent need in flowery paragraphs.

I. The Virtuous Pastor (vv. 1–4)
   A. John's Devotion to Him (v. 1)
   B. John's Desire for Him (v. 2)
   C. John's Delight in Him (vv. 3–4)
      Because of:
      1. The Reputation Gaius Had (v. 3)
      2. The Relationship Gaius Had (v. 4)
II. The Visiting Preacher (vv. 5–8)
   A. Recognizing Him (v. 5)
   B. Refreshing Him (vv. 6–7)
      1. A Privilege Extended (v. 6)
      2. A Principle Extolled (v. 7)
   C. Receiving Him (v. 8)
III. The Vainglorious Pope (vv. 9–11)
   A. His Pride (v. 9)
   B. His Presumption (v. 10a)
   C. His Practice (vv. 10b–11)
      1. Condemned (v. 10b)
      2. Contrasted (v. 11)
IV. The Valued Partner (v. 12)
V. The Vigilant Presbyter (vv. 13–14)
   A. He Had So Much to Say (v. 13)
   B. He Was Coming That Way (v. 14)

We learn from both of John's last two letters that because of his age he was reluctant to sit down and write letters, but he was still able to get around. This last letter of his is addressed to a man named Gaius.

I. The Virtuous Pastor (vv. 1–4)

Gaius was evidently a person of some prominence in the local church where he resided. He was a man with a pastor's heart, a true shepherd of the sheep—in glaring contrast with the man in the church who fought for position and authority.

John begins the letter by telling of his *devotion to Gaius*: "the wellbeloved Gaius, whom I love in the truth" (v. 1). The name Gaius was common enough in the Roman world. F. F. Bruce says it was one of a dozen and a half names from which Roman parents could choose a *praenomen* for one of their sons.[2] We meet the name several times in the New Testament besides here. There was a Gaius of Corinth (Rom. 16:23; 1 Cor. 1:14), who was Paul's host when he was in that city and who sent greetings to the church at Rome. He was one of the few people Paul baptized in person. There was a man of Macedonia by the name of Gaius, who was with Paul at Ephesus (Acts 19:29) at the time of the Ephesian riot. There was a Gaius of Derbe (Acts 20:4), who was Paul's traveling companion when, after the Ephesus riot, Paul made his way to Jerusalem. Some think that "Derbe" should read "Doberus" and that the last two named are the same individual. We have no way of knowing whether the Gaius addressed by John was one of these, but it could well be. In any case, he was a man much loved by the aged apostle John.

Next we note John's *desire for Gaius*. He desired that "thou mayest prosper and be in health, even as thy soul prospereth" (v. 2). A good prayer! Many of us would have to put the prayer the other way around—that we might be just as prosperous spiritually as we are physically.

Then comes John's *delight in Gaius* (vv. 3–4). Gaius had a widespread reputation for faithfulness to the truth, both in creed and conduct. John says, "I have no greater joy than to hear that my children walk in truth" (v. 4), which some have seen to be a reference to John's leading Gaius to the Lord. W. E. Vine points out the emphasis on the word *my* and renders the phrase "my own children" to indicate that John was referring to people he himself had led to Christ.[3]

II. THE VISITING PREACHER (vv. 5–8)

John had felt it necessary to warn the "elect lady" against taking visiting preachers at face value. By contrast, he commends Gaius for his hospitality to visiting preachers, genuine servants of the Lord. The church to which Gaius belonged was influenced by Diotrephes, who for his own selfish reasons refused to receive itinerant ministers of the Word. Gaius had risked the menacing displeasure of Diotrephes in order to be a help and blessing to the Lord's servants. It was, and is, a Christian duty to extend hospitality and help to such. These believers had gone forth "taking nothing of the Gentiles" and they did it trusting the Lord to meet their needs "for his name's sake" (v. 7). What a rebuke to those today who shamelessly beg all and sundry, saint and sinner alike, to support their work and their programs! As if the Lord needed or wanted His work to be financed by the unsaved! John underlines the responsibility of the Lord's people and the local church to receive and support those who are engaged in full-time Christian work.

IV. THE VAINGLORIOUS POPE (vv. 9–11)

In contrast with Gaius is Diotrephes, who had usurped the position of a kind of monarchical episcopate, a lord over the local church, a tyrannical ecclesiastical despot. This man had assumed such power that he could repudiate the authority of the oldest and last surviving apostle of the Lord Jesus. He had the power to suppress a letter that John had previously written to the church. He refused to receive traveling preachers and was able to browbeat others into compliance with his views, excommunicating those who opposed him.

John denounces his pride and presumption and what he calls his "prating"—the word used simply means "to talk nonsense" (v. 10). But his nonsense was malicious nonsense, and he had assumed the power to enforce it. John warned Diotrephes that he would deal with him when he came that way. It is interesting to compare Paul's "if I come" (2 Cor. 13:2) with John's "if I come" (v. 10). John, as it were, held the rod over Diotrephes but did not say what he would do to him. The coming of Paul and the coming of John perhaps illustrate the coming of the Lord, when all will get what they deserve. John urged his friend Gaius not to be influenced by the spirit of Diotrephes.

The spirit and ambition of Diotrephes may have received a temporary check by John's letter, but it soon took root and flourished and developed in later centuries into clericalism and papal power.

IV. The Valued Partner (v. 12)

Demetrius was possibly the brother who carried this letter to its destination and who delivered it in such a way Diotrephes could not get his hands on it and destroy it. John commends him to Gaius. He tells Gaius he can trust Demetrius, who had a threefold witness to his character. He had "good report of all men, and of the truth itself; yea, and we also bear record; and ye know that our record is true." Gaius, it seems, did not know Demetrius, but he was just the kind of man Diotrephes would have refused to receive.

V. The Vigilant Presbyter (vv. 13–14)

Thus John brings his letter to a close. He had introduced himself to Gaius as "the elder" (*presbyteros*). Throughout this brief memo breathes the spirit of a man who was a true presbyter, a true elder, a true under-shepherd of the flock of God. His concluding remarks underline his continuing care. He is saying, "I have many things to say, but I won't write any more just now. I hope to see you soon, and then we'll talk face to face. In the meantime, peace be with you. The 'friends' salute you. Greet the friends by name."

That expression "by name," Vine reminds us, occurs only one place elsewhere in the New Testament—in John 10:3, where the Lord says He calls His own sheep by name. John perhaps was conscious that he, himself, was acting as a true shepherd of the sheep in writing this, his last letter. The shepherd's cloak has now been handed on to us.

CHAPTER 28

JUDE

Apostasy Unmasked

The epistle of Jude was written by the "brother of James." The question is raised as to which of the two men by the name of Jude (Judas) was the author of this epistle. Besides Judas Iscariot, there was another apostle Jude of whom little is known. He is sometimes identified with Lebbeus and with Thaddaeus (Matt. 10:3; Mark 3:18), and his words are recorded in the Bible only once. When the Lord was talking to His disciples just before going out to His betrayal, Jude asked, "Lord, how is it that thou wilt manifest thyself unto us, and not unto the world?" (John 14:22).

The other Jude known in the New Testament was one of the brethren of the Lord Jesus (Matt. 13:55; Mark 6:3). Like the others, he remained an unbeliever during the Lord's lifetime (John 7:5), but afterward joined the company of disciples (Acts 1:14).

Hegesippus, sometimes called the father of church history (he lived about the middle of the second century) tells a story about Jude, which has been preserved for us by Eusebius. It is of sufficient interest to be included here. He says,

> There were yet living of the family of our Lord, the grandchildren of Judas, called the brother of our Lord according to the flesh. These were reported as being of the family of David, and were brought to Domitian by the Evocatus. For this emperor was as much alarmed at the appearance of Christ as Herod. He put the question whether they were of David's race, and they confessed that they were. He then asked them what property they had, or how much money they owned. And both of them answered that they had between them only nine thousand denarii, and this they

had not in silver, but in the value of a piece of land containing only thirty-nine acres, from which they raised their taxes, and supported themselves by their own labor. Then they also began to show their hands, exhibiting the hardness of their bodies, and the callosity formed by incessant labor on their hands, as evidence of their own labor. When asked, also, respecting Christ and His Kingdom, what was its nature, and when and where it was to appear, they replied "that it was not a temporal nor an earthly kingdom, but celestial and angelic; that it would appear at the end of the world when, coming in glory, He would judge the quick and dead, and give to every one according to his works." Upon which Domitian, despising them, made no reply; but treating them with contempt, as simpletons, commanded them to be dismissed, and by a decree ordered the persecution to cease. Thus delivered, they ruled the churches, both as witnesses and relatives of the Lord. When peace was established, they continued living even to the times of Trajan.[1]

As Domitian reigned from A.D. 81 to 96, this passage helps us determine the limit of Jude's life.

Probably it was this Jude, the full brother of James (author of the epistle that bears his name), and the half-brother of the Lord Jesus, who authored this little memo on apostasy. If the author were the other Jude, the apostle, it is difficult to see why he should have appealed to his relationship with James rather than to his own apostleship. But as "the brother of James" he established his status, for James was the well-known head of the Jerusalem church. He does not appeal to his own relationship to the Lord, for the resurrection changed all natural ties.

The likelihood is that he wrote from Palestine. The strong Jewish character of the book indicates it was written primarily for Hebrew Christians. Its strong resemblance to parts of 2 Peter do not help us, for we cannot prove that one borrowed from the other nor, if such was the case, which epistle came first. The most probable conclusion is that this letter was composed before A.D. 70.

I. Introduction (vv. 1–4)
   A. His Salutation (vv. 1–2)
   B. His Subject (vv. 3–4)
      1. Chosen (v. 3a)
      2. Changed (vv. 3b–4)
II. Confronting the Apostasy of the Church (vv. 5–13)
   A. How Apostasy Affects Morality (vv. 5–10)

      1. The Pilgrim Age: False Disciples (v. 5)
      2. The Primeval Age: Fallen Dominions (v. 6)
      3. The Patriarchal Age: Fearful Degradation (v. 7)
      4. The Pentecostal Age: Filthy Dreamers (vv. 8–10)
        a. Their Behavior (v. 8a)
        b. Their Brazenness (v. v8b–10)
    B. How Apostasy Affects Mentality (vv. 11–13)
      1. The Men Involved (v. 11)
        a. Cain: Attacking the Salvation of God (v. 11a)
        b. Balaam: Attacking the Sovereignty of God (v. 11b)
        c. Core: Attacking the Servants of God (v. 11c)
      2. The Mistake Involved (vv. 12–13)
  III. Confronting the Apathy of the Church (vv. 14–23)
    A. Holy Spirit Preaching (vv. 14–19)
      1. God's Warning (vv. 14–16)
        a. The Undoing of the Apostates (vv. 14–15a)
        b. The Ungodliness of the Apostates (v. 15b)
        c. The Unrighteousness of the Apostates (v. 16)
      2. God's Word (vv. 17–19)
        a. Remember! (v. 17)
        b. Recognize! (v. 18)
        c. Remove! (v. 19)
    B. Holy Spirit Praying (v. 20)
    C. Holy Spirit Preservation (v. 21)
      1. Our Moral Responsibility (v. 21a)
      2. His Merciful Reliability (v. 21b)
    D. Holy Spirit Power (vv. 22–23)
      1. Compassion in Soul Winning (v. 22)
      2. Caution in Soul Winning (v. 23)
  IV. Conclusion (vv. 24–25)
    A. A Parting Blessing Manward (v. 24)
    B. A Parting Benediction Godward (v. 25)

This fascinating little memo has been called "the vestibule of the book of Revelation." And so it is. It brings us into the antechamber of the Apocalypse and prepares us for the closing scenes in the drama of the end-times. The author of this book, like James, grew up in the same home as Jesus. They knew Him as a lad at school, as a helper in the little Nazareth home, as the village carpenter. True, they had never known anyone so good, had never known anyone so wise, had never known anyone so clever, so compassionate, or so conscientious. But they certainly didn't believe He was the Christ. They were too close for that; they couldn't see the forest for the trees. But after His resurrection, they believed and became important members of the Jerusalem church. Jude describes himself now as "the slave of Jesus Christ" (see v. 1). His greatest wonder, surely, is that he wasn't always His slave, even in those unforgettable Nazareth years.

So then, some time before the fall of Jerusalem, Jude took his pen to write a letter. We watch with keenest interest as Jude reaches for his paper and ink. Surely he is going to tell us about those thirty silent years! He is going to tell us about Jesus as a boy, about Jesus as a brother, about Jesus as a straight-A student in school, about Jesus as the best sportsman in town, as the best craftsman in the country. He is going to tell us some of the things Jesus did and said as a boy, as a teenager, as a young man before He became famous in the world that then was. Nothing of the kind! He tells us that he intends to write about "the common salvation" (v. 3). He wants to take us to Calvary, to tell us more about that "so great salvation" purchased for us with the precious blood of Christ. But even as he dips his pen in the ink, the Holy Spirit changes Jude's mind. Instead of a manuscript, we have a memo; instead of a theology, we have a thunderbolt. For suddenly Jude's eyes are opened to see the terrible condition of the church and the perils that in the end would plunge the world into darkest night.

I. INTRODUCTION (vv. 1–4)

Jude intended to write to his readers of "the common salvation" but, because of an alarming growth in apostasy, felt urged instead to unmask "the acts of the apostates." His main argument is based on analogies from the past, a careful analysis of the current outbreak of apostasy, and a consideration of an ancient prophetic announcement concerning latter-day departure from the faith.

As we begin, let us first draw a comparison between the moon and the church. Like the moon, the church has no light of its own. It shines solely by reflecting the light of the sun. So, too, the church exists simply to reflect the light of Christ upon this dark world. Like the moon, the church shines and ministers only during the absence of the sun. When the sun returns, the moon dims and fades from view. The church's ministry in this world is only during the period of the Lord's absence. When He comes back, He will render unnecessary the present ministry of the church. Like the moon, the church exerts a strong influence on human tides. Twice every day the moon pulls the waters of the sea into the ordered banks of the world's great rivers. So the church exerts an influence upon the surging Gentile seas. There are times when it draws them powerfully into ordered channels; there are times when its influence is gone and the seas rush back again to their wild, lawless ways. Like the moon, the church waxes and wanes. There are times when the moon sheds brilliant light upon the earth; there are times when its light is almost nil. Just so the church.

There have been times of revival in the history of the church when its light has flooded the nations. There have been times of black apostasy when its light has been removed and men have stumbled in darkness. Like the moon, the church can be eclipsed. Then total darkness seizes upon the land. An eclipse of the moon takes place only under one condition—the earth comes between the moon and the sun. The earth then blots out the light of the moon. This is what was happening in Jude's day. The world was coming between the church and Christ. An eclipse of the church's light was threatening the world with utter darkness.

Jude, then, was quickened by the Holy Spirit to warn about and to give us clues to the final end-time apostasy. For his little memo was not restricted to his own day and age. Jude was carried by the Spirit to the end times to see the apostasy of the church just prior to the return of Christ.

This is where we are today, and this is what makes this note so important to us today. Scores of cults parade themselves as Christian, and large segments of the church deny the Scriptures. The church has lost its sovereignty because it has lost its soul—it no longer believes anything. It has been eclipsed. The world has come between the church and Christ.

Jude shows the serious spiritual perils that had surfaced in the church in his day. They had surfaced in the past; Jude says they will surface again. He goes back to Hebrew history and up to highest heaven for his illustrations. He talks of Satan and Sodom, Moses and Michael, Cain and Core, clouds and constellations, seas and trees. Illustrations are everywhere as he makes his points.

II. Confronting the Apostasy of the Church (vv. 5–13)

He begins by showing that apostasy affects both the morality and the mentality of people; it has a social side to it as well as a spiritual side; it attacks our behavior just as much as it attacks our beliefs.

A. How Apostasy Affects Morality (vv. 5–10)

He illustrates this from four different periods of the past, drawing attention to the *pilgrim age*—when Israel journeyed from Egypt to Canaan. Apostasy surfaced at that time, so serious that it called down the judgment of God. He points to the *primeval age*—the days before the flood, when God looked upon a society that had once known Him but that had ruled Him out of all human affairs and that had become so vile that God had been compelled to act in judgment. He looks at the *patriarchal age*—to the time when God again acted in judgment, raining fire and brimstone down from heaven upon Sodom and its sister cities for their unnatural sins. Finally he comes to the *Pentecostal age*—the days in which Jude himself lived and when some of the apostles still lived. Apostasy had again taken root in the very face of apostolic authority, daring even the Holy Spirit to act.

A study of these four great epochal apostasies shows that there is indeed a moral side to apostasy. An apostate age advertises itself by its toleration of gross sin, just as a time of revival advertises itself by the cleaning up of such sin in society.

1. The Pilgrim Age: False Disciples (v. 5)

"The Lord, having saved the people out of the land of Egypt, afterward destroyed them that believed not." Much of the trouble was caused by the "mixed multitude" who had joined the ranks of God's redeemed people, an unregenerate crowd who had no experience of the Paschal lamb, sheltering behind the shed blood, or escape from the avenging angel. They were "fellow travelers" who had joined the movement for its social and secular benefits. They went through the baptism unto Moses and took their place around the table and attempted to keep the law, but they missed the most important thing of all—the blood.

The word "destroyed" is the same one used by Jesus to describe Judas in His upper room prayer: "None of them is lost [destroyed], but the son of perdition . . ." (John 17:12). John uses the word twelve times. It is one of the strongest words in the Greek language to describe the final, irretrievable destruction of the damned. Jude deliberately uses this word—the very word Jesus used to describe the fate of Judas—to describe the fate of these false disciples.

2. The Primeval Age: Fallen Dominions (v. 6)

"And the angels which kept not their first estate, but left their own habitation, he hath reserved in everlasting chains under darkness unto the judgment of the great day." The original fall of the angels appears to have taken place when Lucifer apostatized against the light and glory of heaven. Many of these fallen angels now hold sway as principalities and powers, the rulers of this world's darkness, wicked spirits in high places as we learn elsewhere in the Bible (see Eph. 6:12).

There was a second fall for some of them in Noah's day. They "went after strange flesh." That is, they entered into lustful liaisons with the daughters of men, the women of the house of Cain. As a result, they produced a hybrid progeny, renowned for its enormous size and great wickedness. These were the "giants" of Old Testament times and the "heroes" and gods of mythology.

Jude says they kept not their own "habitation," a word that occurs one other time in the New Testament. Paul tells us that we are to get a different kind of body in the resurrection—he calls it a "house which is from heaven" (2 Cor. 5:2). It will be a body suited for heaven, a glorious spirit body, like that of Jesus. These fallen angels went in the opposite direction. They took to themselves a lower kind of body so that they could indulge in carnal lust. They "went after strange flesh," that is, they committed a sin that was against their nature.

It happened again after the flood. The Canaanites and their dreadful religious

practices stemmed from another incursion of fallen angels, and another race of giants was produced. We remember that ten of the twelve spies were terrified of them
and passed their fears on to the common people. Remnants of this accursed seed
lingered on in the land until the last of them were slain by David and his men. It
seems that a similar demonic penetration of the human race will happen again at
the end of the age and precipitate the end-time events of the apocalypse.

3. The Patriarchal Age: Fearful Degradation (v. 7)

"Even as Sodom and Gomorrha, and the cities about them in like manner,
giving themselves over to fornication, and going after strange flesh, are set forth for
an example, suffering the vengeance of eternal fire." This is the supreme mark of
an apostate society. It is a society that tolerates the sins of Sodom. In the end, God
simply overthrew Sodomite society in flaming fire and burning brimstone. The
practitioners of those shameful horrors went straight from the fires of judgment to
the fires of hell. That is what God thinks about the sin of sodomy. God does not
see this as "gay"; He simply sees guilt.

The fact that these ancient sins—going after "strange flesh"—continue to appear in our age, with the approval of society, indicates how far the latter-day apostasy has already gone. God has already begun to visit guilt with judgment. In this
modern promiscuous society there are an estimated 45 million Americans suffering
from herpes disorders. Every year 36,000 cases of syphilis are reported and an estimated 700,000 persons get new gonorrheal infections.[2] Beginning in the early
1980s, the lethal killer AIDS reared its head, especially among promiscuous homosexuals. This sexually transmitted virus destroys the body's immune system and
leaves its victims a prey to all kinds of opportunist diseases.

In the early onset of the AIDS epidemic, medical professionals seemed to send
confusing signals. They were baffled by the complexity of the virus that causes this
killer disease; they feared it would become epidemic, yet at the same time they
urged us not to be alarmed. Activist decried any suggestion of quarantining AIDS
victims and carriers.

Society was pressured to accept sexually deviant lifestyles as if they were perfectly
normal and right. Widespread acceptance of homosexuality, however, is always the
mark of an apostate society. The sexually transmitted diseases now rampant in our
society are only the initial penalty for shameless sin, the down payment. Society
cannot be permissive of the sin and hope to avoid the physical and spiritual consequences. God's eternal judgment is the ultimate end for those who refuse to repent.

4. The Pentecostal Age: Filthy Dreamers (vv. 8–10)

"Likewise also these filthy dreamers defile the flesh, despise dominion, and
speak evil of dignities." Those who practice these abominations scoff at the laws

of society made to enforce goodness and morality. They make mock of God. They take their bodies, intended by God to be the temple of the Holy Spirit, and make them vehicles for unbridled lust. God calls these people "filthy dreamers." This is a very significant expression. The word for "dreamers" occurs only one other time in the New Testament—in Acts 2:17. In explaining to Jerusalem the significance of Pentecost, Peter quoted from Joel: "In the last days . . . I will pour out of my Spirit upon all flesh . . . and your old men shall *dream dreams* [same word]." On the day of Pentecost men dreamed Spirit-inspired dreams; these "filthy dreamers" dream Satan-inspired dreams.

This underlines the significance of this whole little book. It is not that these sins are to be found in unregenerate society. Reprehensible as they are, such sins can be expected among people so perverted, so lost to shame, so satiated with ordinary sin that mere fornication is a tame worm compared with the dragon-lusts they have cultivated. The point is that these sins have now *come into the church*. That was the ultimate mark of apostasy. It was happening in Jude's day, and it called forth this letter, brief, urgent, impassioned, Holy Spirit-inspired, along with Peter's second epistle. And it is happening in our day. The apostate church is welcoming homosexuals into its communion and ordaining them to its ministry. It is a final insult to the holiness of God.

So Jude, confronting the apostasy of the church, shows how apostasy affects morality.

B. How Apostasy Affects Mentality (vv. 11–13)

1. The Men Involved (v. 11)

We must remember he is speaking now of the demise of the church as an effective voice for God in an apostate age. He summons on stage three men from the past—Cain, Balaam, and Korah. He uses these three representative men to illustrate how the apostate church thinks.

Cain attacked the *salvation of God*. He introduced into the world a bloodless salvation, a way to approach God without the cross. He denied the efficacy of the blood and the need for Calvary. He came up with a gospel of personal merit.

Balaam attacked the *sovereignty of God*. He denied that there was any future for the nation of Israel—and he did it for money. He was a paid preacher, interested only in a well-paying job, and quite willing to deny the truth of God in order to keep his pockets lined. Korah attacked the *servants of God*. He denied that Moses and Aaron were God-ordained men, and claimed he had as much right in the ministry as they.

The demoralization of the church's morality was linked with the depreciation of the church's message.

2. *The Mistake Involved (vv. 12–13)*

Jude now shows the utter emptiness of the way of life chosen by the apostates. They are hidden rocks; clouds without water, carried about by winds; trees without fruit, twice dead; raging waves of the sea, foaming out their own shame; wandering stars "to whom is reserved the blackness of darkness for ever" (v. 13).

It is worse than useless for the church to accept such people into its fellowship and to consecrate them to its ministry. They have nothing to offer, their lives are utterly empty, and they are dangerous. They have no place in the fellowship of the church at all. What they need to do is repent of their sin first—if they can.

III. Confronting the Apathy of the Church (vv. 14–23)

He sees a fourfold solution to the problem of apostasy. There needs to be a revival.

A. Holy Spirit Preaching (vv. 14–19)

We need the kind of preaching that characterized Enoch in his day. Enoch preached the coming of the Lord in judgment: "Behold, the Lord cometh with ten thousands of his saints, To execute judgment upon all" (vv. 14–15). Two things about Enoch's preaching stand out. It was *confident preaching*: "The Lord cometh. . . ." Enoch's emphasis was not on the Lord's coming for His church, for he knew nothing about that and nothing about the rapture. The church was not in his line of vision. He leaped over 1,000 years, to the flood; over 2,500 years more, to Bethlehem; over 2,000 years of the church age. He leaped over five and a half millennia because he knew nothing about the *time*, just the *truth*—"The Lord cometh!"

It was *convicting preaching*: "The Lord cometh . . . to execute judgment upon all, and to convict all that are ungodly." The Lord is going to convict the ungodly, make them see the horror of their lost estate. Conviction and sentencing are on the way.

That was God's first answer to apostasy—Holy Spirit preaching, the preaching of judgment, the preaching of the second coming of Christ. It did not stem the tide in Jude's day, but it left people without excuse.

Yet other things are needed.

B. Holy Spirit Praying (v. 20)

"But ye, beloved, building up yourselves on your most holy faith, praying in the Holy Ghost." There was still a remnant in the church. There always is a remnant in the church. God never leaves Himself without His "seven thousand who refuse to bow the knee to Baal" (see 1 Kings 19:18). They are a minority, but they are there, and their job is to pray, to pray in the power of the Holy Spirit.

The "most holy faith" is God's answer to a most unholy sodomite society, to an infected church, to an unregenerate pulpit, to unbelieving church members, to general compromise.

What we have is a faith—and what a faith! It is a faith centered in the second person of the Godhead. It takes its stand on the virgin birth of Christ; on His immaculate, miraculous life; on His vicarious, atoning death; on His resurrection and ascension; on His ministry as Great High Priest; on His coming again as King; on the presence of the Holy Spirit on earth to convict, regenerate, restrain, fill, baptize, indwell, and anoint. What we have is a faith!

What we have is a *holy* faith. It makes profligate people pure, drunken people sober, crooked people straight, filthy people clean. It regenerates. It makes people to be new creatures, makes them children of God, Spirit born, clean-living, God-fearing, heaven-bound. It is a holy faith.

We have a *most* holy faith. There can be no compromise with sin, no matter in what persuasive terms it is garbed, no matter how great a majority it commands.

C. Holy Spirit Preservation (v. 21)

"Keep yourselves in the love of God, looking for the mercy of our Lord Jesus Christ unto eternal life." How does one keep oneself? The answer is in Acts 20:32—"I commend you to God, and to the word of his grace, which is able to build you up." We build up ourselves by allowing the Spirit-breathed Word of God to be the rule of our lives. This is God's own antidote to the poison of apostasy. Along with that is the steady anticipation of the return of the Lord Jesus and the dawn of eternal life in His presence.

D. Holy Spirit Power (vv. 22–23)

"And of some have compassion, making a difference" (v. 22). There are souls to be saved. There are people who are caught up in sin who long with all their hearts to be set free.

"And others save with fear, pulling them out of the fire; hating even the garment spotted by the flesh" (v. 23). Recently I was sharing services with the pastor from a very large church. In the course of his preaching, he stated that his church had a ministry to "gays." I asked him if he "made a difference." He wanted to know what I meant, and bristled at what followed. "Do you warn your people that this person here and that person there is a homosexual?" He said, "No, that would be discriminatory."

He has missed the whole point of Jude 21–23. We are told by God to be discriminatory. Nothing could be worse than to introduce sodomites into a congregation without warning people about who and what they are. Not only are many of them carriers of a deadly virus, but their proclivities make them a possible moral danger to boys and to others. Even when they profess to be saved, they need to be watched, unless some extraordinary work of grace is done in their souls. Once it is entrenched, homosexual behavior is very difficult to eradicate. Jude warns that there are some who must be held at arm's length even as we seek to minister to them.

IV. CONCLUSION (vv. 24–25)

Jude concludes with a word of practical encouragement and with one of the most magnificent doxologies in the Bible.

On every hand today the great apostasy, so frequently mentioned in the New Testament, is making its advance. Every believer needs to know what God has to say about this subject. Hence, as a textbook of apostate religious belief and abnormal moral behavior, the book of Jude is unsurpassed.

CHAPTER 29

REVELATION

The Future Unveiled

The book of Revelation is given its divine title in the first verse; it is "The
Revelation of Jesus Christ." The language of the book is Greek, but its
thoughts and idioms are Hebrew, and it is saturated with Old Testament language.
Indeed, there are about 550 references to Old Testament passages in the book. It is
closely related to the book of Daniel, to which it forms a sequel.

Many interesting comparisons and contrasts can be made as well between
Revelation and Genesis. Genesis tells of paradise lost, Revelation speaks of paradise
regained; the Garden of Eden in Genesis gives way in Revelation to the City of
God; the tree of life in Genesis is seen again in Revelation; the serpent appears in
Genesis and meets his doom in Revelation; sin, sorrow, tears, the curse—all begin
in Genesis and all vanish in Revelation. The book of Revelation naturally com-
pletes the circle of revealed truth begun in Genesis.

Four main schools of interpretation have been applied to this book. The *preter-
ists* maintain that the greatest part of the book has already been fulfilled in the early
history of the church. The *historicists* claim that the book of Revelation covers the
whole period of history from the apostolic period to the present time. The *idealists*
spiritualize the teaching of the book and say that it does not set forth actual events
at all but that its symbols depict spiritual realities. The *futurists* believe that the
major part of the book has to do with what is still future.

The great theme of the book of Revelation is Christ. Christ in all His glory
controls the factors of time and space, and precipitates and determines the events of
the last days. It was written by the apostle John who was an old man when a second
great wave of pagan persecution broke out against the church during the reign of

Domitian. John was exiled to the island of Patmos off the coast of Asia Minor, where he received the visions of this book.

The scenes in the book alternate between heaven and earth. In chapter one we are in heaven; in chapters two and three we come back down to earth again for the letters to the seven churches; in chapters four and five we go back to heaven to see the Lord Jesus step into the spotlight of eternity and receive the scroll, the title deed of earth; in chapter six we come back down to earth to see what happens when the seals are broken; in chapter seven we are back in heaven for the sealing of the witnesses; in chapters eight and nine we are back on earth for the blowing of the trumpets, and so on.

The book, though, begins in heaven and ends in heaven. It gives us the full and final answer to the Lord's prayer: "Thy kingdom come, thy will be done *on earth*, as it is in *heaven*" (see Matt. 6:10). In this book we see God's will being decreed and declared in heaven; then we see His will being done on earth.

The structure of Revelation is somewhat unusual. There is a chronological sequence to the book, but the chronology is constantly interrupted by commentary, by parenthetical passages that give added details to the major chronological events. Some of these commentary sections are brief, some are quite lengthy. For the most part they concentrate on action precipitated by the trumpet judgments. It is during this period that the Beast, the Devil's messiah, comes into his own and takes over the affairs of this planet. The commentary sections shed much light on how he accomplishes this, and reveal what use he makes of the world power that is finally concentrated in his hands. It is one of the expositor's hermeneutical challenges to determine just when and where these commentary sections begin and end, and just where they fit in relation to the rest of the book.

Then, too, significant use is made of symbols. Symbolism is not unusual in Scripture, but proper rules for interpreting them must be implemented. Thus, the presence of symbols is certainly not meant as merely an opportunity for the interpreter to exercise his ingenuity. To state, then, as one author does, that the creatures freed from the abyss in chapter nine are helicopters is contrary to the context of the passage. Such an "interpretation" is highly imaginative, completely false, and without any support from the text itself or from the rest of Scripture.

The primary rule for handling Bible symbolism is simple—God is His own interpreter! That is, the Holy Spirit invariably interprets His own symbolism. Thus we find that symbols are either explained in their immediate context, elsewhere in the book in which they occur, or somewhere else in the Bible. In chapter one, for instance, we are told that the "stars" and the "lampstands" symbolize angels and churches. In chapter seventeen we meet a scarlet woman sitting upon many waters and also upon a scarlet beast recognizable by its seven heads. We do not have to leave the chapter before we are told that the seven heads are seven mountains, that the waters represent "peoples, and multitudes, and nations, and tongues" (17:15), and that the woman herself is "that great city, which reigneth over the kings of the earth" (17:18). That city is Rome, clearly identifiable from these clues.

    I. Introduction (1:1–3)
   II. Visions of God (1:4–20)
       A. The Position of God the Son (1:4–6)
       B. The Purpose of God the Son (1:7–8)
       C. The Providence of God the Son (1:9–11)
       D. The Person of God the Son (1:12–16)
       E. The Power of God the Son (1:17–20)
  III. Visions of Grace (2:1–3:22)
       A. The Practical View of These Letters
          1. Conditions Present Then
          2. Conditions Prevalent Still
       B. The Prophetic View of These Letters
  IV. Visions of Government (4:1–20:15)
       A. Hallelujahs in Heaven (4:1–5:14)
       B. Horrors on Earth (6:1–20:15)
          1. The Seals: A World Ruined by Man (6:1–7:17)
             a. Particular Details (6:1–17)
                (1) The Four Horsemen of the Apocalypse
                   (a) Seal 1: Successful Propaganda
                   (b) Seal 2: Sanguinary Policies
                   (c) Seal 3: Severe Privations
                   (d) Seal 4: Spreading Plagues
                (2) The Further Horrors of the Apocalypse
                   (a) Seal 5: Immense Persecution
                   (b) Seal 6: Impotent Panic
                   (c) Seal 7: Imprecatory Prayer
             b. Parenthetical Details (7:1–17)
          2. The Trumpets: A World Ruled by Satan (8:1–14:20)
             a. Particular Details (8:1–9:21)
                (1) The War Trumpets (8:1–13)
                   (a) Trumpet 1: The Brewing Storm
                   (b) Trumpet 2: The Boiling Sun
                   (c) Trumpet 3: The Banished Star
                   (d) Trumpet 4: The Blackened Sky
                (2) The Woe Trumpets (9:1–21; 10:7; 11:15–19)
                   (a) Trumpet 5: Misery Endured

As stated above, the basic underlying structure of Revelation is that of chronology interrupted by commentary,[1] some brief, some embracing several chapters. This constant fluctuation can be confusing. In the major portion of the book, the chronology is carried by the seals, trumpets, and vials. Once we are through with the vials, the recurring expression "and I saw" marks the onward march of events. The chart on the following page shows how some of the chapters are chronologically related.

The more vital parenthetical sections in the book are those describing the sealing of the 144,000 (chap. 7); the incidents of the little book and the two witnesses (chaps. 10–11); the preliminary description of the great tribulation (chap. 12); the description of the two beasts (chap. 13); the events that anticipate the final judgments (chap. 14); the description of the two Babylons (chaps. 17–18).

I. Introduction (1:1–3)

John gives us at once the great theme of the book—it is the "revelation [apocalypse, unveiling] of Jesus Christ." He is the key to the book—it is all about Him. A special blessing is given to those who read, hear, and obey its revelations. Satan hates this book because it magnifies the Lord Jesus, and also because it describes his own fall and eternal doom.

II. Visions of God (1:4–20)

The visions of chapter one are visions of God the Son, the glorious second person of the Godhead. John tells us the circumstances under which he received these particular visions. He was a prisoner on Patmos, an island offshore from the mainland of Asia Minor, where the churches John addresses were located.

CHRONOLOGICAL RELATIONSHIP
OF REVELATION CHAPTERS

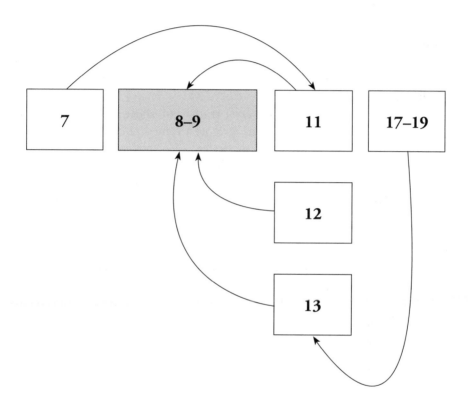

We are left in no doubt as to who is in control, or as to how it is all going to end. Everything is to climax with the coming again of the Lord Jesus in power and glory, in visible and awesome splendor. The end is so good that God puts it on the very first page!

These opening visions set before us the absolute *deity* of the Lord Jesus. He is seen as coequal with the Father and with the Spirit in bestowing blessing. He is called "the Almighty." They set before us, too, the absolute *determination* of the Lord to come back, in power and great glory, to the scene of His former rejection. They set before us, moreover, the absolute *dominion* of the Lord, as the Controller of all the forces of time and space. John fell at His feet as one dead.

III. VISIONS OF GRACE (2:1–3:22)

Chapters two and three present matters dealing with the age of grace in which we live. They contain a series of seven letters dictated by the ascended Lord, written down by John, and sent to the churches themselves.

These letters contain *practical* truth. That is, they were addressed to seven churches actually existing in a geographical and historical context, and they deal with practical issues in those churches. And they paint an excellent portrait of the Christian church as it was at the end of the first century.

They also contain *perennial* truth. There have always been churches, in all the centuries since Pentecost, that have needed the specific promises and warnings contained in these letters.

But, further, they contain *prophetic* truth. For those seven churches, in the order in which they are addressed, give us a cameo of church history from Pentecost to the rapture. In each of the letters a key phrase can be found that highlights its prophetic significance. With Ephesus it is the phrase "Thou art fallen"; with Smyrna it is the expression "tribulation ten days"; with Pergamos the key phrase is "the doctrine of Balaam"; with Thyatira it is the phrase "that woman Jezebel"; with Sardis it is the statement "a name . . . but dead"; with Philadelphia it is the phrase "an open door"; and with Laodicea it is the comment "thou art lukewarm."

We can summarize the prophetic aspect of these seven churches as follows:

1. *Ephesus*: The Post-Apostolic Age. This period was marked by a rapid cooling of love for Christ. The heresies, which were already beginning to raise their heads in apostolic times, flourished. Gnosticism took such rapid root that the very life and existence of the church was threatened.
2. *Smyrna*: The Persecution Age. There were ten distinct outbursts of Roman persecution directed against the church, the last of which, under Diocletian, lasted ten years.
3. *Pergamos*: The Patronizing Age. The accession of Constantine marked the beginning of a new era. Satan had attacked the church as a serpent in the post-apostolic age; then as a roaring lion under the persecuting Caesars. In this age he becomes the bear seeking to smother the church with the warm embrace of the world. It was the most successful of all his devices.
4. *Thyatira*: The Papal Age. The reference to Jezebel is significant. In the Old Testament she was a pagan princess who used the secular arm in Israel to impose an idolatrous religion on God's people and to persecute those who resisted. In the church the advent of Constantine led to swift decline. Paganism took the seat of power, immorality was condoned by religion, the secular arm was used to persecute the true church. As time went on, scarlet

and purple and imperial power, idolatry and spiritual adultery reigned supreme in the name of God.

5. *Sardis*: The Protestant Age. For all its initial vitality and reform, the Protestant movement soon lost its momentum. It leaned too heavily on the arm of princes. Soon, all it had was a name and a reputation.

6. *Philadelphia*: The Productive Age. This was the day of the open door, when revival, evangelistic activity, world missions prevailed.

7. *Laodicea*: The Present Age. This age is seen as one of material prosperity, worldly pride, great outward success, and compromise (lukewarmness). It is what we have today in a church marked by evangelism without the offense of the cross, conversion without conviction, preaching without power, salvation without separation, love without truth, "churchianity" without Christianity, religion without the Holy Spirit, organization without spiritual life.

IV. VISIONS OF GOVERNMENT (4:1–20:15)

A. Hallelujahs in Heaven (4:1–5:14)

A brief survey cannot be expected to unravel the complex structure of the book of Revelation. Here we can only give an overall view of these chapters.

This long section begins in heaven, where all judgment is fittingly handed over to Christ. We are given a magnificent glimpse into heaven in chapters four and five. Probably nowhere else in the Bible do we have a greater emphasis on the throne of God (it is mentioned sixteen times[2]) or on the invincible power and sovereignty of that throne. But we soon come back down to earth. The Lord takes the seven-sealed scroll into His hands, begins to break the seals, and thus precipitates the end-time judgments that now engulf the globe.

B. Horrors on Earth (6:1–20:15)

1. The Seals: A World Ruined by Man (6:1–7:17)

A discernible escalation occurs from one series of judgments to another in the book of Revelation. Under the seals, it is very evidently *man* who fills the picture. The scenes are familiar and the symbols used are simple and easily explained. With the breaking of the seals, divine restraint is increasingly removed from the earth.

The church has gone, and the Holy Spirit takes up a position relative to earth similar to the one He occupied in Old Testament times. Man is allowed to have things his own way. As a result, he reduces the earth to a state of utter chaos. One horror follows another. There is "cold war" and global conflict, famine and pestilence, persecution and panic. Many of the things already at work in today's world are simply given free rein. They sweep the earth from end to end.

Events under the seals closely parallel the end-time events chronicled by the Lord Jesus in the first part of the Olivet discourse (Matt. 24). But these things are only "the beginning of sorrows" (Matt. 24:8). The things we see all about us today are not the actual events predicted to take place when the seals are broken, but they are heralds of things to come. They are shadows cast forward upon our age by oncoming events.

Conditions under the seals impel men to look around for a man, for someone with enough genius and charisma to bring some sort of sanity and order out of the universal chaos.

2. The Trumpets: A World Ruled by Satan (8:1–14:20)

This man now steps forward and takes over the planet. A world ruined by man becomes now a world ruled by *Satan*. The beast comes up out of the sea and Satan is flung down from the sky. The upheavals on the planet so prevalent today, intensified by the breaking of the seals, produce a moral climate ideal for the coming of the Devil's messiah and his propaganda agent, the false prophet. The commentary chapters shed light on Satan's strategy for openly ruling the world.

The Beast, for instance, has two comings. When he first surfaces, he is "the beast out of the sea" (see 13:1); later on, he is "the beast out of the abyss" (see 17:8). In the first stage of his appearing, he is an ordinary human being, a genius no doubt, in league with Satan and demon-possessed assuredly—but still, a human being. In the second stage of his career he is superhuman, more than a mere man.

In the early stages of his career he uses the religious system centered at Rome to help him gain control of the West. He unites the nations of western Europe, revives the Roman Empire, and possibly brings all the western hemisphere together in a grand alliance dominated and controlled by himself. Then he uses the ten confederate kings of his empire to destroy the religious system.

Next, he turns his attention to Israel and signs a seven-year pact guaranteeing her security and promising to rebuild the temple. It is at this time, too, that a massive war is fought (under the sixth trumpet), engaging armies numbering two hundred million (perhaps a symbolic number). There are good reasons for equating this conflict with the one described in Ezekiel 38–39, which brings an end to Russian power in the world.[3] In any case, the beast wins control of the world. The nations exclaim, "Who can make war with the beast?" (see 13:4) and agree to accept his sovereignty over the world and to worship him and the dragon (Satan) who gives him his power.

The Jews and Israel have now become expendable. The beast seizes their rebuilt temple and his prophet sets up an image of the beast in the Holy Place. He gives this image breath and it performs miracles. All men are commanded to receive "the mark of the beast" and worship his image. Those who refuse are boycotted, persecuted, and killed. The Jewish people in particular now face the beast's wrath and are exposed to the blood bath of the great tribulation.

During this whole period, God still has a testimony to Himself on earth. First, it is the two witnesses; then it is the 144,000 witnesses; after that it is a "multitude, which no man could number" (7:9), who are the fruit of their testimony. The 144,000 are raptured to heaven as a body, but the vast host of their converts have to face the undiluted wrath of the beast. This whole period will be one of terror and unequalled horror for mankind.

3. The Vials (Bowls): A World Rescued by God (15:1–20:15)

When the vials of God's wrath are outpoured, Satan's empire begins to break up. First, the beast's power structure is weakened and the eastern half of his empire, never fully assimilated, breaks away. The nations of the East mobilize against the West, pour across the Euphrates River, and deploy on the plains of Megiddo, where armies have fought from time immemorial. The Jews will be in their last extremity, and their country, invaded by the beast's armies, and Jerusalem, will be lying prostrate at his feet. The final purge of Jews will be in its last stages when news comes of the now very present threat from the East. The West, mobilized by the beast, will already be deployed at Megiddo when the Lord returns from heaven to make a full end of all His foes. A terrible carnage follows. The Beast and the false prophet are taken and are hurled headlong into the lake of fire, and Satan is incarcerated for a thousand years in the abyss. The long-awaited reign of Christ begins.

The slumbering Old Testament prophecies regarding the millennial age awaken to glorious, magnificent, and literal fulfillment. The age ends with one final rebellion as Satan is loosed from his prison, deceives the nations once more, and leads them in a final, futile march on Jerusalem.

V. Visions of Glory (21:1–22:5)

Only eight verses (21:1–8) are devoted to a description of the new creation—we could wish it were eight volumes! The Holy Spirit, for the most part, remains silent about what we will be doing in eternity, but we can be sure God has marvelous plans to make eternity an exciting experience for His own.

We have a detailed description, however, of the new capital, the heavenly Jerusalem. It seems best to view this as a real place (John 14:1–3). It would seem that this celestial city will be brought into a meaningful relation to the earth during the Millennium—probably by being placed in stationary orbit over the earthly Jerusalem.

The millennial age will end in rebellion, as we have seen. Before God detonates the universe, the celestial city will, seemingly, become another "Noah's ark" for those of earth's people who love the Lord. They will probably be transported to the celestial city, which will then be taken back out of time into eternity, from whence it came. Then flaming fires will embrace the earth, the solar system, and all of space. The new heaven and the new earth, which will replace the old ones, will probably orbit forever around the Holy City (21:2).

VI. CONCLUSION (22:6–21)

This remarkable book ends with a fresh assurance to John that "these sayings are faithful and true" (v. 6). They are not idle dreams. They deal with realities—realities now coming rapidly into focus and awaiting only the rapture of the church before coming to a head.

Again the Lord assures us of His coming. "Surely I come quickly!" He says. "Even so, come, Lord Jesus" is the response of His waiting people (v. 20).

Appropriately enough, the last word in the book and the last word in the Bible is "Amen"—a name for the Lord Jesus (Rev. 3:14). Thus the Holy Spirit leaves us where the disciples found themselves on the Mount of Transfiguration when, the visions and visitation all over, "they saw no man, save Jesus only" (Matt. 17:8).

The Talmud's Slow Evolution

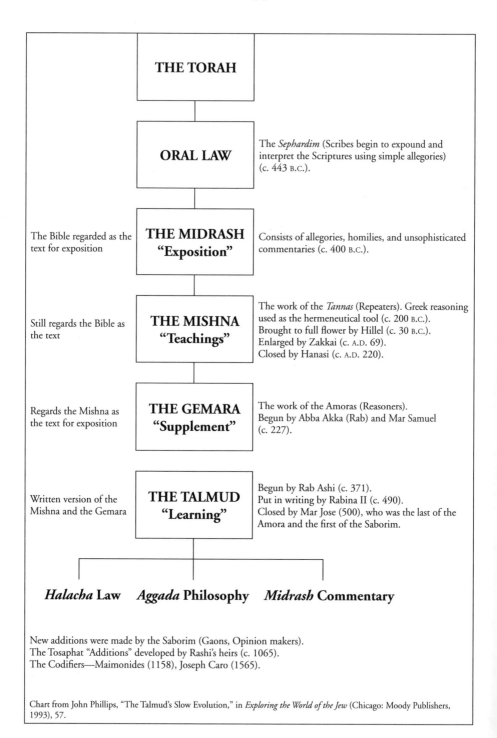

THE TORAH

ORAL LAW

The *Sephardim* (Scribes begin to expound and interpret the Scriptures using simple allegories) (c. 443 B.C.).

The Bible regarded as the text for exposition

THE MIDRASH
"Exposition"

Consists of allegories, homilies, and unsophisticated commentaries (c. 400 B.C.).

Still regards the Bible as the text

THE MISHNA
"Teachings"

The work of the *Tannas* (Repeaters). Greek reasoning used as the hermeneutical tool (c. 200 B.C.). Brought to full flower by Hillel (c. 30 B.C.). Enlarged by Zakkai (c. A.D. 69). Closed by Hanasi (c. A.D. 220).

Regards the Mishna as the text for exposition

THE GEMARA
"Supplement"

The work of the Amoras (Reasoners). Begun by Abba Akka (Rab) and Mar Samuel (c. 227).

Written version of the Mishna and the Gemara

THE TALMUD
"Learning"

Begun by Rab Ashi (c. 371). Put in writing by Rabina II (c. 490). Closed by Mar Jose (500), who was the last of the Amora and the first of the Saborim.

Halacha **Law**   *Aggada* **Philosophy**   *Midrash* **Commentary**

New additions were made by the Saborim (Gaons, Opinion makers). The Tosaphat "Additions" developed by Rashi's heirs (c. 1065). The Codifiers—Maimonides (1158), Joseph Caro (1565).

Chart from John Phillips, "The Talmud's Slow Evolution," in *Exploring the World of the Jew* (Chicago: Moody Publishers, 1993), 57.

NOTES

Chapter 2: The New Testament
1. Rom. 1:17; 2:26; 3:5, 21, 22, 25, 26; 4:3, 5, 6, 9, 11 (2x), 13, 22; 5:17, 18, 21; 6:13, 16, 18, 19, 20; 8:4, 10; 9:28, 30 (2x), 31; 10:3 (2x), 4, 5, 6, 10; 14:17.
2. Acts 1:2, 5, 8, 16; 2:4, 17, 18, 33, 38; 4:8, 31; 5:3, 9, 32; 6:3, 5; 7:51, 55; 8:15, 17, 18, 19, 29, 39; 9:17, 31; 10:19, 38, 44, 45, 47; 11:15, 16, 24, 28; 13:2, 4, 9, 52; 15:8, 28; 16:6, 7; 19:2, 6; 20:23, 28; 21:4, 11; 28:25.
3. Handley Carr Glynn Moule (1841–1920) was a prominent evangelical clergyman who wrote several books. H. C. G. Moule, *Philippian Studies: Lessons in Faith and Love from St. Paul's Epistle to the Philippians* (New York: Hodder and Stoughton, n.d.), 134.

Chapter 3: The Four Gospels
1. Simon Greenleaf, *A Treatise on the Law of Evidence* (New York: Arno Press, n.d.), 13.

Chapter 4: Matthew
1. Matt. 1:22; 2:15, 17, 23; 4:14; 8:17; 12:17; 13:35; 21:4; 22:31; 27:9, 35.

Chapter 6: Luke
1. Luke 1:11, 13, 18, 19, 26, 28, 30, 34, 35, 38; 2:9, 10, 15, 21; 4:10; 9:26; 12:8, 9; 15:10; 16:22; 20:36; 22:43; 24:23.

Chapter 7: John
1. William Graham Scroggie (1877–1958), pastor of the famous Spurgeon

Metropolitan Tabernacle, London, and author of the *Unfolding Drama of Redemption.*
2. John 1:6, 15, 19, 26, 28, 29, 32, 35, 40; 3:23, 24, 25, 26, 27; 4:1; 5:33, 36; 10:40, 41 (2x).

Chapter 8: Acts
1. Acts 1:2, 5, 8, 16; 2:4, 17, 18, 33, 38; 5:3, 9, 32; 6:3, 5; 7:51, 55; 8:15, 17, 18, 19, 29, 39; 9:17, 31; 10:19, 38, 44, 45, 47; 11:12, 15, 16, 24, 28; 13:2, 4, 9, 52; 15:8, 28; 16:6, 7; 19:2, 6; 20:23, 28; 21:4, 11; 28:25.
2. John Phillips, *Exploring Acts* (Grand Rapids: Kregel, 2001).

Chapter 9: Romans
1. For a full treatment of this important book, see John Phillips, *Exploring Romans* (Grand Rapids: Kregel, 2002).

Chapter 11: 2 Corinthians
1. Archimedes, "Doric Speech of Syracuse," in John Tzetzes, *Book of Histories (Chiliades)*, trans. Francis R. Walton, 2:129–30.

Chapter 12: Galatians
1. From the introduction to the book of Galatians, E. W. Bullinger, *The Companion Bible* (Grand Rapids: Kregel, 1999).
2. Gen. 1:11, 12 (2x), 21 (2x), 24 (2x), 25 (3x).
3. Martin Luther, *A Commentary on St. Paul's Epistle to the Galatians* (New York: Carter & Brothers, 1860).

Chapter 13: Ephesians
1. Eph. 1:2, 6, 7; 2:5, 7, 8; 3:2, 7, 8; 4:7, 29; 6:24.
2. See John Phillips, *Exploring Ephesians and Philippians* (Grand Rapids: Kregel, 2002).

Chapter 14: Philippians
1. Samuel Whitlock Gandy, *The Believer's Hymnbook* (n.p., 1800s).

Chapter 15: Colossians
1. James Hopwood Jeans, "The Dying Sun," *The Mysterious Universe* (Cambridge, MA: Cambridge University Press, 1931), 1.
2. Alexander Maclaren, "The Epistles of St. Paul to the Colossians and Philemon" in *An Exposition of the Bible*, ed. Marcus Dods, R. A. Watson, Dean F. W. Farrar, et al. (Hartford, CT: n.p., 1903), 6:280.

Chapter 16: 1 Thessalonians

1. Isa. 2:12; 13:6, 9; Ezek. 13:5; 30:3; Joel 1:15; 2:1, 11, 31; 3:14; Amos 5:20; Obad. 1:15; Zeph. 1:7, 14; Zech. 14:1; Mal. 4:5; Acts 2:20; 1 Cor. 5:5; 1 Thess. 5:2; 2 Peter 3:10.

Chapter 17: 2 Thessalonians

1. Not "the day of Christ" as in the King James text—the day of Christ is the day of verse 1; the day of the Lord is the day of Old Testament prophecy already mentioned by Paul in his first letter, 1 Thessalonians 5:1–9.

Chapter 19: 2 Timothy

1. For a fuller discussion of this, see John Phillips, *Exploring the Future* (Grand Rapids: Kregel, 2002).

Chapter 23: James

1. Martin Luther, "Preface to the New Testament," *Works of Martin Luther: The Philadelphia Edition*, trans. C. M. Jacobs (Grand Rapids: Baker, 1982), 6:439–44.

Chapter 24: 1 Peter

1. Peter's first epistle strikes at the roots of many of the cherished dogmas of Rome, as do Peter's other writings and speeches. They strike at Rome's claim that Peter was the Rock on which the church was built (2:6); Rome's historic suppression of the Scriptures (2:2); Rome's claim that we should pray to Mary rather than directly to God (1:17); Rome's sale of indulgences (1:18); Rome's claim that the Scriptures are to be supplemented by tradition (1:18); Rome's teaching that salvation is by works (2:24); Rome's craving for temporal power (2:13–17); Rome's hierarchy of one man lording power over the church (5:3–4); Rome's practice of giving her priests special status over others (2:5–9); Rome's claim that only ordained people can minister (4:10–11); Rome's desire for money (5:2; Acts 3:6); Rome's desire for adulation of men; Rome's concept of baptismal regeneration (3:20–21).
2. Tacitus, *Annals*, 15.
3. Ibid., 55.

Chapter 25: 2 Peter

1. William Martin, "Waiting for the End," *Atlantic Monthly* 249, no. 6 (June 1982): 31–37.

Chapter 26: 1 John

1. D. M. Panton (1870–1955) ministered at Surrey Chapel, Norwich, England. He was founder, as well as editor from 1924 until his death in 1955, of *Dawn* magazine, a strong voice for deep scriptural and prophetical truth.

Chapter 27: 2 and 3 John

1. A friend of mine suggested to me that "the elect lady" might be Mary, the Lord's mother. This raises some interesting speculations. She was John's aunt. James and Jude were his cousins. If there is anything at all to this speculation, she must have been a very old woman indeed.
2. F. F. Bruce, "The Full Name of the Procurator Felix," *Journal for the Study of the New Testament* 1, no. 1 (1978): 33–36.
3. Likely source for this quote is W. E. Vine, *Vine's Expository Dictionary of New Testament Words* (Glasgow: Pickering & Inglis, 1941).

Chapter 28: Jude

1. Eusebius, *Ecclesiastical History*, 3.20.
2. Statistics are from the Department of Health and Human Services, Centers for Disease Control and Prevention, http://www.cdc.gov (accessed June 25, 2009).

Chapter 29: Revelation

1. For a complete commentary, see John Phillips, *Exploring Revelation* (Grand Rapids: Kregel, 2001).
2. Rev. 4:2, 3, 4, 5 (2x), 6 (3x), 9, 10 (2x); 5:1, 6, 7, 11, 13.
3. See John Phillips, *Exploring the Future* (Grand Rapids: Kregel, 2002).